Globalization and Reform in Higher Education

SRHE and Open University Press Imprint
General Editor: Heather Eggins

Current titles include:

Peter G. Taylor: *Making Sense of Academic Life*
Richard Taylor, Jean Barr and Tom Steele: *For a Radical Higher Education*
Malcolm Tight: *Researching Higher Education*
Susan Toohey: *Designing Courses for Higher Education*
Paul R. Trowler (ed.): *Higher Education Policy and Institutional Change*
Melanie Walker (ed.): *Reconstructing Professionalism in University Teaching*
David Warner and David Palfreyman (eds): *Higher Education Management of UK Higher Education*
Gareth Williams (ed.): *The Enterprising University*
Diana Woodward and Karen Ross: *Managing Equal Opportunities in Higher Education*

Globalization and Reform in Higher Education

edited by Heather Eggins

Society for Research into Higher Education
& Open University Press

Open University Press
McGraw-Hill Education
McGraw-Hill House
Shoppenhangers Road
Maidenhead
Berkshire
England
SL6 2QL

email: enquiries@openup.co.uk
world wide web: www.openup.co.uk

First published 2003

Copyright © Heather Eggins 2003

A catalogue record of this book is available from the British Library

ISBN 0 335 21396 0 (pb)   0 335 21397 9 (hb)

Library of Congress Cataloging-in-Publication Data
CIP data has been applied for

Typeset by RefineCatch Limited, Bungay, Suffolk
Printed in the UK by Bell & Bain Ltd, Glasgow

This book is dedicated to
Jack Alexander Simmons
and
Ragheed Abdulwahab Mohammed Al-Mufti

Contents

Contributors

Rosemary Deem is Professor of Education at the University of Bristol and Director of the UK Learning and Teaching Support Network Education Subject Centre, ESCalate. She is also joint managing editor of *The Sociological Review* (Blackwells).

Heather Eggins is Director of the Society for Research into Higher Education and Visiting Professor at the University of Strathclyde.

Elaine El-Khawas is Professor of Education Policy at The George Washington University and Director of the ERIC Clearinghouse on Higher Education.

D. Bruce Johnstone is University Professor of Higher and Comparative Education and Director of the Center for Comparative and Global Studies in Education at the State University of New York at Buffalo. He is also the former Chancellor of the State University of New York system.

Mary-Louise Kearney is Director of the Division for Relations with National Commissions and New Partnerships in UNESCO's Sector for External Relations and Co-operation. She was involved in the WCHE of 1998 and is a Vice President of the SRHE.

Adrianna Kezar is Assistant Professor at The George Washington University.

Elisabeth Lillie is Faculty Head of Collaborative Courses and Chair of Faculty Teaching and Learning Committee (Arts) at the University of Ulster. She has participated in the work of the European Thematic Network Project and is a member of the Scientific Committee on Quality Enhancement in Language Studies.

Simon Marginson is Professor and Director of the Monash Centre for Research in International Education at Monash University, Australia. He edits the *Australian Journal of Education*.

Ann I. Morey is Distinguished Research Professor and Director of the Center for Educational Leadership, Innovation and Policy at San Diego State University, California.

Preeti Shroff-Mehta has a Masters degree in Development Studies from the University of Sussex and a Masters in Urban Planning and a Ph.D. in Comparative Education from the State University of New York at Buffalo. He does international consulting and lives in Chevy Chase, Maryland, USA.

Dr. Barbara Sporn is Associate Professor at Wirtschaftsuniversität Wien, Austria.

George Subotzky is Associate Professor and Director of the Centre for the Study of Higher Education (formerly the Education Policy Unit) at the University of the Western Cape, Cape Town.

William Taylor's fifty-year career in education includes ten years as Director of the University of London Institute of Education, and another ten as a University Vice Chancellor and Principal. He continues to serve as a Governor, Visiting Professor and consultant to universities and colleges in the United Kingdom and overseas.

List of abbreviations

AACSB	The Association to Advance Collegiate Schools of Business
ANC	African National Congress
ASTEC	Australian Science, Technology and Engineering Council
CNAA	The Council for National Academic Awards
CAE	Colleges of Advanced Education
CHE	The Council on Higher Education
CIHE	Council for Industry and Higher Education
COSATU	The Congress of South African Unions
CRC	Cooperative Research Centre
CVCP	Committee of Vice-Chancellors and Principals
DETYA	Department of Education, Training and Youth Affairs
DFID	Department for International Development
DoE	Department of Education
EFC	Expected Family Contribution
ENQUA	European Network for Quality Assurance in Higher Education
EQUIS	European Quality Improvement System
ESRC	The Economic and Social Research Council
EUA	The European University Association
FIBAA	Foundation for International Business Administration Accreditation
GCCA	Graduate Careers Council of Australia
GEAR	Growth, Employment and Redistribution
GNU	The Government of National Unity
HDI	Historically disadvantaged institution
HECS	The Higher Education Contribution Scheme
HEFCE	Higher Education Funding Council for England
HEFCW	Higher Education Funding Council for Wales
HoDs	Heads of Department
ILT	Institute for Learning and Teaching
IMF	International Monetary Fund

LTSN	Learning and Teaching Support Network
NAB	National Accreditation Board
NCA	North Central Association
NCHE	National Commission on Higher Education
NEASC	New England Association of Schools and Colleges
OECD	Organisation for Economic Cooperation and Development
PRCS	Premature Retirement Compensation
PVC	Pro-Vice Chancellor
QAA	Quality Assurance Agency
RDP	Reconstruction and Development Programme
SACP	South African Communist Party
SHEFC	The Scottish Higher Education Funding Council
TAFE	Technical and Further Education
TQM	Total Quality Management
VC	Vice Chancellor
VET	Vocational Education and Training
WASC	Western Association of Schools and Colleges

Foreword

It is a pleasure to write the Foreword to *Globalization and Reform in Higher Education* in my capacity as a Vice-President of the Society for Research into Higher Education. For many years, SRHE has been a close and dynamic collaborator of UNESCO in the field of higher education. For this reason, it seems fitting to situate these remarks in relation to UNESCO's current priorities in this domain.

Today, UNESCO's activities in higher education are located near the sub-programme entitled *Building Learning Societies*. Action is focused on promoting diversity and co-operation and on responding to the opportunities and challenges generated by globalization and its impact on education. However, this present vision has been shaped by the outcomes of the 1998 World Conference on Higher Education (WCHE). This book is timely because it coincides with the five-year evaluation of the WCHE convened by UNESCO in 2003, to address the rapid and far-reaching changes that have occurred in the intervening years as a result of accelerating globalization and its singularly complex impact on sustainable human development.

The WCHE constituted a worldwide debate on major issues facing the sector in the years ahead, namely *access on merit, enhanced management of systems and institutions* and *closer links with the world of work*. The debate was organized around four key areas requiring renovation and innovation: *quality, management and financing, relevance* and *international co-operation*. As these domains merit ongoing analysis, it is no surprise that they figure prominently in this new book since they remain cornerstones of sound higher education systems and institutions in every region of the world. However, the influence of globalization on these domains has resulted in a new set of challenges for which bold and creative solutions are required.

The WCHE links the past to the present for two reasons. Firstly, it flagged certain emerging issues that have now moved centre stage in the intervening half decade during which the world has entered the era of the 'Knowledge Society' and its critical component, the 'Knowledge Economy'. In this regard, higher education has become recognized as the catalyst for social and economic progress because this sector creates, disseminates and applies all forms of knowledge. In this evolving context where the role of advanced human capital has gained critical ground, developing and transition countries are facing fresh challenges and high risks as they struggle to compete in an increasingly sophisticated global economy. The advent of the Knowledge Society has affected the development agenda of each and every nation in multiple ways. Consequently, there is serious pressure on each country to ensure that the state's responsibility is to support higher education institutions so that they may effectively respond to the escalating pace of social change. In a world where education has become borderless, countries must learn to operate in dual mode because national issues assume global ramifications. The loss of local capacity via the Brain Drain, the need for quality assurance frameworks at national and international levels, the urgency for codes of conduct to regulate educational services and to protect intellectual property rights, and the dangers of the growing digital divide are some of the pressing problems for which sound yet adaptable solutions are vital.

Secondly, perhaps the most forward-looking feature of the WCHE was its involvement of all relevant stakeholders in the deliberations. As a result, the principal outcomes, notably the *World Declaration* and the *Framework for Priority Action and Development,* gained a special legitimacy because they were adopted by the many and diverse publics represented amongst the 5000 participants inter alia Member States, policy-makers, academics, teachers and researchers, students, parliamentarians, inter-governmental and non-governmental organizations and the business community. Over the past five years, in many social, economic and cultural contexts, there has been growing recognition of the fact that the scale and complexity of current challenges cannot be adequately resolved by governments alone. Thus, there is a new emphasis on partnership and its potential for stimulating fresh and effective action because the actors involved are strongly motivated to co-operate and to benefit from the diverse expertise brought to such alliances. The synergy accruing from these linking arrangements is considered as a source of creativity, experimentation and advancement. The principle of partnership received special attention from the United Nations during the preparations for the Third Millennium. In 1999, the *Global Compact* invited the business community to become a full partner in seeking solutions to development issues. In 2000, the *Millennium Goals* included the forging of global partnerships as a *sine qua non* for social progress in the new century. In 2003, the UN established a *High Level Panel on Civil Society* in acknowledgement of the fact that social decision-making must involve multiple and diverse stakeholders. This spirit of solidarity is already well known in higher education through modalities such as academic networking, outreach to industry and town-gown relations. These strategies need to be adopted on a global scale so that the many beneficiaries of higher education can bring their optimal contribution to the development of the sector at a time of global change.

As the first decade of the 21st century unfolds, the major issues in higher education, though perennial to some extent, now possess a radically different dimension due to the new context of globalization. This necessitates genuinely innovative approaches both to reflection and to co-operation modalities by policy-makers, by the academic community and by society at large. The contributors to this book, who are well aware of these new imperatives, bring their rich experience to this latest phase of enquiry and development-oriented action. In assembling these diverse views on higher education, the SRHE is supporting UNESCO's commitment to peace and development in an era of globalization, which is the unifying theme of its current Medium Term Strategy (2002–7).

Mary-Louise Kearney
UNESCO

Preface

This volume is the result of two streams of development in which the editor has been involved in her capacity as Director of the Society for Research into Higher Education.

The first began with the Annual Conference of the Society held at the University of Lancaster in December 1998 on the theme of 'The Globalization of Higher Education'. Peter Scott edited a volume of precedings, which all delegates received. The book has remained a useful compilation of thinking on the topic, and is frequently cited by the authors of the present volume.

The second theme to emerge was that of higher education reform, and the British Council approached the Director of SRHE to ask if she would put together an international conference on the topic. The Society was fortunate in having a number of leading scholars as members, who were able to speak with authority on such topics as funding, access and participation, governance, management and quality.

It was following this week-long seminar held in February 1999 that the editor was invited by John Skelton, the then owner of Open University Press, to consider editing a volume on the topic of higher education reform. The idea was accepted, and was metamorphosed into a volume that would include a number of international contributors, so that a wide range of responses to higher education reform could be garnered.

At this point, the ideas around the concepts related to globalization came to the fore, and the Society decided, in tandem with the Association of Commonwealth Universities and the Education Policy Unit of the University of the Western Cape, to mount a major international conference in South Africa in March 2001 on the theme of 'Globalization and Higher Education: views from the South'. The conference proved to be an exciting intellectual event which attracted some 350 delegates and provided a platform for several of the world's leading researchers in higher education. Support was provided by UNESCO, the World Bank, the UK Department for International Development, the Anglo-American Corporation and several other trusts to enable bursaries to be provided for those from less developed countries to attend. All the higher education institutions in the region contributed actively to the conference. Two publications have appeared relating to that conference: *SRHE International News*, November 2001, which is a collection of some keynote addresses and some papers; and the Proceedings of the Conference also published by the Society, which contains edited transcripts of the symposia presented at the conference, with the keynotes.

The interest in the topic of globalization has continued unabated. Indeed, a further major international conference is planned in 2005. The international conference and its publications have necessarily concentrated on the effects on less developed countries. It seemed proper that, alongside these publications, there should also be discussion on the effects of globalization on developed countries.

The present volume therefore seeks to examine higher education reform in the light of globalization, concentrating mainly on the developed countries, but with one of the case studies drawn from South Africa. The issues are global; the case studies, of Australia and South Africa, explore in some detail how the broad issues are being applied in particular situations.

It is the hope of the Editor that you will find this a stimulating and enjoyable volume.

Heather Eggins
London
June 2003

Acknowledgements

I wish to thank my many friends and colleagues who have given me inestimable support, over several years, in the production of this book. Their continuing encouragement was much appreciated when the volume had to be delayed because of surgery.

Particular mention should be made of the members of the Council of the Society for Research into Higher Education, its Fellows and its past President, Sir William Taylor. Valued assistance has also been received from my colleagues at the University of Strathclyde, for which I remain most grateful.

Much thanks, as ever, is due to the support of my family, my husband and daughter, who remain encouraging and helpful, however trying the circumstances.

I would like to thank Agnieszka Trzcinska, whose painstaking work on the bibliography and help with the preparation of the text has been much appreciated.

Particular thanks go to Rachel Johnson, in relation to Rosemary Deem's chapter, who not only collected a great deal of the data used here but whose paper on 'Tales of Management and Change in UK Universities', presented to the Consortium of European Education Researchers meeting at Bowness on Windermere in September 2000, was invaluable in writing this account. Thanks also to the rest of the research team: Sam Hillyard, Mike Reed, Oliver Fulton and Stephen Watson, as well as Heidi Edmundson, project administrator, and the sixteen universities where much of the research was conducted.

Finally, I would like to thank my contributors, who have waited patiently for the volume to be finalized, and have dealt patiently with me when I harried them. I have enjoyed their company in the making of this volume.

1

Globalization and reform: necessary conjunctions in higher education

Heather Eggins

The last ten years has seen the issue of globalization moving from one in which it was incumbent to prove that there was such a phenomenon as globalization (Castells 1996; Giddens 2001) to a situation where there is broad acceptance that there has been a fundamental change in the environment in which humanity finds itself, in comparison with the world of our ancestors.

Globalization, as Giddens puts it 'is a shift in our very life circumstances; it is the way we now live' (Giddens 1990). Changes in those life circumstances are far-reaching, comprehensive and move at a faster pace. Indeed the speed of change is closely allied to the growth of communications. Developments in information and communication technologies have been exponential: it seems extraordinary to consider how basic and crude were the transatlantic cables in place before the 1950s, that the first radio transmission by satellite took place in 1962 and that now the numbers using the Internet exceed 70 million.

Sociologists perceive globalization in terms of flows of people and services, both globally and locally (Giddens 1990; Castells 1996). Modern communication technology enables people to transcend space with ease. At points the flows bring about convergence; at points they diverge. This makes for an uneven process that can bring about on the one hand growing global inequality (Kraak 2000), and on the other a capacity for harmonization. Castells (2000) argues that the new social forms of space and time, 'space of flows' and 'timeless time', coexist with traditional forms of space and time, setting up a 'new economy' in which the global networks of the information society are key concepts.

The effects have been considerable, for society at large, and for higher education in particular. There have been undoubted advantages. Joseph Stiglitz, writing in his influential book, *Globalization and its Discontents* (2002) says:

> Globalization has brought huge benefits – East Asia's success was based on globalization, especially on the opportunities for trade, and

increased access to markets and technology. Globalization has brought better health, as well as an active global civil society fighting for more democracy and greater social justice.

(Stiglitz 2002: 214)

Much of the earlier debate, during the 1990s, concentrated on the economic aspects of globalization, aspects which are referred to by a number of authors in this volume (Sporn, Marginson, Johnstone, Subotzky). Marginson's case study in particular, of developments in Australian higher education during this period, traces how the neo-liberal trends associated with globalization were called into play in Australian policy-making. Sporn argues that the effects of globalization on Europe can be mainly discerned in two respects: the introduction of the market, and the withdrawal of the state. 'The introduction of a common currency, the Euro, has accelerated the need for standards. Accordingly, state budgets have to meet certain requirements regarding deficits and spending, unemployment has to be low, and inflation has to be under control' (Sporn's chapter, p. 117). Thus, within Europe, the economic effects of the creation of the European Union, itself a response to the new levels of interdependence among peoples created by globalization, have clearly brought about major change.

A number of commentators have pointed out that the trends commonly associated with globalization, such as the promotion of free trade, competition and the ascendancy of market forces, can be viewed as threats to the role of the nation state (Guillen 2001). Indeed Stiglitz castigates the IMF for forcing on developing countries a particular view of economics – 'market fundamentalism' – which has in some cases brought disaster, e.g. Argentina.

However, he argues that the discontents caused by this market approach to globalization can be overcome. Globalization is a fact of life from which we cannot retreat. His argument is that 'globalization can be reshaped to realise its potential for good' (Stiglitz 2002: 215). He argues that the role of government is crucial in that 'government can, and has, played an essential role not only in mitigating [. . .] market failures but also in ensuring social justice' (Stiglitz 2002: 218).

The notion of social cohesion as a necessity in a nation if its economy is to function is emphasized. Stiglitz argues that in the most successful countries, such as the United States and East Asia, 'governments provided a high-quality education for all and furnished much of the infrastructure'. He also stresses the importance of openness and transparency, thereby enabling citizens to understand government policy decisions and hence become more involved in those decisions.

The reforms carried out at the World Bank are discussed, and Stiglitz notes with approval that a change of philosophy has occurred. The Bank recognized that successful development 'came not just from promoting primary education but also from establishing a strong technological basis, which included support for advanced training. It is possible to promote equality and rapid growth at the same time' (Stiglitz 2002: 241).

The issues for higher education

Higher education, as a consequence, has moved from a peripheral to a central position in the responses of governments to globalization; it is a key factor in the developing countries, evidenced by the World Bank's 'Task Force Report on Higher Education in Developing Countries' (2000); it is undoubtedly viewed as crucial to the developed countries, as illustrated in a number of chapters in this book (Lillie, Sporn, Marginson *et al.*).

Peter Scott (writing in *The Globalization of Higher Education*) pointed out that 'all universities are subject to the same processes of globalization – partly as objects, victims even, of these processes, but partly as subjects or key agents of globalization' (Scott 1998b: 122). They are positioned within national systems 'locked into national contexts' and the majority are still state institutions. Yet globalization 'is inescapably bound up with the emergence of a knowledge society that trades in symbolic goods, worldwide brands, images-as-commodities and scientific know-how' (Scott 1998b: 127). The tensions generated by such a dichotomy necessarily lead to change and reform. Governments are moved to 'steer' higher education in the hope of repositioning it to increase effectiveness and efficiency (El Khawas, Lillie, Marginson). University Councils bring about changes in governance to meet the same ends (Deem).

Marijk van der Wende, in her inaugural address entitled 'Higher Education Globally: towards new frameworks for research and policy', suggested that there are four rationales for globalization, each of which resonates in higher education. These four, namely the economic rationale, the political rationale, the academic rationale and the cultural rationale, provide a useful framework for exploring the different ways in which globalization has engendered reforms in the higher education sector.

The economic rationale

The economic rationale, different aspects of which are considered by a number of authors (Marginson, Johnstone, Morey, Sporn *et al.*) was particularly dominant in the 1990s. The emphasis on financial-economic issues has been marked. The cutbacks in public funding to universities have forced much consideration of where new sources of funding are to be found.

Johnstone and Shroff-Mehta offer a detailed discussion of international tuition and financial assistance policies. The 'cost sharing' of higher education with students and parents contributing growing sums to their own or their children's education is shown to be a worldwide phenomenon. The range of methods employed may vary from country to country – for example, in Australia, China, USA – but the notion of buying into what is seen by many as a private good now has universal acceptance.

Considerable interest has been shown by government in support of the claim that a graduate education brings with it enhanced earning power, but the drivers from government for an expansion of the higher education systems (c.f. Marginson) stem much more from a concern to be economically competitive in international terms. In 'The Future of Higher Education', published by the UK Department for Education and Skills (2003), it is clear that 'a higher education sector which meets the needs of the economy in terms of trained people, research, and technology transfer' (2003: 21) is a central concern.

In line with this the UK government has announced a 50 per cent participation target for young people aged 18–30 in England by 2010. However, as Ewart Keep's work has shown (Keep 2003), there is no proven direct correlation between numbers of graduates and economic success. Charles Clarke, Secretary of State for Education and Skills, claimed 'demand for graduates is very strong, and research shows that 80% of the 1.7 million new jobs which are expected to be created by the end of the decade will be in occupations which normally recruit those with higher education qualifications' (2003). Labour market studies, however, do not necessarily bear out that assertion. There will certainly be a demand for more skilled workers at technician level (DfES 2001) but forecast of future graduate demands are not so certain (Keep 2003).

Other researchers, however, point out that globalization has fostered a new typology of graduate jobs (Elias and Purcell 2003). Within the UK alone there is now a wider range of occupations and new occupations that can absorb graduates, and although a number may be underemployed at the inception of their careers, almost all are assimilated into the labour market within seven years. The three characteristics of graduates, namely expertise, strategic skills and negotiating/interpersonal skills can arguably be advantageous throughout the labour market. Kate Purcell noted that 'there is little evidence to support the argument that there is an oversupply of graduates. Over the past 25 years the number of jobs which can accommodate graduates has increased by three million. Forecasts suggest this trend will continue' (Elias and Purcell 2003).

The economic imperative continues to drive governments to believe that more graduates with more knowledge and skills will make for more wealth creation in the country (De Corte 2003). Charles Clarke, in the foreword to *The Future of Higher Education*, urged his readers 'to make better progress in harnessing knowledge to wealth creation' (Clarke 2003). Each of the UK's research councils is charged with wealth creation. The vision of a competitive society whose innovative and creative researchers place the country high on the list of achievers recurs regularly in government documents, as it does in those of other countries (cf. Marginson, Chapter 9). With the growth of emphasis on the market has come a new interest in the universities to collaborate closely with business. In Britain there are a considerable number of courses specifically designed to meet the needs of a particular company or group of companies, and a majority of these (58 per cent) are offered as bespoke courses at company premises.

The Higher Education-Business Interaction Survey (HEFCE, 2001) showed that 51 per cent of universities attached high priority to the economic development of their region (87 per cent of the new universities did so) and all had well-developed business strategies. It is notable that the new universities are particularly attuned to fostering relationships with business: almost half of these institutions have more than 50 per cent business representation on their governing bodies.

One could argue also that the way in which universities are now managed owes much to the influence of business. Managerialism is mentioned by other contributors, Sporn, for example, and is considered in detail in Rosemary Deem's chapter. She notes that 'much of what was found appears to have initially been introduced from outside, principally by government policy agendas and funding regimes'.

The academic rationale

The academic rationale cannot be entirely divorced from the desire to make money for the university from international endeavours. Internationalization was perceived, from the 1980s, as a means of enhancing the quality of education and research. The 'brain drain' of top academics from one country to another, in search of optimum conditions for their research, and improved economic reward, is still with us. The worry now is that less developed countries may lose their leading intellectuals to developed countries, with potentially massive damage to their own systems.

Strategic international alliances between universities in different countries are referred to by several chapter authors. International research projects, international degree offerings, international exchange of academic staff and students, has become commonplace. The flows of people and ideas around the world are seen as generating additional institutional and national income (c.f. Marginson, Sporn).

However, the dominance of English worldwide, particularly promoted by the Internet, has meant that, within Europe at least, the flows of students have been towards the UK rather than out from it. Increasingly, indeed, English is used as a second language for university teaching, thus enabling countries such as the Netherlands and Denmark to attract students from Asia and elsewhere to study in particular colleges.

Some would argue that foreign students act as 'ambassadors for their country'. Although this assertion might well be questioned, there is no doubt that future leaders of less developed countries develop strong ties with the country where they studied as graduates. That can be very valuable, thirty years down the line.

Internationalization, considered in detail by Peter Scott (1998b), is undoubtedly of strategic importance. It has been developed further by the growth of the Internet. The capacity of academics to access information from all points of the globe in pursuing their own research and preparing their own teaching is a recent and much appreciated boon.

The cultural rationale

The cultural rationale is a recurring theme in many of the chapters. At one end of the spectrum, critics of the way in which globalization has been managed point to the cultural change in institutions where one sees a 'tightly integrated regime of managerial discipline and control' (Deem's chapter, p. 55) alongside a loss of discretion and trust.

The new culture is all-encompassing: 'What is new is that current UK higher education policies ... increasingly privilege the modernization of public services and the sweeping away of old ways of doing things' (Deem's chapter, p. 55). A related characteristic is the 'continuous monitoring and audit of performance and quality' (Deem's chapter, p. 55). This is explored in considerable detail in the chapters by Kezar and El Khawas and Lillie. Kezar and El Khawas see performance currently being used in the States 'as a tool for external review of universities' (Kezar and El Khawas chapter, p. 85). They chart the rise in pressure on accrediting agencies 'to examine effectiveness and efficiency as important goals'. Student outcomes are seen 'as a hallmark of quality', 'value added' is emphasized, and institutions are expected to prove that they are becoming more effective. Performance goals are set, and these may include in some States improved graduation rates for low income and minority students as well as data on employment rates and employer feedback.

Elisabeth Lillie considers quality assurance practices throughout Europe in the light of the creation of a European space for higher education, as set out in the Bologna Declaration (June 1999). Here too is surveyed a movement towards the maintenance of standards, often brought about by a shift from self-regulation to 'a somewhat greater measure of national control and conformity'. However, the writer points out the 'strong sense of the importance of transparency and the adherence to generally understood national norms'. The argument is that the review process itself leads to greater transparency, which is to be welcomed. The cultural shift from the secrecy of earlier days is marked.

A second characteristic is the enhancement of quality and sharing of good practice between institutions, which can meet the demands of governments for information and the many stakeholders – students, employers, parents, government – who are interested in the results. One can discern that 'a certain harmonisation is being effected as Europeans engage in a process of interaction and inter-learning'. Problems still exist, but there appears to be a willingness to work positively in the spirit of the Declaration. As such, Stiglitz would argue that this indicates the constructive aspect of globalization where cooperation is valued.

Several authors, for example Taylor, Morey, Deem and Lillie, recognize that academic morale is low in a number of countries. Taylor argues that this might be owing partially to 'the erosion of trust' engendered by the growing bureaucratization that the institution is caught up in.

William Taylor welcomes the emphasis now laid on effective teaching and the focus on the experience of the students. For him the academic is still central to the success of the enterprise: 'official interventions cannot succeed unless they come to be "owned" by those whose practice they are intended to improve. The ultimate safeguard of academic standards is still the conscience of the individual teacher.'

Barbara Sporn touches on a related, important topic, that of academic freedom. Philip Altbach (2001) has noted that a major cultural swift being evidenced worldwide is the whittling away of the individual academic's rights to pursue their research without fear or favour. The need to maintain academic freedom is paramount.

The demand for access to higher education and to participation in it is a characteristic of the cultural rationale. The growth in demand in recent years has been phenomenal. A report presented to the Universitas 21 Global Experience Conference in October 2002 in Singapore claimed 'an estimate of 100 million qualified students who will not be able to find places in conventional universities by the year 2010, even assuming a 40% growth in those universities'. (The Universitas 21 group is itself a collaborative group of universities from all over the world whose formation owes much to globalization.) The demand for higher education is fuelled by the Internet, by the ways in which the knowledge economy works, and by the urging of governments who see it as essential to produce a highly skilled workforce to meet the needs of the international labour market.

One other aspect of the cultural rationale is important: that of gender. Women have responded to the opportunity to study: indeed, over half of the students in many developed countries are now female. Likewise those women who have chosen career paths in academia have found themselves in a traditional environment where breaking through the glass ceiling was a daunting prospect. Studies on the problems faced by such women are numerous (Glazer-Raymo 1999; Eggins 1997).

The global imperative is towards equity and inclusiveness. The aspirations of women sit squarely in the globalization debate. Carmen Luke, writing in *Globalization and Women in Academia* (2001), considers the cases of women academics in Singapore, Hong Kong, Thailand and Malaysia. She explores the sociocultural and political issues related to women and education in Southeast Asia and notes women's under-representation in higher education management: 'Exclusion from powerful senior networks', she argues, 'limits women's visibility and access to crucial information, influential alliances, and promotional prospects' (Luke 2001: 233).

However, governments are beginning to be supportive of studies in this area. An interesting research project on 'Gender Equity in Higher Education' was launched in the UK in May 2003. The aim of the study, which involves Nigeria, Uganda, Tanzania, Sri Lanka and South Africa, is to research the action that the universities in the case study are taking with regard to gender equity. Three categories will be examined: access, for example women entering non-traditional subject areas; staff development, for example women into management programmes; and curriculum transformation, for example gender mainstreaming projects. The project will also be considering social processes and the effects gender equity strategies have had on organizational development and institutional strengthening. What is noteworthy about the project is that it is the first such to be funded by the UK Department for International Development (DFID), along with the Carnegie Corporation of New York.

The political rationale

Marijk van der Wende (2002) writes that the political rationale is a 'response to support the process of reconstruction, nation-building and economic and democratic reform through co-operation, capacity building, knowledge transfer and the education of a local intellectual cohort to modern and international standards' (Van der Wende: 33).

The case studies by Simon Marginson and by George Subotzky examine in some detail the political rationale at work in Australia and in South Africa. Both consider the government's efforts to 'steer' higher education in their respective countries. The theme is echoed in a number of other chapters, (for example Taylor, Kezar and El Khawas). The ways in which steering is undertaken differ in detail, but the overall aim is the same. The response to globalization has been and continues to be perceived in a drive by government to reform the national higher education system to deliver the ends they crave (Kogan and Hanney 2000; Marginson and Considine 2000). Subotzky's study shows that change takes place despite rather than because of government interventions. The assumption that large-scale planning can produce intended outcomes cannot always be relied upon.

Conclusion

Globalization is itself a complex force that affects all aspects of our global and national education systems. On the one hand is the pull towards cooperation, social cohesion, social harmony, transparency, equity and to enabling greater numbers to participate in higher education. On the other hand are the financial issues, the neo-liberal agenda that calls for competition, free trade, the dominance of the market. The flows of change move first in one direction, then in another: equity, inequality; convergence, divergence; change, non-change; inclusion, exclusion; the global, the local. The recognition that higher education reforms are necessarily intertwined with the effects of globalization may enable us to understand more clearly the higher education systems and their relationship to society as a whole.

Part 1

The issues

2

Steering change in tertiary education

William Taylor

The tertiary stage

In the last hundred years first primary and then secondary education have became universal in the industrially developed world. Before the 21st century is many years old, we can expect the same to become true of tertiary education, seen as a stage of post-secondary provision that embraces work hitherto defined as higher and further education, vocational training and adult education.

The process whereby this will come about will almost certainly be appropriated by politicians and policy-makers as a 'reform'. But in large part it will be the consequence of policies already in place and trends already under way. Despite the form of continuing growth being problematic – for example the balance of degree and sub-degree programmes – high levels of participation in tertiary education achieved as a result of recent expansion are unlikely to be reversed.

This still leaves issues to resolve and choices to be made of a kind that constitute the stuff of 'reform'. In particular, attempts to plan and to control the internal diversity and institutional differentiation that will best serve the purposes of universal tertiary education, and to reconcile the interests concerned, are likely to give rise to strenuous political and professional debate.

Although the philosophy and shape of primary education have changed over time – the impact in many countries of 'progressive' ideas is one of the best documented of such changes (Rohrs and Lenhart 1995; Darling 1994; Herbst 1997) – its content and scope have remained remarkably uniform (Tyack and Cuban 1995; Hampel *et al.* 1996). Primary education is neither diversified nor differentiated.

It was not until the second half of the 20th century that the term 'secondary education' was used to describe a *stage* of schooling in which a whole age group participated. Earlier forms of education defined as 'secondary' had been selective in intake and elitist in orientation. When universal secondary education arrived it was marked in most countries (although not all) by differentiation of both curricula and institutions. The social and economic factors that played a part in this differentiation, and its consequences for individual life chances, have been actively debated for decades (Simon 1994; Paris 1995).

Universal participation moves this debate into the tertiary sphere. Governments need to decide how far they can and should influence the scale and the shape of tertiary participation. The questions to be asked and answered are not about growth or stability but about what types of courses and qualifications will best satisfy social demand, facilitate economic development, and minimize the 'risk to social structure and cohesion ... if a significant proportion of the population is excluded or discouraged from participation in a stage of education which clearly confers benefits' (OECD 1997: 8).

The social and economic context of change

Education policy both reflects and reinforces national values, beliefs and purposes. Yet it is arguable that what unites developed countries is more important than the historical, cultural and social differences among them. In their thinking and approach to problems, tertiary education policy-makers often have more in common with their cross-border counterparts than with fellow nationals from outside their speciality.

Most developed countries are multi-party democracies. Their cultural and linguistic pluralism is sometimes more strongly entrenched in legislation than in habit, but is nonetheless of growing importance in the social experience of citizens, especially in urban areas. In a manner consistent with their economic structures, social values tend towards individualism, although strong internal communities and identities – both regional and national – persist. In recent years such identities have shown signs of becoming more significant factors in economic and social policy.

Within the market economies of developed countries competition is encouraged, monopoly and oligopoly frowned upon and, to varying extents, legislated against. All are seeking to improve their competitive position in regional and world markets and committed to the economic growth on which healthy capitalism depends, although exposed to expressions of increasing concern among their populations and international organizations about environmental hazards.

Within economically advanced countries, significant inequalities persist in income, housing, quality of life, health, life expectancy and access to education. While changes in employment patterns, in social structure and the allocation of esteem make simple longitudinal comparisons unreliable, such inequalities have proved resistant to ameliorative measures put in place over the past four decades (Archer *et al.* 2003).

A commitment to reducing economic and social inequality is shared by political parties of very different persuasions. The objective of greater equity features in the tertiary education mission statements of many of them, and is especially prominent in those of the left and centre, although as Papadopoulos (1994) shows, its importance as a policy imperative has varied over time. There remains much disagreement as to how equity might best be achieved and the price it might exact in terms of individual liberty and control over private assets.

Current political, social and economic conditions give the state an important but by no means hegemonic role in setting objectives and regulating the conduct of individuals, corporations and organizations in the direction of justice, fairness and efficiency. Legislation exists in most countries to ensure equal treatment before the law and within employment of both men and women and of members of minority ethnic and linguistic groups, although this is not always easy to enforce.

Considerable scope remains for differences of opinion about core values, how they might best be served, the roles of central, regional and local government and the costs and benefits of institutional autonomy.

Until recently, makers of educational policy talked mainly to each other. If in the future nearly everyone will be participating in tertiary education in some way, and few aspects of the economy and of society will be unaffected by its successes and its failures, then the range of stakeholders wishing to participate in policy discussions will widen. Tertiary education policy statements inevitably have little to say about many issues that affect the quality of life of the populations they serve, such as (to pick out a few at random) national and regional identity, immigration, environmental damage, drugs, conflict resolution, inter-generational relations, over-crowded roads and food safety. Nonetheless, the work of tertiary institutions has both immediate and long-term relevance to these and to many other problems. In the United Kingdom, the term 'joined-up thinking' is being used to characterize attempts to achieve greater integration between educational, social and economic policies.

Reconciling equality and quality

Trow's (1989) categorization, rooted in US experience, of the prodigious expansion of student numbers and institutions that has taken place since the Second World War, as a movement from elite to mass and then to universal higher education, has been widely used in discussions of tertiary growth in other industrialized countries. Age participation ratios in the 1950s and 1960s in the United States were not matched elsewhere until a decade or more later. In many countries, the most rapid phase of expansion has been since the end of the 1980s. With enrolment ratios for full-time undergraduate study already in the order of 30 to 40 per cent, and overall enrolment in all kinds of full and part time, pre- and post-work experience tertiary education in excess of 65 per cent, some countries can claim that they are already well on the way to universal participation.

Although the concept of tertiary education is not new, its current scope is both more inclusive and more broadly defined than in the past. In so far as a tertiary sector could have been said to exist, it was dominated by the universities. In those aspects of their work in which they competed directly with the universities, the institutions that had developed in the 1960s and early 1970s – polytechnics, fachhochschulen, regional colleges and their like – were often less successful in recruiting the ablest students. Their role did not customarily include research. Generally, but not universally, their graduates went into less prestigious employment with poorer long-term earnings potential. Colleges teaching post-secondary qualifications below the level of the degree or diploma were in many instances not regarded as being within the orbit of tertiary education at all – terms such as 'further education' and 'continuing education' were, and still are, employed. Post-secondary education was differentiated rather than diversified. And with differentiation went hierarchy.

Hierarchy is characteristic of all forms of social organization (Wright 1994). To recognize this does not imply insensitivity to the enormous importance of culture, or despair concerning the possibilities of social change. The forms that hierarchy takes are responsive to political and administrative intervention. What matters is not the fact of hierarchy but ensuring that its forms are consistent with and sustain the values of pluralist democracies.

Today's slogan of choice is *diversity*. Higher education has either been redefined to embrace a broader range of institutions and programmes or abandoned in favour of a more all-embracing concept of life-long tertiary education. It is unsurprising that politicians and policy-makers played down the extent to which institutions, courses, curricula and outcomes have been differentiated. They have had good and honourable reasons for doing so. Among these have been:

- The desire to emphasize a sense of common citizenship in societies divided by social class, income differentials, life style and cultural origins. Strong institutional differentiation sharpens the sense of hierarchy and thus the possibility of conflict. Diversity, on the other hand, carries less negative political weight.
- The need to ensure that a larger proportion of the population than ever before have the means to acquire knowledge and skills relevant to types of work in which they are likely to succeed, without these means being felt to be inferior to the education provided by older, high-status institutions.
- The wish to meet the labour market needs of increasingly mobile and technological societies.
- Avoiding the appearance of institutionalizing differences in ability, potential and performance in political climates that dispute or deny concepts such as 'general intelligence'.
- The importance of maintaining a commitment to equality as a countervailing value to the de facto outcomes of individual and institutional competition.

- The desire to avoid conceding claims on public resources that arise exclusively from identification with traditional high-status institutions such as universities.
- Awareness of the substantial influence still exercised within political, social and economic networks by the alumni of elite institutions such as Oxford and Cambridge, the Grandes Écoles, and Ivy League universities in the US, and the need to channel this influence in socially beneficial ways.

As well as seeking to emphasize equal esteem for diverse institutions and outcomes, governments are also concerned with efficiency and effectiveness, with the best use of scarce public resources, with motivating individual and institutional effort. This has been seen to require overt and explicit identification of success and failure – course assessments, institutional ranking, even the naming and shaming of backsliders.

The apparent contradiction between equality and efficiency has been resolved by redefining 'quality'. Success and failure are not to be measured along a single hierarchical continuum, but in terms of 'fitness for purpose' (a phrase conveniently resonant of evolutionary rigour). Esteem is to be associated more with the extent to which such fitness is achieved, less with 'irrelevant' distinctions between purposes.

Growth and change

It is easy now to forget that a decade before the late 1980s expansion there was serious anxiety about the educational consequences of demographic decline. In the event, where it did occur, its effects were largely nullified by larger proportions of high school students qualifying for continuing study, stronger secondary transition ratios, additional demand for places from women, part-time students and post-graduates, and the perception that advanced qualifications conferred better employment and career opportunities.

The failure of the recruitment shortfall to materialize was partly a consequence of external factors, but also owed something to measures universities had already taken in its anticipation. External and internal forces, working together, produced a faster rate of growth than would otherwise have occurred. During periods of economic stringency in higher education in the late 1970s and 1980s, and in preparation for what they believed might be the lean years of demographic downturn, many higher education institutions looked for, and found, sources of finance other than the state. They became more entrepreneurial. They recruited larger numbers of overseas students and ceased to be sensitive about pricing their services at private sector rates.

The metaphor of the 'tipping point' has long been employed in studies of social and institutional change. Slow initial take-up, requiring much external effort, may eventually enable a point to be reached at which resistance is so reduced that adoption accelerates rapidly, perhaps even to the point of becoming universal. The metaphor offers a misleading representation, however, of conditions in which internal forces generated during earlier stages of a change process increase its speed and tendency to universality. Chaos theory, with its ideas of phase transition, critical states, self-similar patterns (in which at a certain stage sub-systems organize themselves in a manner similar to the whole) may yield further useful metaphors for understanding change in higher education. In particular, it may be necessary to look more closely at how the development and implementation of tertiary education policies relate to the internal dynamics of institutions.

Studies of imperfections in information flow within hierarchical systems suggest that a fifth or a quarter of all 'commands' are ignored, misunderstood or misapplied (Buchanan 1997). Work of this kind may provide fruitful insights about why, for example, some governments have persistently failed to control university wastage and drop-out or to reduce the time that students take to obtain their diploma or degree. Legislation or administrative fiat may decree open entry, but the internal dynamic of academic life is highly selective. If selection cannot be applied on entry, academics themselves can make sure that in the interests of quality, it operates within the courses and programmes for which they retain most of the responsibility.

Much of the most recent growth has taken place within an institutional framework only shaped during the 1960s and 1970s. There is today little enthusiasm among academics for radical structural reform (some might ask if there ever was). Yet a dynamic capitalism encourages entrepreneurial stances, rewards innovators, celebrates change. Capitalist economies need growth, and growth means change. Within tertiary education, the fact that change benefits some people more than others affects its pace and direction. It is also reflected in the tensions that exist in nearly every country between, on the one side, academics and their organizations and, on the other, the politicians who vote funds and administrators who distribute them.

In pursuit of economically and socially advantageous goals, current policy seeks to harness the self-interest of diverse constituencies. To conceptualize the whole of post-school education in terms of a 'tertiary system', without significant institutional re-ordering, benefits hitherto 'less noble' institutions and teachers of lower-status courses without seriously threatening those who have traditionally occupied the commanding heights of university higher education. Less favourable staff–student ratios may be especially unwelcome to the latter, but if they occur within a context of overall growth, the creation of more job and promotion opportunities may compensate for having more students to teach.

In devising future policy, attention has to be paid to how the internal dynamics of tertiary education systems, and of their institutional microsystems, are likely to support or to subvert national prescriptions. National governments are likely to find it helpful to continue playing down the hierarchical characteristics of tertiary systems. Unified nomenclature (as when in Australia the Colleges of Advanced Education and in England the polytechnics all became universities); a common basis of 'ownership' (as in New Zealand); common funding formulae; similar entry requirements – all these promote a sense of institutional and outcome equality that reflects long-standing aspiration rather than present reality.

This is not to suggest that governments are acting dishonestly or that institutions and academics are solely concerned with their own benefit at the expense of the general good. It is to argue that if they are to succeed, tertiary policies need to take greater account of the internal dynamics of academic systems and institutions, seeking to enlist the latter in support of policy objectives rather than encourage defensive action that will subvert these objectives.

If the libraries, laboratories and medical schools of elite universities generate outcomes that benefit the health and well-being of the population as a whole and it can be shown that such outcomes are unlikely to be produced as economically and efficiently by other means, the elite status of these institutions is justified. Real life is, of course, never so simple. Claims to superior conditions or better funding or more favourable staff–student ratios, based on the utilitarian principle that such privilege will ensure the greatest good of the greatest number, are difficult to establish and easy to challenge.

While most of the hierarchies that feature in tertiary education have some rational justification, others do not. The latter are sometimes the hardest to change. Discussions about tertiary education tend to focus on its higher echelons, usually research-intensive universities and other high-status institutions such as the Grandes Écoles in France, specialist technical and scientific institutions in other countries that serve a national and international clientele, and some of the more prestigious liberal arts colleges in the United States. The literature of tertiary education focuses heavily on the universities. It contains far fewer works about other institutions that have and will continue to play a major role in universalizing tertiary provision.

The reasons for this imbalance are obvious enough. However valuable it may be to talk and to write about tertiary education as embracing all the many forms of post-secondary education now available, there is still little sense on the part of administrative and academic staff in being part of a single system. Different types of institutions are subject to separate funding, governance and administrative arrangements. There is no uniformity in salaries and conditions of service. Even where institutions such as colleges of advanced education and polytechnics have been redesignated universities, teachers have remained members of separate trade unions and professional organizations. The proportion of part-time students and those from disadvantaged backgrounds is far smaller in some institutions than in others. Cultural identities ('the idea of a university', 'the technical tradition') remain distinctive.

Differences that owe more to history than to current policy are not invariably dysfunctional. Policy-makers with a strong commitment to egalitarian values often deplore the seemingly conservative selection practices of high-status institutions. But where such status rests upon high academic standards and research reputation, care has to be taken to ensure that these are not undermined by more liberal admissions.

The diversity of current tertiary provision means no simple answer is possible to the question of the direction and scale of further growth. The Higher Education Funding Council for England has identified six factors that might increase student demand (quoted in Goddard 2001):

- improved educational attainments on the part of secondary school leavers
- population increase within social classes with currently high rates of participation
- greater diversification of routes into higher education
- employment prospects
- a perceived increase in the rates of return to individuals of higher qualifications
- success in policy initiatives designed to widen participation.

Not all such factors are within the control of policy-makers. The provision of places is seldom driven by careful analysis of employer and societal demand, which the organization and content of courses then aims to fulfil. In practice, demand tends to be driven by students' perceptions of their own interests and needs. But students are not always well informed about whether particular courses will be satisfying in these respects. Those who advise them are seldom able to predict the state of job markets three, four or five years hence.

It is sometimes suggested a time will be reached when the economic, social and political benefits of extending post-secondary opportunities will fall below the direct and indirect costs of such provision. The value added will not be enough to justify the expense. Whether this is so depends on the criteria that define 'value'. A broader conception of the economic benefits of tertiary education is emerging. Furthermore, if the current trend to give students and their families direct responsibility for at least a proportion of the costs of higher education continues, it is less likely that controversial policy decisions will be required. Individuals rather than governments will determine the point at which the benefits, however broadly conceived, exceed the costs of investing in higher education.

'Client-focused' change

The report of the OECD ten-country thematic review (OECD 1997) finds sufficient evidence of student-focused policies in member countries to adopt an explicitly 'client-centred' position. It is emphasized that 'client' is not synonymous with 'student'; there are other stakeholders whose interests must be considered – employers, social partners, and other economic and social actors with vital interests in tertiary outcomes. Furthermore, the institutional perspective should be respected. A balance of attention is required. Despite these caveats, the thematic review does differ from earlier OECD work in focusing on the individual student as the source of demand for tertiary education and as the principal 'customer' for the services it offers.

Client-centred or student-focused tertiary policies are an aspect of the market revolution that has taken place over the last two decades. The ideological features of this revolution are more marked in the United Kingdom, Australia and New Zealand than elsewhere, if only because of discontinuity with earlier welfare and public service traditions in these countries. In the United States and, to a varying extent among its Provinces, in Canada, the market has intensified values that were always prominent in their cultures and economic arrangements. In Germany, France and some other European countries, market concepts are still a relatively modest element in tertiary policy-making, and their importance is politically contested. There are a number of reasons why both national and cross-national policy statements and analyses have adopted this student-focused emphasis.

- The last three decades have seen major structural changes in tertiary education. Past experience does not encourage the view that changes in structure invariably produce outcomes universally perceived as beneficial. There appears to be neither need nor appetite for a further round of structural change. A focus on the experience of students emphasizes the importance of process rather than structure. There may be more scope for adjusting and developing relationships among existing institutions. In the UK, the many different forms of 'strategic alliance' have replaced mergers as a focus of attention. Such alliances are also being forged with universities in other countries through bodies such as the Global University Alliance, Scottish Knowledge, UNext, Universitas 21 and the Worldwide Universities Network.
- In a climate of reduced per capita public expenditure and lower direct taxes, funding problems consequent upon rapid growth direct attention to the possibility that a higher proportion of the costs of tertiary education should be a charge against the future earnings of individual student beneficiaries.
- If individuals are to contribute, immediately or prospectively, to the costs of tertiary education, they are likely to be more concerned about the quality of the teaching and learning opportunities they are offered. They will be less tolerant of poor lectures, tardy and unhelpful assessment, dilatory supervision and so on. Failures in these areas will cause discontent among what is now a much more substantial proportion of the electorate than when tertiary education catered principally for an intellectual and social elite. Governments are sensitive to such discontent, and to the inefficiencies and lack of effectiveness that cause it. In the interests of enhancing teaching quality, they support the work of bodies such as the UK Institute for Learning and Teaching (ILT) in accrediting individual teachers.

- To focus on students rather than institutions is consistent with an emphasis on the possibilities of progression between study levels and mobility between institutions.
- While a high proportion of tertiary institutions designated as universities undertake research as well as teaching, it is neither feasible nor affordable that every tertiary provider should have a research role. Within tertiary education as a whole the emphasis has to be on the opportunities for individual students to experience good teaching and to advance their own learning.
- Students of selective elite institutions readily assume responsibility for their own learning. Many of them succeed despite inadequacies in the teaching they experience. It cannot be assumed that this will be the case in a mass system. Students in tertiary education today are on average less able and less well prepared than smaller and more rigorously selected cohorts in the past. Staff–student ratios are also less favourable. All this underlines the importance of effective teaching and of student-centred emphases.
- At a time when students are being asked to shoulder greater financial burdens, it is advantageous to governments to present policies in terms of the benefits to the individual of the open access, flexible course structures, progression between levels and equality of esteem that characterize student-centred approaches.
- The conceptualization of tertiary education in market terms, which is an increasingly important (although by no means universal) feature of policy, puts a premium on student choice. For such choice to be exercised effectively, individuals need much better information about the range of opportunities open to them than was necessary in a smaller and more selective system, thus further emphasizing the student perspective.

The idea that tertiary provision should focus on students' needs is not uncontested. Many tertiary teachers remain to be convinced that students are in a position to exercise meaningful choices. Pigden (1997) suggests that

> . . . many students come to university with no very clear idea of what they want or what interests them. They do not have a determinate set of preferences that are already there to be catered to. Rather their preferences are shaped in the course of the education process . . . With consumer goods, the customer is always [or almost always] right. With education, it is often a case of 'Teacher knows best'.

Influence and control

Tertiary provision based upon client demand and a sense that university or college is 'the place to be' is in important senses out of control. Governments can, however, seek to influence the volume, speed and composition of change. How can such influence be exercised?

During the last two decades, governments have adopted a wider range of methods of maintaining control and exercising influence, among which the application of quality criteria to the distribution of resources is of central importance. The possibilities and forms of official intervention owe much to the history and statutory *basis* of tertiary education provision in the countries concerned. Interventions are obviously easier to plan (although by no means always easier to implement) in systems in which student numbers, institutional provision, finance and staffing are all determined centrally. But even here, tertiary education may not be all of a piece. Some of its forms – vocational and technical education at sub-degree and sub-diploma levels, adult and continuing education other than for formal qualifications, post-experience study for skilled operatives and qualified professionals – may be the responsibility of regional and local governments which are not always willing or able to dance to the tunes that national ministries and legislatures compose and attempt to conduct. Provision at some levels may depend to a greater or lesser extent on private finance – either directly through the training activities of employers, or indirectly by willingness to meet the substitution costs of staff who take advantage of government-funded opportunities. The legal status of universities, or long-standing and valued practice, may limit the extent to which government can dictate how the funds that it makes available are used.

Formal descriptions of constitutional and funding arrangements seldom convey an accurate impression of the distribution of power and influence and how this has changed over time. The subtleties and nuances of in-country arrangements defy ready generalization. Inevitable recourse to such generalization in international gatherings is a frequent source of frustration for participants.

The most ubiquitous and effective form of influence that government can exercise over tertiary education is the power of the purse. Although there are considerable variations between countries in the extent to which tertiary provision depends upon public funds, they remain everywhere the principal source of institutional support. Even where there are large numbers of private institutions, as in the United States and Japan, these depend to some extent on public funds in the form of student support, research grants and other specific disbursements. As expansion has progressed, so governments have become more sophisticated in the ways in which they use funding to support some trends and initiatives and to inhibit others. Funds have been linked not only to policies, but also to performance. The quality movement has been tightly harnessed to the process of resource distribution, nowhere more so than in the United Kingdom, where both research and teaching assessments have financial consequences for the institutions concerned (Turner 1996; Brennan 1997b; Davies 1997).

Given the multiplicity of sources from which tertiary institutions now derive support – education ministries and 'arms-reach' funding councils, other departments of government, employers, research foundations, students, entrepreneurial activities, the renting out of accommodation and so on – it is important for governments to identify those areas in which maximum policy leverage can be exerted, without direct involvement being sought in, or responsibility accepted for, every aspect of an institution's affairs. Thus per capita income may be separated from capital provision, with institutions themselves being obliged to find the latter by means of loans; teaching and research income may be treated separately, sometimes as a means of concentrating research in centres of excellence, sometimes in order to build up research capacity in hitherto underprovided locations or poorly resourced specialities; money may be moved from one part of the tertiary sector to another, in accordance with new policies and priorities; and per capita payments may be adjusted in order to encourage the provision of courses in shortage areas and to diminish the incentive to offer those where there is oversupply.

Student contributions to the cost of their tertiary education is an issue of such political salience that in some countries its discussion has overshadowed other aspects of tertiary finance. Such payments have been customary in the United States for a very long time, although there are many scholarships available to promising candidates who might not otherwise be able to afford continuing study. Within recent years a decision to require all students to make up-front, on-course or deferred contributions to their own tuition costs has been acted upon in a few countries, notably Australia and New Zealand. There have been fewer movements in this direction in Europe, except in the United Kingdom.

In principle, tuition fees offer a potent means of steering. It would be possible by setting differential fees to stimulate applications for courses leading to qualifications of which there are shortages in the labour market or for which there exists social demand. By rigorous means-testing a form of positive discrimination could be exercised in favour of candidates from underprivileged backgrounds. Charging fees might also encourage shorter courses and earlier completion, where government pressure has hitherto seldom been successful.

Against this has to be reckoned the time that it might take for signals about differential costs to reach school students whose subject choice at 13 or 16 may determine the programmes for which they are qualified at 18; the difficulty of medium- and long-term labour market forecasting; the outcry from those subject interests that would see themselves as marked down in value and importance; and the likelihood that factors other than cost could be predominant in affecting the flow of demand (UniversitiesUK 2001).

Equity considerations have broadened the debate about tuition fees to embrace all those costs that students incur in pursuing tertiary education – earnings foregone, living expenses and, given the wide age span of the student population, the support of dependants. Grants and bursaries are capable of being used by governments to influence demand in the same way as tuition fees; changes in existing arrangements tend to generate similar kinds of opposition. More hard evidence is needed about how the manipulation of fees and student support affects access and equity. A commitment to monitoring such effects needs to accompany any proposals that governments make to steer demand and take-up by these means. This is particularly important at a time when future growth is increasingly dependent upon increased levels of participation from groups that have not hitherto aspired to higher education. In England, government has for several years offered universities a funding premium for each student admitted from low income and socially deprived areas, based on postcode analysis. In line with the emphasis being placed on wider participation in higher education, it was proposed in 2003 that this 'postcode premium' increase from 5 per cent to 20 per cent.

The postcode premium increase was one element in a wide-ranging set of proposals, including abolition of the means-tested, flat-rate, fee contribution put in place following the 1997 Dearing Report on higher education. Instead, students would be able to obtain loans at favourable rates for both tuition and maintenance, which they would begin to repay after graduation when their annual income reached £15,000. The tuition contribution would be set at £1100 per year at 2003 rates, but universities would have discretion to charge fees of up to £3000 (Department for Education and Skills 2003). Students from poor families would be granted fee reliefs. Earlier, Scotland had replaced up-front fees by payments after graduation to a 'graduate endowment' scheme.

Although the fees issue has been raised in some other European countries, few governments are pursuing the matter with real vigour. Proposals to charge substantial fee contributions or full-cost fees generally encounter strenuous opposition.

Earlier efforts at rational planning sought to steer demand by a combination of work-force planning and student number quotas. The former still applies in some expensive to provide subjects where the majority of graduates enter public employment or are paid largely from public funds – medicine is the most obvious example. Quotas also continue where governments are responsible for an adequate supply of qualified people, such as teachers and nurses. In the majority of subject fields, the market now reigns. It is assumed that if too many Masters of Business Administration (or their equivalent) are produced, then salaries will fall, individual rates of return to the extra years of study will decline, demand for the qualification will slacken, and the number of courses will diminish. And vice versa. The qualifications market, however, is plagued by many imperfections in information flow. New courses can take many years to design, implement and produce their first graduates. Institutional inertia, academic tradition and uncertainties about current and future trends protect existing courses from closure. But since experience has shown that other means of steering can be just as prone to these difficulties, it is now more often left to tertiary institutions to decide how many students to admit to each programme – and to bear the financial consequences of their decisions.

It is no longer sensible to contrast centralized and decentralized patterns of control of tertiary education. There has certainly been a general tendency to move towards what in the USA is called 'building level management'. But this has been accompanied by new and demanding requirements for accountability. These now constitute a significant part of the means available to governments to monitor policy compliance and maintain control over tertiary provision. Although institutions may no longer have to apply to a central Ministry for permission to appoint junior members of staff or obtain approval for every item of expenditure, however minor, they are subject to increasingly numerous codes of practice and increasingly complex levels of financial, administrative and academic audit. In some cases, these have pro-liferated to such an extent as to cause concern about the proportion of resources that institutions and individuals devote to surviving within what has been called 'the compliance culture'. While the ratio of academic teachers to students deteriorates, larger numbers of administrators are employed to ensure that a multiplicity of returns are duly completed, audits are conducted in a regulation manner, and the penalties associated with non-compliance are avoided. Suggestions that in several countries academic morale is low may have something to do with the erosion of trust that this bureaucratization implies.

Governments also steer by attempting to control the flow of information and engineering support for their policies through the media. One of the ways in which 'post-modern' research and theorizing has added to our understanding of political action and of educational change has been in showing how both positive and negative climates of opinion are created and maintained, and how they influence the perception and implementation of policy. Ministers, administrators, specialized agencies and organized interest groups today pay much more attention to information and public relations than even two decades ago. A variety of ways exist for obtaining professional and public reaction to tentative ideas and draft proposals, without having to incur the opprobrium that attaches to failed policies. So-called 'Big Ideas' – such as *Life-Long Education* or the *Learning Society* – strengthen the impression of policy coherence, furnish positive rhetorical opportunities and play down the costs inherent in political choice. In complex, plural societies all this is a necessary way of minimizing the risks of ungovernability, keeping conflict within bounds and making change manageable.

Finally – but by no means exhaustively – governments steer by influencing the views and actions of voluntary organizations and interest groups in the field of tertiary education. To appreciate fully how this works would require an understanding of the contacts that exist in each country between politi-cians and administrators and the key figures and organizations of the field. These extend well beyond the formal means of consultation that may be written into statute or blessed by long practice. The participation of policy-makers and public servants in professional conferences; the exposure of draft documents to individuals whose opinion is valued, who can be trusted to keep their involvement to themselves but who are capable of influencing others; off-the-record briefings; friendly phone-calls; the ubiquitous working lunch – all these contribute to policy formation and decision-making in democracies, no less in tertiary education than in other fields. There are subtle rules and understandings as to what does and what does not constitute appropriate and acceptable conduct. Such rules are seldom codified. They must be learned and updated on a continuous basis. They need to be evaluated in terms of an ethically defensible conception of the general good.

Discussion of these mechanisms seldom takes place in formal gatherings, partly because these are not normally regarded as appropriate venues for such discussion, partly because knowledge and understanding of the rules requires considerable 'native speaker insight', partly because the processes involved are vulnerable to facile criticism. Yet it would be a mistake to ignore the part that such informal exchanges play in the ability of governments to devise, draft, legitimate and implement their tertiary policies. Without such informal mechanisms, good government would be impossible.

There are important differences between governments in the way in which they undertake steering, and in the reactions to which such action gives rise. Tuition fees have been among the most controversial. Even where they have been introduced, there is as yet little attempt to employ them to steer enrolments or to reflect differential rates of return. Elsewhere, the political costs involved have discouraged rapid action. Nonetheless, it seems doubtful if academic standards and the quality of the student experience can be safeguarded unless the costs of mass tertiary education are better shared than at present. Funding higher and vocational education for a small proportion of the 18–24 age group is a very different task from funding tertiary education for whole populations. Especially so at a time when other demands on public resources are increasing and policies concerning levels of direct and indirect taxation can determine the fate of governments.

Changing courses and curricula

There are several reasons why, if the full benefits of the expansion and diversification of tertiary education are to be realized, courses and curricula must be a central concern for policy-makers.

- The combined effects of institutional inertia, differential subject status and academic drift can undermine relevance, discourage attempts to relate content and qualifications to labour market needs and raise the unit cost of tertiary provision.
- At some levels there are long-standing conventions that preclude the direct involvement of governments in the determination of institutional objectives and design of programmes. Government funding is provided in response to plans drawn up by staff of the institutions. There are few specific quotas, except in fields that are high cost (e.g. medicine) or politically sensitive (e.g. teacher training and supply). Such steering as may be necessary has to be accomplished by other means.

- Expansion has brought into tertiary education large numbers of students without recent experience of independent study. Their working and living conditions often militate against traditional modes of learning. Their success depends on the willingness and ability of staff to make significant adaptations to teaching, supervision and assessment.
- Such adaptations would be greatly facilitated if additional resources could be made available and favourable staff–student ratios maintained. When neither is possible, morale is damaged and unwelcome political pressures generated.
- However strong the wish of policy-makers and administrators to intervene in what goes on in lecture room and laboratory, they remain dependent upon the voluntary cooperation of subject specialists.

A coherent system-wide pattern of qualifications and awards is an essential feature of any successful attempt to operationalize the concept of tertiary education. In making institutional boundaries permeable, such a pattern shifts the balance of attention from differentiation towards diversity. There is no longer a series of sharply distinguishable institutional types, each with their own class of awards – certificates, diplomas, bachelors degrees, taught post-graduate and research qualifications. Upper secondary schools can offer courses hitherto part of the first year, curriculum of universities and colleges. Vocational and general 'short-cycle' institutions can teach for qualifications that carry full credit towards a 'long-cycle' award elsewhere. Universities can provide sub-degree and sub-diploma programmes, especially where these are prerequisites for the higher-level study of subjects that do not feature in the school curriculum, where a student is 'converting' or where elements of a multi-disciplinary field of study need reinforcement.

For awards to be portable and to carry full external credit requires some form of common accreditation. In some countries no institution can award a degree of any kind without state or agency recognition. Elsewhere a combination of market forces and self-regulation make state intervention unnecessary. In such systems, the possession of a degree or diploma in itself means little and conveys little employment advantage; it is from where it was obtained that matters. Professional bodies can exert strict control over the teaching and assessment of awards – down to the number of minutes devoted to each aspect of the programme. A great variety of such quality assurance and quality assessment mechanisms now exist, including national inspectorates for higher education.

There have been important moves in several countries from syllabuses to modules. The former specify a programme that extends over the whole three, four or five years of work required for an award. Such a programme may offer certain alternatives and options, but for the most part its content is determined in advance by the teachers of the faculty or department to which the student 'belongs'. Modular structures, on the other hand, emphasize flexibility, cross-disciplinarity and the ability to construct programmes tailored to individual needs and interests. To maintain academic coherence and to ensure common standards within such structures can require a formidable internal bureaucracy.

Modular arrangements facilitate credit accumulation and transfer. While mutual recognition of qualifications and awards between institutions is more common than heretofore, it depends essentially on the willingness of one institution to recognize that another teaches and assesses to a similar standard. But in a mass system the existence of a single 'gold standard' can no longer be taken for granted. In the UK, responses to a report that argued the case for a national system of credit accumulation and transfer suggested that universities, colleges and professional bodies were not yet ready to agree on a unified framework with a common unit of academic currency (Tysome 1995). However, in 1999 the Quality Assurance Agency in the UK began undertaking consultations on a common framework of qualifications, designed to ensure that terms such as 'Diploma', 'Bachelor's degree' and 'Master's degree' refer to similar levels of achievement. A two-year foundation degree has also been established, contributions to the teaching of which can also be made by colleges of further (as distinct from higher) education. Students who perform well and wish to continue can go on to qualify for a full honours degree after a further period of study. In 2003, the British government proposed that the future expansion of higher education should be mainly by means of such two-year courses (Department for Education and Skills 2003). It remains to be seen if the demand for such awards is equal to the hopes that policy-makers have invested in their development (Robinson and Piatt 2000; Goddard 2001).

Changing teaching and learning

Over the past decade there have been significant developments in the provision of systematic training for university teachers (Moses 1993). Few universities are now without specialist units for this purpose, the establishment of which has often been encouraged by funding agencies and other official bodies. There are numerous Internet sources of teaching materials for staff development.

These developments have not been without their critics. But the suspicion that in some places still greets the work of the increasing number of specialists in teaching at tertiary level is not because what they are doing is unimportant or of poor quality, but because of the implications it is perceived to have for the nature and role of the academic profession and of the institutions in which academics are employed.

It is argued that the basis of a teacher's professionalism is their subject, not the teaching of that subject. Academic staff identify themselves primarily as physicists, linguists, chemists, historians, statisticians, not as tertiary teachers. To focus on the teaching role can be seen to threaten the basis of their identity, or to imply the need for a formal distinction between research and teaching responsibilities that would be resisted by those whose *de facto* contribution to research is minimal or non-existent as much as by active researchers. Academics are unlikely to be persuaded that the improvement of teaching quality really matters unless staff development is subject-focused. The quality of teaching is not to be measured only by the care with which material is assembled, the number of computer-based and audio-visual aids used in its presentation, the ability of students to recall the exact details of what was said. Teaching and learning are seen as complex, even mysterious, processes, the outcomes of which cannot be reduced to formulae and check-lists of competences.

Even a cursory examination of the relevant journals would suggest that a very wide range of teaching methods are now in general use, and the tra-ditional lecture is somewhat outmoded. In practice, the evidence that indi-vidualized audio-visual, computer-assisted and planned instruction methods improve learning is not always heeded. This is partly due to the investment of resources that such methods require (high development costs also tend to limit flexibility), partly due to the pressures of deteriorating student–staff ratios, partly due to staff conviction that lecturing, for all its limitations, remains a cost-effective means of communicating information. Lecturing has long been a very common method of instruction. Terenzini and Pascarella (1994, p.29) quote a study by Pollio, which found that in a typical classroom or lecture hall, staff spend about 80 per cent of their time addressing stu-dents – who were attentive to what was being said for only about 50 per cent of the time.

A great deal of academic work – even in the sciences and technology – is solitary. Sitting in front of a computer display is just as solitary as reading a book. High standards depend on a willingness to give sustained attention to difficult material. Peer pressure, formal evaluation and rewards more closely related to performance will only make for improved teaching and learning, more productive research and effective service if they influence the devel-opment of an individual academic's own commitments to the highest stand-ards of quality and professionalism, enable them to judge in a particular instance whether these standards have been upheld, and provide the motive and the means to remedy shortfalls.

The strategies, the policies, the codes of practice and the procedures that governments, institutions and academic departments use to direct change and secure improvement need to be judged by the extent to which they encourage and enable individual academics and administrators to embody the culture of quality into every personal encounter, every meeting chaired or serviced, every lecture given, every practical session supervised, every seminar led, every essay graded or examination paper marked. Official inter-ventions cannot succeed unless they come to be 'owned' by those whose practice they are intended to improve. The ultimate safeguard of academic standards is still the conscience of the individual teacher.

Re-engineering change

The comprehensive reordering and realignment of systems implied by the concept of re-engineering and featured prominently in recent management literature is not often open to those who seek to change tertiary education. Change is for the most part organic and incremental. Past experience suggests that apparently radical institutional change can leave educational fundamentals untouched. Major reform – such as the redesignation of British polytechnics and Australian colleges of advanced education as universities – is often the culmination of a process extending over years, if not decades.

The impracticability of system re-engineering does not, however, remove the need to ask fundamental questions. It is important to identify decision points that offer choices between reinforcing a trend that may as a consequence become irreversible, or of calling a halt and changing direction.

The diversity of the tertiary enterprise, especially on an international scale, encourages attempts to formulate generalizations that encompass everything from part-time short-cycle technical and vocational education in local centres to full-time long-cycle programmes in the sciences, arts and humanities in prestigious universities. Drawing such all-inclusive maps is a necessary element in conceptualizing and operationalizing tertiary education. But it is important that the scale of such maps should not be too small. Otherwise important detail is lost, and the significance of differences missed.

The governance of multi-cultural capitalist democracies, exposed to rapid technological change and intense international competition, is not facilitated by explicit institutional and individual categorizations that appear to limit access to power and to status. It has been argued earlier in this chapter that institutional and course differentiation has given way to diversification. But even within diversified systems there are complex patterns of institutional difference, based less on statute and regulation (which require political legitimation) than on reputation, competitive success, fashion and market position (which do not).

The employment value of a first degree or diploma increasingly depends on both explicit and implicit criteria – on the relevance of the knowledge and skills acquired to undertake the tasks involved, but also on judgements about the way in which the institution from which a candidate has graduated selects, teaches and assesses its students. Such reputational factors can be particularly important when job vacancies are few and applicants many.

Despite all the attention given to management and data collection in recent years, the statistical basis for policy-making is still very patchy. One example is the definition of what constitutes a full-time student. In some countries a large proportion of students classified as full-time undertake significant amounts of paid daytime employment (Neave 1998). Without such earnings they would be unable to study.

There is still much to be done if research is to inform fully policy formulation and implementation, to improve the contribution that universities and colleges make to the quality of social, political and cultural life and to enhance the employment prospects and satisfactions of individual citizens.

Tertiary education as a new educational culture

The changes in the culture of post-school education necessary to operationalize the concepts of tertiary education and of life-long learning are still at an early stage in most countries (Scott 1995; Parry 2001a; Watson and Bowden 2001). Only a relatively small proportion of the population see education in terms of life-long involvement. Going to school, getting a degree, are too frequently perceived as phases of life through which individuals pass. They have a beginning and an end. Once complete, they do not have to be repeated – 'We did that last year'. Successful course completion may help to open doors but offers little guidance as to choices to be made and directions to be taken. Education is not everywhere well integrated with work and with life in family and community. Hence the still frequent references to absent-minded professors, ivory towers and the 'real world' being beyond the walls.

The idea of a 'Learning Society' is not new. It was frequently discussed within countries and in international bodies a quarter of a century ago, in the guise of *education permanent, recurrent education* and *lifelong learning*. At that time neither the technological developments that would revolutionize employment prospects nor the educational opportunities that would give most of the population some experience of education after school had taken off. In both respects the position today is very different (Eggins 2000). There is also greater awareness of the complex inter-dependence of what have hitherto been educationally and administratively distinct kinds of post-school and adult provision. Political stability and social cohesion in rapidly changing, urbanized and multi-cultural societies call for an emphasis not on the limitations imposed by genetic endowment, but on the cognitive, motor and moral improvement of all citizens, however diverse their potential. The Learning Society is a present reality for those groups well equipped to take advantage of the multitude of opportunities that exist for participating in education at all levels and acquiring the initial, post-experience and advanced qualifications relevant to employment and to the conduct of a fulfilled life. The policy problem lies elsewhere. It is that of responding to the needs of the significant proportion of the population who failed at school, who have no worthwhile qualifications, who find learning difficult and who have few incentives to improve their lot. Such people place a heavy burden on welfare support, tend to be more likely than their better placed contemporaries to get into trouble within their local communities and with public authorities and possess little 'social capital'. There are signs that democratic and libertarian sensitivities about imposing life styles no longer readily extend to those who, often through no fault of their own, constitute a major drain on society's resources.

No single measure will ensure that tertiary education reaches parts of the population that other forms of education have hitherto failed to reach. Access issues in the UK are currently receiving a great deal of attention (CIHE 1997, 1999; CVCP 1998; Callender and Kemp 2000; House of Commons 2001a, 2001b). There is interest in such initiatives as individual learning accounts, into which government will put money that can be used to pay for further education (Millns and Piatt 2000); levies upon employers to help pay for enhanced training; literacy and numeracy campaigns; freephone helplines to provide better information; informing choice through improvements in careers guidance and advice; the extension of credit accumulation and transfer (which impinges on tertiary provision at all levels); changes in welfare benefit rules that encourage the unemployed to enrol for further study; and the much more extensive use of information technology, including the setting up of new institutions that work largely through this medium but with different emphases to existing distance learning facilities.

Although IT and multi-media-based learning attract more attention than traditional face-to-face teaching, it remains the case that at its best, the latter remains a highly effective means of motivating underachievers. Hence the importance of ensuring that tertiary-level staff are equipped to employ the whole range of teaching methods and approaches appropriate to what is for many a new clientele.

If attempts to satisfy demands for greater equality of access and fairness in public funding are not to erode high standards of scholarship and research, then active links have to exist between institutions at different levels. If course credits are to be cumulative and transferable, there has to be some publicly attested assurance of their quality. If vocational and professional colleges are to remain true to their missions and best serve the occupations and enterprises with which they are linked, then they have to be funded and administered in ways that minimize taints of underprivilege, and to offer routes to other types and levels of education for all those who can benefit. If diversity is not to be seen merely as the acceptable face of differentiation, then all the institutions and programmes that offer education and training to school leavers and to adults need to be seen as elements in a single tertiary network, as universal in its scope, and coverage at post-school and adult level as is primary and secondary education for younger students. It is in these directions that, if they are to succeed, tertiary education policies need to be steered in the 21st century.

3

Higher education finance and accessibility: an international comparative examination of tuition and financial assistance policies

D. Bruce Johnstone and Preeti Shroff-Mehta

Recent years have seen a dramatic, albeit uneven and still contested, shift in the burden of higher education costs from being borne predominantly by government, or taxpayers, to being shared with parents and students. This 'cost sharing', as articulated in Johnstone (1986, 1992, 1993b), may take the form of tuition, either being introduced where it did not hitherto exist, or being rapidly increased where it already does – 'filling in', as it were, for diminishing governmental/taxpayer support. (China and the UK, although with totally different social-political-economic systems and at totally different stages in their expansion of higher educational participation, are both examples of a recent introduction of tuition fees.) 'Cost sharing' may also take the form of public institutions charging more nearly 'break even' or 'full cost' fees for room, board, books and other costs of student living that may formerly have been covered mainly by government. In other cases, the shift of the cost burden from government to student and family may come in the form of a reduction in student grants, or in the 'effective grants' represented by student loan subsidies in the form of very low rates of interest. Finally, the shift may come about through public policies shifting enrolments from a heavily subsidized public sector to a much less subsidized, tuition-dependent private sector. But in all these ways and in combinations thereof, the burden of higher educational costs worldwide is being shifted *to* students and families *from* governments or taxpayers.[1]

In light of this apparent phenomenon, this chapter explores five questions:

1. What are the theoretical and practical rationales for shifting some portion of the higher educational cost burden from governments and taxpayers to students and families?
2. What are the theoretical, political, ideological, practical and/or strategic bases for resistance to this shift?
3. What is the impact of increasing cost burdens (mainly tuition and related fees) on access, or participation? Or, what is the impact of increasing

student and family-borne costs on student enrolment behaviour – that is, enrolment, persistence to a degree, continuation to a higher degree, and the decision of where, or in what kind of higher educational institution, to enrol? (In this connection, we will be particularly interested in whether enrolments might be dampened for those whose access is already compromised by (a) low income; (b) racial, ethnic, religious, or linguistic status; (c) gender (most often 'being female'); or (d) isolation – especially from good secondary schools and the cultural enrichment generally associated with urban areas, as well as from institutions of higher education close enough to allow living at home.)

4. What is the higher education cost (or more properly, the *expenditure*) burden currently being borne by the student and family in various countries, and what is the recent increase in these costs being borne by students and families, as opposed to governments or taxpayers? (This question must consider any offsetting effects of means-tested or otherwise targeted grants and student loans.)

5. What policy tools – for example need-based grants, loans, loan subsidies, very low or no tuition, subsidized lodging and food – are being employed to increase accessibility, and what is known of their efficacy?

Rationale for the shift of costs to parents and students

The principal causes for, or rationales behind, this shift are three, and they differ considerably in their underlying economic, political and ideological assumptions. The first rationale is the sheer need for other-than-governmental revenue. This need begins with the dramatic increase in most countries in both the public and private demand for higher education, recognized as a major engine of national economic growth and provider of individual opportunity and prosperity. This demand pressure is a function of the sheer demographic increase in the traditional college-age cohort, compounded by the increasing secondary school completion rates, which in turn increases the number of those wanting to go on to higher education, further compounded by an expansion of what may be considered a college-going age cohort to include adults formerly bypassed by the system. This demand pressure is especially felt in low-income countries that are still trying to change from 'elite' to 'mass' tertiary-level participation, at the same time as they are trying to become more economically competitive in an increasingly global economy. But the increase in demand for higher education can also be found in countries already at mass or even near-universal participation rates, as the average student 'consumes' ever-increasing amounts of higher or (at least post-secondary) education over their lifetime.

However, the institutions delivering higher education are also nearly everywhere – and especially in most developing or low-income countries and in those countries in transition from command to market-driven economies – suffering from a severe and worsening austerity. This austerity is a function of at least three forces. First is the demand pressure, mentioned just above. Second is the high – and likely to be increasing – per-student costs on top of the increasing numbers of students.[2] Per-student costs in higher education generally rise faster than unit costs in the general economy due to the traditional resistance on the part of the academy (institutions and faculty alike) to measures that would increase productivity by substituting capital for labour or by shedding existing, but lower-priority, programmes and their associated labour costs.[3]

A third cause of increased austerity, especially in the low-income and 'transitional' countries, is the decline in available public (taxpayer-based) revenue. This decline, in turn, may be a function either (or both) of an increased difficulty of taxation, or of competition from other, often more politically compelling, public needs. For example, taxes were relatively easy to collect in centrally-controlled economies such as the former Soviet Union and Eastern Europe before the so-called collapse of Communism, where purchasing power could be siphoned off at each level of the state-owned production processes via 'turnover', or other forms of value-added taxes. The state could also control – and thus tax – all international trade. Privatization and globalization have essentially eliminated these largely invisible and easy-to-collect taxes, and the alternatives – such as taxes on income, retail sales, property and the sales of luxury goods – are visible, unpopular, expensive, relatively easy to avoid and, technically (in addition to politically), difficult to collect. Furthermore, for the limited taxes that can be collected (or the limited deficit financing that the economy can tolerate), higher education increasingly has a lower priority than other public sector needs such as primary and secondary education, public health, housing and public infrastructure, welfare and the social and economic 'safety net', and internal and external security.

It is in light of these forces and of the consequent financial struggles that national systems of higher education and institutions nearly everywhere in the world are having to supplement their governmental revenues, not only with 'cost sharing', as noted above, but with entrepreneurial activities such as the sale of faculty services, the sale or lease of university facilities, the vigorous pursuit of grants and contracts, and fund raising from alumni, corporations and friends. Thus, tuition and other fees from students and families have the potential for substantially augmenting the increasingly scarce public revenues. Tuition also has the advantage of doing so without simultaneously adding new cost or diverting faculty from their core teaching responsibilities (as is the case with supplementing revenues via grants and contracts or other forms of faculty entrepreneurship).

The objection that imposing tuition fees or increasing them at a rapid rate might exclude potential students from poor or rural or otherwise disadvantaged families can be met, it is argued, by the promise of *generally available loans* (that is, loans that do not depend on the creditworthiness – and thus the financial worth – of the family), or by *means-tested student grants*, paid for, at least in part, by the augmented tuition revenue. In fact, the proponents of cost sharing are likely to argue that the alternative to some form of substantial public revenue supplementation is continued or worsening austerity in the public higher education system, the likely result of which would be limitations on enrolment and/or increasingly shabby and underfunded universities. And because the sons and daughters of the wealthy will always have alternatives (in the private sector or higher education abroad), the students, or potential students, who will be hurt most are the very disadvantaged students that the resistance to tuition is supposed to protect.

The second rationale for tuition and other forms of cost sharing, based less on need or expediency than on principle (however ideologically contested), is the notion of equity: the view that those who benefit should at least share in the costs. The principle is made more vivid and compelling by four observations. The first is that 'free' higher education is actually paid for by all citizens, whether or not they know that they have been taxed (or have had their purchasing power effectively confiscated by inflation brought on by the printing of money). Second, most taxes – public policies to the contrary notwithstanding – are collected through regressive, or at best proportional, taxes on sales, production, or individual incomes that cannot be otherwise hidden (or through the even more regressive governmentally-induced inflation, as mentioned above). Third, a very disproportionate number of the beneficiaries of higher education are from middle, upper middle, and upper income families who could and would pay at least a portion of the costs of instruction if they had to – thus demonstrating the value to them of the higher educational opportunity and signalling the benefits that are thought to be private as opposed to public. Such students and families would probably prefer that much or all of this particular benefit be paid for by the general taxpayer. But whether higher education is subsidized or not – that is, whether tuition fees are zero, moderate, or high – should make little or no difference in the enrolment behaviour of the student from more affluent families. In this instance, the higher public subsidy required by low or no tuition fees can be said (at least by the proponents of 'cost sharing') to resemble a transfer payment from the public treasury to middle and upper middle class families. Fourth and finally, to the extent that there are potential students who would be excluded from higher education by the presence of tuition fees, a portion of the fees collected can easily (at least in theory) fund the means-tested grants and loan subsidies that can (again, at least in theory) maintain and even enhance accessibility.[4]

A third rationale for cost-sharing in higher education is the neo-liberal economic notion that tuition fees – a price, as it were, on a valuable and highly demanded commodity – bring to higher education some of the virtues of the market. The first such virtue is the presumption of greater efficiency: that the payment of some tuition fees will make students and families more discerning consumers and the universities more cost-conscious providers. The second virtue attributed to the market is producer responsiveness: the assumption that the need to supplement public revenue with tuition fees, gifts and grants will make universities more responsive to individual and societal needs. A variation on this theme is directed at the alleged problem of *academic malingering* – that is, students alleged to be taking more years or more courses (or both) than are necessary or even useful, merely or largely because the courses and sometimes even the living expenses are paid for, and because the alternative may be either unemployment or an unappealing job out in the real world. Germany, the Netherlands and the US have responded in part by eliminating or reducing student aid after insufficient progress toward the degree, and some US states have begun charging the higher out-of-state tuition fees after so many 'excess' credits.

Resistance to cost sharing

All of this is admittedly contested ideological ground, and not all policy-makers, observers, or stakeholders share the notion that increased cost sharing – that is, a further shift of the cost burden to the student and family – is correct, necessary, or even 'good expediency'. The shift in the higher educational cost burden from governments and taxpayers to students and families may not be easily accepted, especially in countries with dominant socio-political ideologies that hold higher education to be another social entitlement: to be free, at least for those fortunate enough to make it through the rigorous academic secondary system. This ideology, in turn, can stem from a view that society is the major beneficiary of higher education, and that this observation ought to override the demonstrably high private benefits received by the graduates and their families.

This economic rationale provides good theoretical cover to student, parent and faculty self-interest in the preservation of low or no tuition fees. Students, regardless of ideology, tend (understandably enough) to resist the imposition of, or increase in, tuition fees. Students can be a formidable political force, particularly in left and radical politics, especially in Europe and Latin America and in some countries in Asia. Also, parents of students and would-be students, especially in low-income countries, may be politically powerful elites who just happen to benefit most from the free higher education. This may explain why many students and families, both affluent and low-income, and both 'left' and 'right', often tend to oppose tuition fees, while most economists and many political scientists, including those on both the political left and right, tend to approve at least some degree of 'cost sharing'.

In opposition to efficiency and market responsiveness as rationales for greater cost sharing, many academic leaders assert that a proper higher education is *supposed* to be removed, or at least substantially insulated, from commercialization and market forces. Slavishly following what students think they want, or what politicians or business think they want students to take, according to many academic traditionalists, is the road to academic mediocrity. Furthermore, there is no evidence, at least in the US, that academic responsiveness, educational quality, or efficiency improves with higher tuition fees. However, this traditionalist position is increasingly viewed by governments and many citizens as academically self-serving as well as costly to the taxpayer.

The view that higher education ought to be 'free' or at least very highly subsidized may also be mainly *pragmatic* and *strategic*, regardless of ideology or politics. For example, many opponents to the view of cost sharing, as presented above, accept the notion that means-tested financial assistance and loans might *in theory* preserve accessibility in the face of rising tuition fees and diminishing taxpayer subsidies to the 'well-off'. However, they claim that children of the poor may not understand that the high tuition fees can be offset with grants and hence might not aspire to a university education during the middle and secondary years when the absence of such aspiration may effectively preclude the option of any higher education. It is also alleged that children of working class or peasant backgrounds resist borrowing, less from personal economic calculations than from a cultural aversion to debt. Finally, while a policy of high tuition combined with generous means-tested aid might be more efficient, in the sense that the available public subsidies can be more effectively targeted, the high tuition fee can be imposed by short-term political expediency, while the high aid requires a longer-term ideological commitment – and the result can easily be a de facto policy of 'high tuition–*low aid*' or 'high tuition–*high loans only*' (Johnstone 1993a).

Resistance to the shift of costs from governments and taxpayers to students and parents may be based on a recognition that scarce taxpayer dollars are allocated by political authorities not necessarily on a rational assessment of the costs and benefits of all competing claims, but on the basis of which claims can muster the greatest political pressure. To 'critical' or neo-Marxist opponents of neo-liberalism, both the market and the so-called 'liberal democratic' politics prevailing in most of the West mainly perpetuate the existing unequal distribution of power, status, wealth and economic opportunities. A major plank in the critical opposition to higher educational cost sharing and marketization is the assertion that, contrary to the prevailing neo-liberal position, taxes *can* be raised, both substantially and progressively, if there is but the political will and leadership. Doing so, they assert, would obviate the need for tuition fees and other forms of cost sharing, and would also avoid the danger of losing enrolments (particularly among the poor) and risking failure in possibly ineffective and expensive financial aid and loan schemes (Colclough and Manor 1991; Buchert and King 1995).

In keeping with this strictly strategic resistance to cost sharing, even otherwise staunch neo-liberals may worry that increases in tuition may lead neither to more resources for the university, nor to additional need-based aid and greater participation among the hitherto bypassed, nor even to a shift in public resources to other socially worthwhile programmes, but simply to a shift of taxpayer resources from higher education to some other claims that may be more politically forceful, including tax cuts for the wealthy. Thus, it is not necessarily irrational nor irresponsible for stakeholders (even if they be strong believers in most of the typical neo-liberal agenda) to advocate for one particular object of public expenditure – say, high subsidies and low or no tuition fees for higher education – to the exclusion of other public purposes (or tax cuts), which can be assumed to have their own fierce advocates.

However, if the political authorities do not or cannot provide sufficient public revenue to higher education in spite of advocacy for additional tax funds and resistance to tuition fees (and this is the essential plank of the prevailing neo-liberal, cost-sharing advocacy typified by the World Bank), the continuing austerity at some point will become sufficiently damaging – to the point of severe enrolment limitations and increasingly inadequate numbers and/or quality of faculty, books, equipment and physical plant – that more and more parents, students, university rectors and faculty will accept the inevitability, and even perhaps the desirability, of cost sharing through tuition fees and other means.

Cost sharing in higher education

For the reasons cited above, some increased costs borne by parents and students are probably both inevitable and economically rational. The tenets of neo-liberal economics seem to be ascendant in most countries at the opening of the 21st century, including China and much of Eastern and Central Europe, as well as the highly industrialized countries of the West. In the US, UK and Germany, the embrace of market solutions, privatization and fiscal discipline – long the hallmarks of Conservative parties – have become central to the political planks of what traditionally had been the parties of the left, particularly when these parties took over their governments in the 1990s. Although public higher education in the US is the province of the several states, the 1980s and 1990s saw very great increases in public sector tuition fees in most states. Britain in 1997, under a Labour government, became the first European country to adopt public higher education tuition fees as official government policy. And Germany, at the turn of the century once again under a Social Democratic government, in 1999 conspicuously failed to reiterate the traditional Higher Education Framework Law guarantee of free higher education to all successful graduates of the German academic secondary school.

The supplementation of higher educational revenues by nongovernmental sources – primarily students and family – is one of the major recommendations from the World Bank and most other development experts as one important solution to increasingly underfunded and overcrowded universities in the developing world (Johnstone 1991, 1993b; Woodhall 1992; World Bank 1994; Ziderman and Albrecht 1995; Johnstone,

Table 3.1 College and/or university public sector tuition first degree, various countries (academic year: 1997–1998)

Country	US$	
	High tuition	Low tuition
United States	4500	1500
Canada	2668	1350
China	442	0
Japan	2500	2500
Kenya	316	132
Namibia	884	238
Britain	1205	1205

Source: Information gathered by the Higher Education Finance and Accessibility Project, University at Buffalo Center for Comparative and Global Studies in Education

Arora, and Experton 1998). We can see the beginnings of tuition and various kinds of fees in such countries as China, Vietnam, India, more and more countries in Latin America and Africa. We see the dilemma of Russia, East Europe and countries of the former Soviet Union, all struggling with the need for tuition fees to supplement increasingly inadequate public revenues for higher education, looking for loopholes in their present constitutional guarantees of free higher education (Bain 1997). We see a mature, even if unbalanced, private higher education sector, mainly tuition-supported, in Japan, Korea, the Philippines, Chile, Brazil and elsewhere in Latin America, and private higher education sectors emerging in the countries of the former Soviet Union and the rest of Eastern Europe. Representative public sector tuitions in a number of countries are shown in Table 3.1.

In the face of these increasing expenses borne by students and parents, national systems and individual institutions face the challenge of maintaining higher educational accessibility, especially for poor, minority, rural and other traditionally underserved populations. (This challenge is particularly compelling in light of the increasing income disparities being experienced in most of the countries of the world.) In the US and many other countries, the principle of expanding higher educational opportunity and accessibility is being met, among other ways, with means-tested student financial assistance and/or with governmentally guaranteed and generally available student loans (or other forms of delayed payment, such as graduate taxes).

What is most problematic about this shift, at least in the developing world and in the nations of the former Soviet Union and Eastern Europe, is that many of these countries may lack (in addition to a sufficiently affluent middle class that can afford tuition fees) such beliefs and traditions as:

- A belief in the very appropriateness of tuition fees: that is, that parents and/or students *should* contribute to the instructional costs of higher education, at least to the limit of their abilities, even in the acknowledged 'public' institutions. (Families in many cultures expect to pay for their children's *living costs*, although not the *instructional costs*, or tuition fees, which is why the ability to attend university and live at home is important, and why higher education is so much more accessible in urban areas.)

- The tradition of revealing incomes and assets, honestly, in response to tax laws or requests for the documentation of financial need for the obtaining of student assistance. (The difficulty of income verification is becoming more of a problem in developing and 'transitional' economies with the spread of *private employment*, particularly among the middle and professional class, where employment has traditionally been mainly governmental, and incomes easy to track.)
- The tradition of philanthropic giving to higher education, which can build up scholarship funds at colleges and universities, public as well as private. (Some cultures have strong traditions of charity, or of giving to religion, but not necessarily to higher education, which is considered either a private good, appropriately affordable to the elite, or the responsibility of the government.)

It is because of these traditions (together with the nearly $56 billion dollars in student aid and loans, most of it 'need-sensitive') that the US, in the face of very high costs of higher education, both public and private, can still hold to the claim that access to higher education, to the limits of a student's ability and interest, need not be precluded by family financial status. Elsewhere, in the absence of these traditions, and of public policies to maintain accessibility, there is reason to believe that higher education will become increasingly unattainable to all but the affluent.

But policies such as means-tested financial aid and generally available student loans at moderate interest rates are financially, politically, technically and sometimes culturally difficult. For example, 'financial need' is exceedingly difficult to ascertain and verify, especially in non-Western countries, where private sector incomes may be neither reported nor even recorded (or certainly underreported) and where tax evasion is prevalent everywhere (McMahon 1988). Whatever parental financial responsibility may exist may be limited to sons, or may be handled by extended families. Sections of the population may subsist on largely non-monetary income, making 'financial need' even more difficult to assess. Yet without some way of assessing 'need', either very large segments of the population must effectively be denied access to higher education, or tuition fees must be kept zero or low for all students – which, in the absence of alternative public revenue, would mean either that the colleges and universities would have to limit enrolments (and continue to serve only a small elite), or would be maintained at such levels of overcrowding and shabbiness that all students may be denied a decent higher education.

A 'proper tuition fee': the many dimensions of cost sharing

In response to recognition of the need for, and even the inevitably of, greater 'cost sharing' – which is frequently merely a euphemism for the introduction of, or sharp increase in, tuition fees – ministries and higher educational leaders frequently inquire: 'What is the proper level of tuition fees?' They are generally looking either for a monetary amount, or a percentage of instructional costs, that would be 'appropriate', or at least acceptable in some kind of international higher educational mainstream.

But the question of 'a proper tuition fee' cannot be given any kind of useful answer apart from within a context of other policies and contextual circumstances. The principal ones are the following.

1. The existence of other kinds of non-discretionary 'fees' in addition to tuition fees

These 'other-than-tuition' fees may be so-called 'up front' or 'one time' fees, or other mandatory fees for things such as application, registration, student programmes, athletics and recreation, technology. The state of California was notorious for maintaining very low tuition fees only because of the very high other fees. Japanese universities charge 'application fees' as high as $350, which for the major private universities can provide in excess of $15 million in operating revenue with almost no offsetting cost. Indian universities are known for their myriad of small fees.

2. The per-student costs of the particular higher educational institution or programme in question

Costs vary substantially across institutions and sectors, and especially across programmes. If 'cost sharing' – generally meaning the charging of tuition fees – is established by policy as some percentage of per student instructional expenditures, then it matters greatly in making international comparisons how these per-student costs, or institutional expenditures, are calculated. But these costs depend on assumptions or accounting conventions: for example, how so-called indirect costs, or institution-wide expenditures, are apportioned among first-degree or graduate instruction, or how pension costs, or the costs of health insurance, or the costs of capital are handled. In addition, per-student costs vary considerably among degree programmes in accordance with prevailing faculty–student ratios, equipment needs and other programme-specific costs – as, for example, among programmes in science, history, or undergraduate teacher education.

3. The private benefits believed to be attached to certain institutions or certain degree programmes

Regardless of the underlying instructional cost differences, it is commonly thought appropriate (or perhaps merely expedient, or just more feasible) to recover a higher percentage of these costs from those programmes and degrees believed to bring the greatest private return to the student (or parents) – either in future earning capacity, or in prestige, job security, or anything else valued in a profession or vocation. Thus in the world of private higher education, and in public higher education where tuition fees are permitted, tuition and other associated fees for medical and other advanced health professional programmes are generally high, reflecting not only the greater instructional costs of such education, but the high market value of the degree (in turn reflecting the high income and high status associated with these professions). Also, as much of the world that was formerly dominated by Socialist/Marxist central economic planing has given way to private enterprise and market forces, the demand for higher education in economics, management, law, computer and information science, and the English language has risen greatly – and so, too, tuition fees for such programmes.

The establishment of a 'proper tuition fee' is made even more complicated by the interaction and the inter-country variations between these two factors of (1) instructional costs and (2) the mix of public and private benefits. For example, it is conventionally thought that research, or 'classical', universities are more costly per student than shorter-cycle, more vocationally-oriented, less research-intensive institutions, so that a common per cent of costs to be charged to students and their parents will generally yield a higher tuition fee in the classical, research university. However, although the presumably higher unit costs of the classical university may be true for medicine, it is probably not true for other programmes such as law or business that frequently have higher tuition fees, but that can be rather inexpensively delivered, at least at the first degree level.

A higher tuition fee in the classical university is also reinforced by the notion that there is generally greater prestige – and thus greater private benefits and future income prospects – attached to a degree from the classical university (France, with its Grandes Écoles, being the conspicuous exception). In addition, the university student is more apt to be from a wealthier family, and thus likely to be both willing and able to pay a higher tuition fee. And if the student is not from a wealthy family, the greater private benefits and income prospects of the student should still be sufficient – in the economically rational world – to support student loans, and thus the payment of a higher tuition fee.

However, except for the medical and related degrees, which continue to be associated with classical universities, most of the programmes that are coming under greatest demand in much of the world – economics, management, computer and information science, law, and the study of the

English language – can be taught and learned just as (or more) easily in a non-university context. In fact, it can be argued that it is more likely to be the university student – more than the student at a short-cycle, non-university institution – who is more likely to be bringing substantial public, as opposed to mainly private, benefits. Under this construction, it would be the *classical* university that needed (or deserved) the greater public subsidy (and the lower tuition fees) more than the non-university institution that is more apt to be creating predominantly private benefits.

So, in many of these traditionally high tuition fee programmes, the high tuition fee may be less a function of higher instructional costs, and more a function of the market demand for places – which correlates nicely with the expected private monetary return, and also with the greater likelihood of being able to repay student loan debts.

4. The costs of student living (especially room and board)

These expenses are in large part a function of the extent to which it is possible to live at home – which, in turn, is a matter of the proximity of the college or university to the home, the availability of inexpensive transportation, and to some degree the 'culture' of acceptability or non-acceptability of living with one's parents well into one's 20s. State policies in America, for example, generally aim at putting at least a community college within the commuting range of nearly every family (which in the US generally assumes automobile ownership). Clearly, this is not possible in rural parts of most countries, where traditional college-going must assume living 'in residence'. But even where living with parents is possible, the general cultural acceptability may vary among countries, with such an arrangement allegedly being more acceptable, for example, in France than in England or Germany.

If the student cannot live at home, the cost of student living is most affected by the extent to which residence halls and/or canteens are publicly subsidized or otherwise made accessible at minimum cost. The tradition of institutionally-provided residence halls is a legacy of the British collegiate model of higher education, reinforced in those countries where university attendance was assumed to be properly free of any student or family-financial responsibility. But these residence halls can be spartan and crowded, as in China, where very low charges might even cover the very minimal real costs – or quite opulent, as in many US college and university dorms, with air conditioning, private bedrooms, and extensive 'common spaces', in addition to the absence of any governmental subsidy, all of which can make living in a university dormitory in an urban area frequently *more* expensive than in surrounding low-cost, unsubsidized private housing. Table 3.2 shows the total combined expenses borne by students and parents for selected countries.

Table 3.2   Total higher education costs borne by students and parents, various countries (academic year: 1997–1998)

	US$							
	Public				*Private*			
	Tuition & fees	*Food & board*	*Other costs*	*Total Costs*	*Tuition & fees*	*Food & board*	*Other costs*	*Total costs*
US	4000	5650	2350	12,000	20,000	6600	2400	29,000
Canada	2668	3750	5547	11,965	n.a.	n.a.	n.a.	n.a.
China	442	973	530	1945	885	973	884	2742
Mexico	16	1775	380	2171	4218	2715	880	7813
Kenya	316	790	540	1646	2236	1184	618	4038
Namibia	884	1301	334	2519	n.a.	n.a.	n.a.	n.a.
Malaysia	3515	2000	1500	7015	4325	3100	1500	8925
Germany	190	2760	1840	4790	n.a.	n.a.	n.a.	n.a.
Britain	1205	5500	1500	8205	n.a.	n.a.	n.a.	n.a.

Source: Information gathered by the Higher Education Finance and Accessibility Project, University at Buffalo Center for Comparative and Global Studies in Education

5. Parental willingness to pay

The willingness to make financial contributions (even sacrifices) to support the children's higher education may be a function of *culture* as well as of *affluence.* This is not intended to impute a special nobility to those cultures where parents typically make large sacrifices on behalf of their children's higher education. But the Swedish parent, for example, has become accustomed to paying very heavy taxes, but then to enjoying the benefit of 'free' university education for their children, as well as the Scandinavian convention of students paying for their living costs through subsidized student loans; the imposition of tuition charges in Sweden could well be resisted, even by parents who by most measures could well afford the tuition. In contrast, the Chinese parent, who probably has only one child to begin with, and who has probably always placed a very high value on education (or else the child would not likely be in a position even to contemplate higher education), is apparently willing to make considerable personal financial sacrifices for their child to go to a university.[5]

Parents may be thought to be more willing to pay in countries with substantial private education, where people are more used to paying for the higher (and sometimes the secondary) education of their children. This seems to be the case in the US, where tuition at private colleges and universities may be in excess of $20,000 a year, and total expenses well in excess of $30,000, and where undergraduate residential tuition fees in the more expensive public universities can now be $4–5000 or more (having been rising more steeply than those in the private sector), and where total expenses in the public sector can easily reach $15,000 a year. However, the expected correlation of public and private sector tuition does not hold in international comparative analysis. Japan, Brazil, India, Korea, the Philippines and other countries with established private higher education sectors still feature low or no cost public classical universities. Furthermore, efforts to increase tuition in the public sector – even modestly and even in light of the pronounced middle and upper income profiles of these advantaged student bodies – seems still to be met with intense political opposition (as in the total shut down of the National Autonomous University of Mexico for most of 1999 over a government proposal to raise tuition fees from a few cents to approximately $70 per semester).

In America, parents have always faced a quite precisely calculated 'expected family contribution' (EFC). But a realistic expected family contribution cannot be derived simply from some *ex ante* rule of what parents at various income levels *ought* to pay, but of what they seem in fact willing to pay at a particular time in a particular culture. The EFC in the US has actually diminished in recent years. Some would say that this diminution reflects a growing middle class hedonism; others would say that the US Congress has pandered to middle and upper middle class tuition fee anxiety by legislatively excluding most of the EFC that used to stem from parental assets, principally home equity. The US case is further complicated by the large number of students from single parent homes where 'parental financial responsibility' is difficult to determine or enforce. Also, there are very many students in America who are both financially needy and academically marginal and otherwise ambivalent about higher education, but who have places in the open admission sectors of American higher education. Such students may say that they would decline to enrol or drop out in the event of large tuition fee increase. Or, they may attribute their dropping out to 'financial factors', but this may also be the most socially acceptable reason to profess – more so, for example, than factors like academic difficulty, boredom, loss of interest, or their parents' unwillingness to pay what other similarly-situated parents might pay willingly. In short, parental willingness to pay, like student willingness to incur indebtedness, is probably substantially culturally determined, and may further differ by social class or family income – but with the true effect of the strictly financial factors associated with cost sharing embedded within other factors, and difficult to identify precisely.

6. Possibilities for student summertime and term-time employment

Working one's way through college is part of the American myth – and is still substantially true (Stern and Nakata 1991). The US student who claims 'financial need' is expected to earn and save at least $1500 during summers. They are also expected to hold down a part-time job, generally about

10 hours a week, for approximately $2000. However, very many American students hold jobs requiring from 20 to 40 hours a week – while at the same time being enrolled supposedly 'full-time' (although in fact frequently taking more than the standard four years to complete a degree). The ability of student summer and term-time employment to contribute substantially towards cost sharing is a function of at least four factors that may be especially prevalent in the US: (1) a culture of acceptance (even expectation) of part-time youth employment, even among affluent families where such employment is not essential to the family's financial well-being; (2) a generally robust economy with an abundance of part-time, unskilled, low-paying but readily available jobs; (3) the encouragement and financial assistance of the Federal Work-Study Programme, which partially subsidizes college and some community jobs for needy students; and (4) collegiate standards (low compared to most countries) and an academic calendar (including extensive evening classes) that allows and even encourages part-time study and 'stopping out'. Taken together, these economic, cultural and structural features combine to allow substantial cost sharing by the student from part-time and summer employment. However, these features may be largely absent in many countries, and seem to be especially absent in those countries that are experiencing the greatest need to supplement governmental revenue. The non-availability of student employment then puts more pressure on grants and loans – to which we next turn.

7. The general availability and sufficiency of 'need-based' or 'means-tested' grants and subsidized loans

In theory, a 'need-based' grant, increasingly in conjunction with a student loan, substitutes for the missing parental contribution from the low-income family. By 'generally available', we mean that a student otherwise interested in and admissible to higher or post-secondary education, would be entitled to a grant or subsidized loan because of their family's low income, or similarly would not be precluded from borrowing by the absence of family collateral or creditworthy parents. Grants and loans not generally available are by definition *rationed*, usually by criteria of academic merit or preparedness and having nothing to do with the ability of the family to provide financial support. The US Pell grants, the former British mandatory grants, the French *bourse sociale*, and the German BAföG, are examples of governmentally-provided student financial assistance to which a student is entitled simply by being accepted by a university, being from a low-income family, and generally maintaining some minimal academic standard or progress towards the degree. Because academic merit or preparedness, at least as conventionally measured, is strongly correlated with socio-economic status, the more 'merit' figures in the awarding of grants and subsidized loans – much of which (to the upper-middle class) is likely to have little or no impact on the student's enrolment decision – the less is apt to be available for low-income students, and the more the imposition of tuition fees is thus likely to be a barrier to higher educational participation.

'Sufficiency' refers to the ability of the need-based grant or loan subsidies to truly compensate for the low income of the family. 'Sufficiency' is a function of the maximum grant or loan subsidy (that is the amount to which the children of the lowest income families would be entitled) and the degree to which that amount can truly compensate for the unavailability of parental contributions. In its most generous formulation, a grant-loan combination is 'sufficient' to the degree to which it can bring within financial reach of the lowest income family the best higher education to which the student would otherwise be entitled. In its minimum formulation, a grant-loan combination might be deemed 'sufficient' if it brought at least the least expensive higher educational alternative (probably a short-cycle, non-university form) within reach of those students able to live at home and perhaps also work part-time (or even full-time) and attend college only part-time.

'Sufficiency' is also a function of the relationship of the grant (or the grant/loan combination) to varying family incomes. This relationship is established by the (low income) *point* at which the maximum grant begins to be diminished (under the expectation that the family can now begin contributing at least something) and the *rate* at which further increments to family income are effectively 'taxed' through higher expected family contributions and further reductions in the need-based grant. Obviously, the more generally available the grant (that is, the more it is based on income alone, without further rationing by some measure of 'merit'), and the more sufficient the grant (that is, the more generous the grant, or the grant/loan combination, in making possible the most costly alternative to which the student would be academically entitled), and the more realistic the expected parental contribution (in the sense of phasing out the grant and phasing in the expected contribution at a level and rate that most families are able to meet), the more the need-based grant-loan system will be able to compensate for enrolment-limiting effects of tuition fees.

In summary, to answer the inquiry about what tuition fees should be – or what the total expense burden borne by the student and family should be – requires a consideration of all of these factors. One can expect to find a very considerable expense burden (in the range of $20,000–30,000) in the presence of very high tuition fees – as in a high-quality private higher education with little or no public support of basic instructional costs, and no 'price discounts' or grant assistance, and living away from home in conditions not unlike one's employed, non-student age peers. The lowest financial burdens upon students and parents may be found in some combination of low or zero tuition fees[6] and the opportunity to live at home. Many countries, as shown in Table 3.3, have a considerable range of total costs/expenses borne by the student and parent before financial assistance in the form of either grants or loans.

Table 3.3 Range of college and university costs or expenses borne by students and parents, first degrees, various countries (academic year 1997–1998)

| | US$ | | | |
| | Public | | Private | |
	High Estimate	Low Estimate	High Estimate	Low Estimate
United States	12,000	6000	29,000	18,000
Canada	8028	3960	n.a.	n.a.
China	1947	390*	2743	1106
Mexico		4350	6828	4793
Kenya	1711	395	4342	2632
Namibia	2540	436**	n.a.	n.a.
Britain	10,000	6000	n.a.	n.a.

* A teachers or military college or college of agriculture
** A short-cycle technical institute
Source: Information gathered by the Higher Education Finance and Accessibility Project, University at Buffalo Center for Comparative and Global Studies in Education

Grants versus loans

To the extent to which financial assistance is to compensate for low family income and to bring higher education within reach of any student of requisite ability, regardless of their family's income, either grants (non-repayable) or loans (repayable by the student, parent, business enterprise, or taxpayer) should suffice – providing that students are willing to borrow, and that banks or other savings institutions are willing to lend to them. Students would presumably always prefer that their assistance be non-repayable – that is, in the form of grants, in addition to no or very low tuition fees, subsidized room and board, and very subsidized loans that are really 'near grants'. However, to the degree to which the rationale for the combination of tuition fees, unsubsidized student living arrangements, and accompanying student financial assistance is avowedly to shift costs from governments and taxpayers to students and parents, then the more this student assistance can be in the form of a 'true' (that is, unsubsidized or minimally subsidized) loan, the more effectively all of the rationales discussed earlier can be met. That is, it is loans (or other versions of deferred payments, like graduate taxes) more than governmentally-provided grants that:

1. relieve the government, and thus the public sector generally, of some of the burden of the high and rising costs of higher education and (at least theoretically) provide more revenue to the university;
2. promote equity by allowing the costs of higher education to be shared between the public, reflecting the not inconsiderable public benefits of

higher education, and the family, reflecting the also considerable private benefits to both the student and the family;
3. engage the forces of the market to enhance both the efficiency and the responsiveness of the university.

However, in order to relieve the public treasury and truly shift the cost burden to the student and parent, the loans must be repaid – and at something at least near the generally prevailing rate of interest. This is as true with 'contingent repayment' or 'income contingent' loans, such as those employed in Sweden and available in the US, as with conventional 'mortgage type' loans (Johnstone 1972, 1986; Woodhall, 1988, 1989; Ziderman and Albrecht 1995). It is also true of other forms of deferred payment where the student presumably bears a share of the higher educational cost burden, but only repays in the future, over time, and only as long as they are gainfully employed. Such repayment schemes include the so-called graduate tax (often advocated, but never fully implemented; see Barr, 1989), the 'income surtax' repayment employed in Australia through the Higher Education Contribution Scheme (HECS), and the 'drawdown' of governmental pension payments employed in Ghana to repay the student loan fund. In all of these repayment schemes, the present discounted value of the stream of future payments (or of income surtax payments, or of foregone pension fund contributions) must equal the original value of the loan, or of any forgiven tuition fees, for the cost burden truly to have been shifted to the student. To the extent that loan repayments are 'lost' through high defaults, lost tax records, emigration or simple disappearance, subsidized interest rates, or excessively high governmentally-borne costs of collection and servicing, the loan does not really shift the costs, and can be more accurately characterized as a 'near', or 'effective', grant – and generally a rather inefficient and politically costly one at that!

Access and participation: 'cost sharing' and enrolment behaviour

Countries differ in the percentage of a traditional tertiary education age cohort that actually goes on to various forms of higher or post-secondary education. Since there are substantially differing private benefits attached to these different forms, it 'matters', for example, whether students choose, or are able to elect, or are tracked into or restricted from:

- any tertiary level education;
- only a short-cycle, minimum status, non-selective form of post-secondary education;
- a selective, prestigious, classical university;
- or even beyond, to the most selective and prestigious university programmes, such as medicine or law or advanced study toward the Ph.D.

Clearly, there are fewer and fewer students towards the more advanced and selective end of this higher educational pipeline. That is, some students are somehow selected or otherwise admitted into (while others are somehow screened or selected out of) the more advanced, remunerative and 'selective' levels or stages of higher education. The question most commonly identified with higher education's 'accessibility' is the extent to which this selection, or 'screening', or 'narrowing of the pipeline', is a function of factors considered in most societies and cultures to be politically or ideologically acceptable or unacceptable. The principal 'acceptable' factors, or correlates, would be genuinely innate intelligence or talent, or interest (especially interest that is itself a function more of something innate than of environment or culture). Factors generally considered 'unacceptable' – and therefore, if possible, to have their association with 'access' lessened by policy – would be, for example: (a) low income or low social status of the parents; (b) region (especially being from a rural or remote area); (c) race, religion, or ethnicity; or (d) gender (although this may be a more culturally contested correlate).

In this construction, higher educational accessibility may be seen as a policy goal, more or less common to most countries, realized to the degree to which the principle correlates with higher educational participation – as well as to participation within the more prestigious or selective forms or levels of higher education – as being due mainly to interest, ability and talent, and conversely not reliant on family income or status, race or ethnicity, gender, or region or rural/urban location.

There exists in virtually all countries a substantial underlying association between low higher educational participation and these above-mentioned unacceptable correlates, particularly family income and status, race and ethnicity, rural or remote location and, at least in many developing countries, gender. The true causation that diminishes the probability of higher educational participation may be subtle and complex, and may have done its work long before the end of secondary schooling, when more fortunate young people and their parents are making decisions to partake of higher education. High income-high status families are apt to place more emphasis early in a child's life on education. They are apt to have more books in the house, to take more of an interest in their children's education, and to be able to afford (or live where there exist) better middle and secondary schools – all in order to better prepare their children for university entrance. In most countries, the correlation between higher educational participation with family income, status, and other 'unacceptable correlates'[7] is well established before the completion of secondary school. Therefore, a reasonable goal for cost sharing might be to be able to pass some element of costs on to students and parents without further accentuating the 'unacceptable correlates' to higher educational participation of high family income, urban location and dominant ethnicity or language.

Accordingly, an investigation of the connection between cost sharing and accessibility must examine the effect of greater higher educational costs (probably in the form of higher tuition fees, or the implementation of tuition fees where they did not previously exist, or the reduction of student living subsidies) passed on to students and families on:

- the decision to apply to, and matriculate in, any institution of higher education;
- the decision to apply to, or matriculate in, a particular form (for example, a university or a less selective non-university) or a particular programme (for example, medicine, law, engineering, or humanities) in higher or post-secondary education;
- the likelihood of degree completion;
- the likelihood of going on to more advanced (and more prestigious and/ or remunerative) levels of higher education.

The empirical research on the effect of both tuition fee and need-based financial assistance on student enrolment behaviour is mainly econometric analyses, either cross sectional or time series, of enrolment and persistence of US students in response to differing state tuition policies (Leslie and Brinkman 1989; Kane 1995; Heller 1999). This research supports the conventional wisdom that net price (that is, the combined effect of tuition discounted by financial aid) has little effect on middle and upper middle income students. However, it can have a measurable discouraging impact on low-income youth, an impact that is only partly offset by increasing need-based aid.

Significantly, there are factors in the US that may serve to blunt the impact of rising tuition fees on enrolment behaviour, or at least diminish the likelihood that the effect will be an outright denial of accessibility.[8] Among these factors are:

- the very great number of open-access, two-year colleges within commuting range of most US homes, where the successful completion (or even partial completion, or passing only several courses) of programmes is generally transferable, or applicable toward a four-year degree;
- a similar widespread availability of very many virtually open admission four-year colleges, both public and private;
- the peculiarly American 'degree-by-credit-accumulation', or 'modular', system that makes possible easy 'stopping out' (for example, to earn and save money), or transfer from an expensive residential college to a less expensive alternative within commuting range of home;
- an economy with abundant part-time employment possibilities;
- the general availability of need-based grants and student loans (without any test of either student or family credit).

The effect of these factors is to cushion the impact of increasing tuition fees, and to present alternatives to not matriculating at all, or to dropping out altogether, in response to an increase in the cost to be borne by the student or family. It is in countries where such factors do not exist – that is, where the two-year alternative is not transferable to a four-year or advanced degree, or where there are no easily accessible higher educational alternatives within commuting range of home, or no generally available student loans, or no practical part-time student employment opportunities – that a sharp rise in tuition fees or other expenses borne by the student or parent can be assumed to be more likely to preclude higher educational participation altogether.

In the end, we know very little still about the impact on higher educational accessibility of the increasing shift of higher educational costs, worldwide, from governments and taxpayers to students and parents. We know that the shift is happening, and we know that most governments officially espouse a concern for the maintenance (or probably the enhancement) of higher educational accessibility. What we do not know, at least not yet by systematic empirical study, is the impact on university enrolment behaviour (or higher educational participation generally) of increasing cost sharing. Nor, even more importantly, do we know from empirical study the ameliorative efficacy of the common access policies such as means-tested grants, loans, or enhanced student employment opportunities.

The worldwide trend toward some greater 'cost sharing' – that is increasing tuition fees and diminishing levels of public subsidies, at least to non-needy students – seems inevitable. The inevitability does not reflect any triumph of World Bank policies, nor of market capitalism, and would not necessarily be the preference of many thoughtful analysts who believe in markets but who also see many problems in the increasing privatization of higher education. But there seems to be no escape from the conclusions that: (1) higher education in the future will need vast additional resources, particularly in the developing countries; and (2) the only alternative to more of the burden being shifted to parents and students is for there to be very large increases in taxes, progressively raised.

And herein lie the two problems that above all underpin the likelihood of a continued shift of higher education costs from governments and taxpayers to students and parents. The first is that substantial increases in progressive taxes – that is, taxes that fall proportionately more heavily on the rich, and thus are levied mainly on income and wealth – are exceedingly difficult to collect (mainly because they are so easy to escape). The second problem with relying on massive tax increases (progressive or otherwise) to avoid the need for greater higher educational cost sharing is that higher education is simply not at the front of the queue, even if taxes were to be significantly and successfully increased. Primary and secondary education, public health and sanitation, environmental restoration and preservation, housing and other public infrastructure, and a social safety net for the elderly, the unemployed and the unemployable are almost certainly ahead of higher education in most countries. Without some additional cost sharing, it is almost certain that enrolments will be restricted, and/or the higher education that is available to the masses and still 'free' will be of increasingly lower quality.

Higher education needs to continue to claim public resources – and more of them. But it also seems incumbent on those who can influence public policy to work towards the construction both of less costly forms of higher education, and also towards the kinds of financial assistance and loan programmes that can combine significant cost recovery with protection to those whose participation in higher education is most at risk from the inevitable need to share in the costs.

Notes

1 'Taxpayers' includes the general citizen/consumer losing purchasing power to the government via the higher prices brought on by hidden business taxes or through inflation brought about by public deficit financing.

2 Specifying (not to mention making international comparisons between) per-student, first-degree, instructional costs is often unreliable for several reasons including: (1) the difficulty of attributing costs to first degree instruction as opposed, say, to the costs of research or service or advanced instruction; (2) great variability in the accounting treatment of pension and other so-called *benefits* expenses, in addition to direct salary costs; and (3) a similar variability in the treatment of capital costs within most of the published international data on the comparative costs of higher education.

3 The resistance to productivity or efficiency is pervasive in the classical university in most countries, although a kind of 'efficiency' is being forced upon many universities in the forms of mandatory enrolment increases, cuts in faculty numbers and freezes or even reductions in faculty salaries. The more purposeful enhancement to higher educational productivity – through application of instructional technology, or radical restructuring of instructional styles and faculty workloads, for example – are more likely in entirely new institutions and sectors (such as 'distance learning universities'), but it may be debated whether these forms are genuinely 'more productive' or are better described as 'different albeit cheaper'.

4 Some classic expositions of this equity argument include W.L. Hansen and B.A. Weisbrod, *Benefits, Costs, and Finance of Higher Education* (Chicago: Markham Publishing, 1969); Carnegie Commission on Higher Education, *Higher Education: Who Pays? Who Benefits? Who Should Pay?* (New York: McGraw Hill Book Co., 1973); J.P. Jallade, 'Financing Higher Education: The Equity Aspects', *Comparative Education Review*, June 1978, pp. 309–25; G. Psacharopoulos and M. Woodhall, *Education for Development* (Oxford: Oxford University Press for The World Bank, 1985); and J.C. Hearn, C.P. Griswold and G.M. Marine, 'Region, Resources, and Reason: A Contextual Analysis of State Tuition and Student Aid Policies', *Research in Higher Education*, 37 (3): 241–78.

5 This observation was confirmed by conversations the senior author had with parents waiting outside the higher education entrance examination sites in Wuhan and Chongqiung in the summer of 1999, with Professor Shen Hong of Huazhong University.

6 Very low tuition fees are sometimes equated with 'public' higher education, but there can in theory be publicly-owned and privately-owned institutions with high or low tuition fees, depending partly on the underlying instructional costs, but mainly on the degree of public subsidization of these underlying costs.

7 Daniel Levy has observed that these correlates, however 'unacceptable', are nonetheless virtually unavoidable; thus 'lamentable' might be a more useful descriptor.

8 Interestingly, the very openness and already very high participation in US higher education may, other things being equal, actually accentuate the dampening effect of tuition fee increases on higher educational participation because of the large numbers of students who are essentially ambivalent about their higher education, and who may be 'trying it out' as long as the debt loads or the burdens on the parents are not too great.

4

New managerialism in UK universities: manager-academic accounts of change

Rosemary Deem

Introduction

This chapter draws on a UK Economic and Social Research Council funded project on 'New Managerialism and the Management of UK Universities', carried out between 1998 and 2000 by a team of researchers based at Lancaster University.[1] An analysis is offered about how and in what ways new ideas about the management of public services may have permeated UK higher education institutions and provided manager-academics[2] in UK universities with new means of steering change in those organizations. 'New Managerialism' is a set of ideologies about organizational practices and values related to attempts by Western governments to bring about radical shifts in the organization, finances and cultures of public services such as local government, health and education. Other studies confirm that new managerialism itself is not confined to the UK system but is also found in countries as different as Australia (Marginson and Considine 2000) and the Netherlands (Van den Bosch and Teelken 2000). The introduction of new managerialism, although partially rooted in domestic economic and social pressures, like HE change in other countries (Mok 2000), is also related to wider global economic pressures on public expenditure and markets for international students (Scott 1998). Furthermore some of its roots can be traced back to student protest movements in the 1960s and 1970s, to rising costs of public services and endeavours to expand elite systems into systems with a mass intake (Veld 1981).

However, new managerialism is not just about organizational change or making expenditure efficiencies. There is also a high premium on cultural change (Du Gay and Salaman 1992; Itzin and Newman 1995; Clarke and Newman 1997; Du Gay 1998a). UK-based empirical studies of change in a range of publicly-funded services have suggested though, that cultural change may be less easy to achieve than organizational change. Hence what often develops is a complex mix of old and new values and practices (Ferlie, Ashburner *et al.* 1996; Exworthy and Halford 1999). The management of universities is part of a wider set of changes affecting academic work, including changes in status and salaries relative to other professions, work-intensification and greater demands for accountability (Halsey 1992; Henkel 2000; Fulton 2001; Shattock 2001). Similar changes have been noted amongst academic workforces outside the UK too (Altbach 1996; Enders 2001). There have also been shifts in the internal differentiation of the UK academic labour force, including not only the traditional disciplinary tribes and territorialism (Becher and Trowler 2001) but also other divisions too. These include: those between temporary and permanent staff, between teaching-only staff and those who are research-active, and divisions based on gender, ethnicity and type of institution (Altbach 1996; Fulton 1996b; Fulton 1998; Enders 2001; Fulton 2001). A recent White Paper on higher education in England (Department for Education and Skills 2003) also raised new issues about the institutional separation of and reward for teaching and research. This included the possibility that university status could be gained by an institution that does no research. Furthermore, some universities were encouraged to become research-intensive while others were urged to concentrate on teaching. The White Paper explicitly made comparisons between the UK HE system, that in the USA and the tendency in India and China to concentrate research in a few institutions. The White Paper referred also to new modes of HE funding and other mechanisms (such as the establishment of Centres of Excellence for Teaching, changes to university human resource strategies and using student satisfaction surveys as a basis for rewarding excellent teaching), which might be used to lever change. However, the question of whether change to and in universities can be steered by academics rather than by career administrators or funding mechanisms is an important concern for manager-academics and it is also this issue that forms the focus for this chapter.

The ESRC 'New Managerialism' project

The study was funded by the Economic and Social Research Council (grant no. R000237661) between October 1998 and November 2000. The remit of the project was to examine the extent to which 'New Managerialism' was perceived to have permeated the management of UK universities. The study also examined the selection procedures used to appoint manager-academics, as well as their roles, practices, training and informal learning. The first phase of the study used focus group discussions with academics, managers and administrators from generic academic organizations and learned societies. Respondents considered what they perceived was currently happening to the management of universities. The second phase involved semi-structured interviews with 137 manager-academics (from Head of Department to Vice Chancellor) and 29 senior administrators from a cross-section of 16 pre-1992 and post-1992 universities. The pre-1992 universities were drawn from those with charters, while the post-1992 institutions were formerly under local authority control until 1988 when they became incorporated institutions. They were given university status in 1992. The interviews explored the backgrounds, current management practices and perceptions of respondents. In phase three, case studies of the cultures and management of four of the 16 universities enabled comparison of the views of manager-academics with those of academics and support staff (porters, technicians, librarians, secretaries, junior lecturers and contract researchers). The three phases offered a very comprehensive picture of the management ideologies, views and practices found in a range of UK universities.

Debates about new managerialism and their application to higher education

The research explored the extent to which 'New Managerialism' (Clarke and Newman 1997) was perceived by manager-academics, academics and administrators to have permeated the management of UK universities. The concept of 'New Managerialism' informing the research project consisted of three overlapping elements. First, *narratives of strategic change* may be constructed in order 'to persuade others towards certain understandings and actions' (Barry and Elmes 1997, p. 433) in relation to the established governance and management of public service organizations. Second, emergent *distinctive organizational forms* such as cost centres, enterprise and quality assurance units, provide the administrative mechanisms and managerial processes through which change can be realized. Third, there are *practical control technologies* through which strategies and their organizational instrumentation may be transformed into practices, techniques and devices that challenge established systems of 'bureau-professionalism' (Mintzberg 1983) by removing discretion and trust, and replacing them with performance management, quasi-markets and target-setting (Clarke and Newman 1997).

'New Managerialism' thus constitutes an alternative model of governmental and institutional order for higher education in the UK to that which existed under the compromise between corporate bureaucracy and professional self-government from the mid-1940s onwards (Smith and Webster 1997; Jary and Parker 1998). This compromise shaped the post-World War II development of British higher education, on the basis of a trade-off between managerial control and professional autonomy, exemplified in the organizational logics and practice of 'professional bureaucracy' (Mintzberg 1979; Mintzberg 1983). This trade-off has itself been subject to a number of changes in policy and there has been increased state intervention in recent years (Henkel and Little 1999; Shattock 1999; Kogan and Hanney 2000; Parry 2001b). 'New Managerialism' is seen as a novel departure because it entails interrelated organizational, managerial and cultural changes leading to a tightly integrated regime of managerial discipline and control (Reed 1995; Reed 1999), which is radically different from bureau-professionalism (Hood 1995; Webb 1999). Professionals are subjected to a rigorous regime of

external accountability in which continuous monitoring and audit of performance and quality are dominant (Kirkpatrick and Lucio 1995; Power
1997; Deem 1998).

New managerialism and manager-academics

Examining new managerialism in UK higher education is not straightforward. First, many changes are still occurring in the funding regimes and
policy arena. The changing external environment has included continued
massification of student intakes at undergraduate level, coupled with
resource constraint, an increase in staff–student ratios and the rise of an
audit culture, through the development of systems of quality assurance for
teaching (Bauer and Henkel 1999; Brennan and Shah 2000; Newton 2000;
Morley 2001) and research (Mace 2000; Lucas 2001; Harley 2002). So if
manager-academics want to use new managerialism as a means of trying to
bring about change within universities, some of the groundwork has already
been laid for them. Second, despite increasing demands for accountability,
academics remain somewhat more autonomous than many others employed
in UK public services and may react in a variety of ways to attempts to impose
new managerialism (Trowler 1998a).

Third, manager-academics themselves may or may not consciously be
adopting the regimes and values of new managerialism. There is a possibility
that some simply become bi-lingual, as found amongst senior teachers in UK
schools after radical policy reform (Gewirtz, Ball *et al.* 1995). Thus manager-
academics might take on the new language of business and performance
management but retain some of the core academic values of teaching
and research as part of their academic identities (Henkel 2000). This
bi-lingualism is far more likely where manager-academics are only temporarily in management positions and face a 'return to the ranks' afterwards
(common in the pre-1992 universities), than if they occupy permanent positions as managers, which is more widespread in the post-1992 institutions.
Fourth, a close look at the backgrounds of senior manager-academics
interviewed for our study suggested that they were more likely to have backgrounds in higher education than other public services or the private sector.
Unlike the UK National Health Service (NHS), where reforms from the late
1980s onwards introduced a new group of senior managers, many of whom
had no previous experience of running health services (Ferlie, Ashburner
et al. 1996), in UK universities there has been little recruitment of manager-
academics from outside education. Though some manager-academics may
have chosen management as a career track, a majority of Heads of Department (HoDs) in pre-1992 universities interviewed for the project described
themselves as 'reluctant managers', taking their turn or responding to a
'good citizen' sense of obligation to their colleagues.

Fifth, manager-academics in the UK are not yet extensively trained for
their work. Only a third of the sample had received significant training

(beyond a few half days) for their management roles. Finally, manager-academics are far from forming a single community of practice. Their different subject and discipline backgrounds ensure differences exist, as well as variations in pay. Typically HoDs in pre-1992 universities receive only a very small allowance (£1–2000 per annum) for their managerial work, whereas Pro-Vice Chancellors (PVCs) and Vice Chancellors (VCs) are often on salaries substantially higher than those paid to ordinary academics, with most VCs now earning in excess of £125,000 (Goddard 2003). Manager-academics are also divided by gender, with men predominant in the more senior levels, and women often paid less for doing the same job (Bett Report 1999). Nearly two-thirds of the manager-academics interviewed thought that gender affected approaches to management. Women interviewed tended to be more concerned with teaching and students, men with research and finance (Deem 2003a). So if this diverse group of manager-academics does not act with one accord, it is hardly surprising.

Overall the research data tended to suggest that changes to the management of universities may involve a recombination of old and new forms of management, establishing hybridized forms of new managerialism (Reed 1999; Reed 2002; Reed and Deem 2002). The externally imposed changes impel institutions towards a new managerial agenda, whether individual manager-academics want this or not. But on the other hand, posts such as Head of Department or Deputy Vice-Chancellors are hardly new to universities. Nevertheless these posts are taking on a new significance as concerns about money, audits and budgets come to the fore, with incumbents wrestling to combine informal and relatively non-hierarchical ways of organizing academic work through collegiality with new ways of doing things under a harsher funding and policy regime. As Marginson and Considine say of change in Australian universities, 'Tradition, purpose and academic culture are subservient to a far more simple and direct set of incentives based almost exclusively on the power of the budget' (Marginson and Considine 2000: 82). Though many manager-academics may not identify openly or consciously with this change in agenda, in practice many are prepared to collude with it (Casey 1995), especially if they are embarked on a career track that does not involve returning to the academic ranks after a period as a manager-academic. What Slaughter and Leslie refer to as the 'academic capitalist', profiting from the selling of their own expert knowledge and associated labour power (Slaughter and Leslie 1997), is certainly not likely to shirk the association with new forms of management.

Is new managerialism in evidence in UK universities?

Both interview and focus group data were examined for evidence of perceptions of a move to a more managerial culture in UK universities. Use was made of Ferlie *et al.*'s four models of 'New Managerialism' arising out of their research on the health service (Ferlie, Ashburner *et al.* 1996). Ferlie *et al.*'s ideas, based on trying to make sense of empirical data about the NHS reforms, proved a more practicable way of exploring the extent of permeation of new managerialism than some more theoretical analyses (Clarke and Newman 1997), which helped shape the initial stages of the research. The four models are not mutually exclusive and to some extent represent different historical stages in the development of 'New Managerialism' in the UK. The efficiency model, often best described as 'doing more with less' and backed up by funding policies as well as by league tables, as introduced to the NHS in the late 1980s reforms, was perceived by almost all respondents as having significantly permeated universities. The second model has as central features downsizing and decentralization. There was no evidence of downsizing in 1998–2000, although the UK higher education sector is just now beginning to experience this. There was evidence of some decentralization. This included devolved budgets and internal markets for space and other services, such as computing. However, according to many of our respondents, devolution was only partially realized in a number of universities, with budgetary autonomy over hiring new staff rare.

The third model is that of the learning organization (Easterby-Smith, Burgoyne *et al.* 1999) in which there is emphasis on cultural change, team-work, empowerment of employees and strategic scanning of the horizon. Many respondents in phase two reported attempts at cultural change. People in senior posts claimed to be engaged in strategic activity, though research on the gap between Vice-Chancellors' claims to do strategic work and their actual practices of more reactive fire-fighting (Bargh, Bocock *et al.* 2000) should be borne in mind here. Team-work was much mentioned in the focus groups but rather less in phase two by manager-academics, although there was some evidence of the kinds of semi-formal structures, such as faculty and senior management teams, which Marginson and Considine (2000) note are becoming increasingly important in Australian universities. Empowerment was scarcely mentioned by manager-academics or by other staff. The final model, an endeavour to provide a new value-basis for public services and greater involvement of service users in deciding what should be provided (Ranson and Stewart 1994), was not mentioned by any respondent. So the features of new managerialism most evident in UK higher education are changes to the funding environment and changes to the internal organization and financial management of teaching and research. In the next two sections, manager-academic accounts of dealing with change will be examined.

Senior manager-academics and accounts of change

Perceptions and accounts of change figured prominently in both the phase one focus groups and in phase two interviews. In the focus groups, many participants suggested that under the influence of changing government funding of higher education and attempts to bring the values and practices of the private sector to academic institutions, universities had become more 'managed' in the last decade or so. There was also a prevailing view in some of the groups that money rather than academic factors was driving many decisions, especially with the introduction of cost centres to most universities, coupled with a lack of trust in Heads of Department over the use of budgets. It was also felt by many that teamwork was more necessary now than before because of the significance to departments of quality audits of teaching and research. Yet somewhat contradictorily, some groups felt that collegial, non-hierarchical forms of running universities were in decline. Of course, it is quite possible that manager-academics and academics interviewed ten years earlier would also have had similar responses (Halsey 1992; Middlehurst 1993).

In phase two, a key feature of the senior manager-academic interviews was the focus on external changes to the higher education system and the challenges these had posed for the management of universities (though these changes were overwhelmingly those affecting the UK system – rarely were more global factors mentioned). Both Vice Chancellors and Pro-Vice Chancellors talked of the expectations government had of universities and the constraints of trying to meet these whilst receiving fewer public resources than before, and also responding to a myriad of initiatives:

> the objectives, the functions, and goals of universities as far as public expectations are concerned have become more and more diverse and we are all expected to perform at some level on all of them . . . One of the ways in which the collapse in confidence in the public sector was manifest – the pursuit of efficiency and effectiveness in the public sector was engineered during the Tory years of course – was by a competitiveness based on league tables and so on, performance.
>
> (VC, post-1992)

> The . . . things that one is working at all the time is how can I win on the surface – the core funding is being squeezed year after year – create a resource which is itself not shrinking anymore.
>
> (VC, pre-1992)

> Change is continuous, is what I say to everyone, there is no steady state . . . the political agenda has altered quite significantly now, the government . . . want value for money, they want quality, you know, they want to see widening participation, they want social inclusion. I mean we have to address these agendas . . . We are in a world where the pay-master is the government.
>
> (PVC, post-1992)

It is not difficult to discern the thread of money working its way through these different accounts. Money is a powerful technology of change in all publicly-funded higher education systems and institutions, its importance heightened by the new managerial agenda of performance management and target setting, and its effects sharpened by the discipline of cost centres, which are usually departments, faculties or research centres with their own budgets. All universities funded at least partially from the public purse cannot avoid a degree of resource dependency, wherever they are located (Slaughter and Leslie 1997). But these accounts don't just tell a story of managers steering change. Rather, in some instances they speak of trying to manage change in a context where the real steering is quite definitely 'at a distance' (Kikert 1991), operated by remote control from governments and from international economic, social and cultural pressures on higher education and other public services. This is not to say that manager-academics and Vice Chancellors, in particular, do not ever instigate change themselves. Vice Chancellors very clearly do so, according to the accounts provided and our respondents spelled out the parameters of such changes, including 'encouraged' staff departures, hiring of new staff and structural re-organization:

> I think we've changed 25% of the staff in my first two years, so we've made huge changes, closed a major department, merged five, restructured them, still doing it now. So there were a lot of changes, a lot of people took early retirement, a lot of people brought in from all over the world and it's a pattern that's continued all the way through.
>
> (VC, pre-1992)

The changes enacted are not always undertaken in conditions of the VCs' own choosing, as the previous extracts show. Nevertheless, the financial constraints and the requirements of quality audits may legitimate Vice Chancellors to do what they would like to do anyway. It allows them to restructure their institutional arrangements and to encourage the early retirement or voluntary severance of staff who are not considered productive or who don't fit with current academic requirements. It was noted during the research that structural re-organization was often undertaken by new VCs, though there are only so many variations on faculties, schools and departments that are possible. Pro-Vice Chancellors will often be involved in this restructuring too:

> Last year, a group of a hundred of my colleagues were offered PRCS3[3], they weren't forced out, they were offered PRCS. And the university is going to get a lot tougher about performance. Now obviously that's tough . . . I would have to say those people have not performed . . . if you are then going to be absolutely blunt about it, they haven't fully done what they are paid for doing.
>
> (PVC, pre-1992)

What the climate of new managerialism makes possible is for VCs and PVCs to undertake their own changes on the basis that 'managers have a right to manage' and that the resource situation and policy agenda requires tough action if the university is to thrive. In this context it may sometimes be possible for senior management teams of VCs, PVCs and senior administrators, a group increasingly becoming remote from other academic staff (Deem and Johnson 2000), to exert a flexibility and speed not hitherto seen as characteristics of decision-making in universities. Interestingly, in the case studies of 'managed staff', very slow decision-making was mentioned more often by non-managerial staff than speedy decisions (Deem 2003b) but that may be because staff are not always fully apprised of what is happening at the top of their institution. The rapid-change approach has some of the features of what Marginson and Considine (2000) call in their analysis of Australian HE, a 'new kind of executive power, characterised by a will to manage and in some respects, a freedom to act greater than was once the case' (p. 9). This power is certainly making its impact felt in a number of other countries too, including North America (Slaughter and Leslie 1997), Europe (Clark 1998) and the Far East (Mok 2000). Exercising executive power does not mean there is no resistance to the changes concerned. Indeed, some staff not holding management roles whom we encountered during the research case studies showed a great deal of resistance to change. But change was sometimes legitimated by manager-academics with reference to aspects of the new managerial agenda, such as the need to live in the real world, because of resource constraints and the necessity of operating efficiently and effectively, with attention paid to individual performance to ensure 'value for money'. Those resisting were labelled old-fashioned professionals, unwilling to respond to changing times. Interestingly, however, the 'real world' was usually the UK, not the whole of the globe.

Middle manager-accounts – steering in smaller circles?

Those interviewed who were working at middle levels of management as Deans or HoDs gave accounts of the current context of UK universities that were quite similar to the stories told by Vice Chancellors and PVCs, with emphasis on externally-driven agendas and the internal effects of these:

> The conflicting pressures, the fact that QAA [UK Quality Assurance Agency] is pulling you in one direction, Research Assessment is pulling you in another, I think make life very difficult. I think as well the whole sector is phenomenally under-paid and I'm amazed at the quality of our young staff, who are prepared to do a very, very, hard job for a level of remuneration which is, I think, miserable.
>
> (Dean, pre-1992)

> We talk about this as an educational business and we don't talk about courses in a sense, we talk about products that we have to sell to students and to industry. Now, that's a cultural shift . . . the days when you were just delivering to students and they liked it or not have gone. You're delivering to clients now. And you've got to deliver on time, to quality or

they walk away. And if they walk away there's no income and if there's no income there's no business. If there's no business, there's no job.

(HOD, Applied Science, post-1992)

The difference between VCs or PVCs and Deans and HoDs is that the latter two groups are less able to exert pressure for any kind of radical change or change outside their own patch. Hence, for instance, there is little or no possibility of doing anything about staff rewards, as mentioned by the Dean above. However, it *is* possible to steer what happens to individual staff in the faculty or department. The two HoDs quoted have firmly seized the new managerial agenda, even if it is not of their own construction, and are prepared to accept the current conditions and work with them rather than challenge them. Devolved budgets, the imminence of external quality audit, imposition by peer pressure of self-governmentality of performances, appraisal and even staff meetings are all used as technologies to steer change. Once embarked upon, such technologies may prove appealing. They can be used by anyone in a managerial role, whatever their value-position. The manager-academics we spoke to expressed a range of values from feminism and liberal humanism to neo-liberalism and libertarianism, which led them also to have a wide variety of views on what the purposes of higher education were and how they wanted to reshape it. But this aside, management, as Whitehead and others have noted, can be seductive for both women and men (Whitehead 2001). Amongst those interviewed, there was evidence that even reluctant managers, as well as career managers, could become enamoured with being a manager-academic:

Interviewer: did you have an ambition to do those kind of management things when you were younger . . .?
HoD: It's something that's come gradually . . . certainly in the first instance . . . but more I do it the more I quite like it.

(HoD, Business, pre-1992)

I like the excitement associated with change because I've always worked in a highly changeable, highly charged environment where change and you know, things we used to call threats, now become challenges and I expect to do those and I expect to be successful in them . . . I've always worked in a climate where one is fighting to survive and I quite enjoy that, it's very tiring, but you get used to it after 20 years.

(male Dean of Science, post-1992)

This enjoyment of fighting to survive or even of trying to move change in a particular direction led in some cases to fairly overtly managerial attempts to bring about change through semi-public 'naming and shaming' techniques:

I feel a lot of people stay in academia because they like the working environment, they want to do research. So we've basically came up with a double attack on staff, I wanted to look very seriously at staff as to whether they could meet the requirements of the research assessment or the quality assessment, which is to do with teaching, what people's plans were for the future, their vision for the future . . . And as a result of those meetings, six people decided to take early retirement.

(male HoD Science, pre-1992)

However, it was noticeable at HoD level (where the majority of female respondents were located) that women were keener to protect staff from external changes by supporting them in dealing with constraints, than were men. Thus 'soft' people management skills were brought into play (Trow 1993). The following was not atypical of those women HoDs we interviewed:

I'm trying to change the culture. I want researchers to be more interested in teaching and those who teach to be involved in scholarship . . . I've also tried to cut down on staff contact time . . . and concentrate more on student learning time . . . The other thing I've done is to improve and develop how secretaries are seen . . . so they are treated better and understand more of what we do.

(female HoD Science, pre-1992)

. . . the human resource and carrying out staff development/career review with my 16 academic staff, which I've been doing over the last few months, is critically important, very, very time consuming.

(female HoD, Applied Science/Technology, post-1992)

At the same time, these softer visions of how to steer change are located in the same register of managerial change (and use similar technologies, though softened) as the 'harder' management strategies used by some male colleagues at HoD or Dean level, even if those concerned think of themselves as bi-lingual. Indeed, 'soft' people and collaborative management skills may prove an ideal building block for the acquisition of more competitive and entrepreneurial skills, as used in some Australian training programmes for women academics (Brooks and Mackinnon 2001). Furthermore, 'soft' management skills may be explicitly drawn upon in a context where they are successful at mediating to other staff the kinds of organizational, cultural and other changes required in the current conjuncture (Ozga and Deem 2000; Deem and Ozga 2000a). The levers of change are used differently but there is still a high emphasis on monitoring of performativity (Lyotard 1984; Cowen 1996), on activity targets, on forming teams to achieve quality audit success and on stressing the increasingly market-led nature of academic life. Being a manager-academic in the contemporary UK university is about steering change, whether institution-wide or in a much smaller circle. But it is steering change to a tune played first by someone else, principally the funders and policy-makers. This is a story also familiar in universities in other Western countries (Slaughter and Leslie 1997; Marginson and Considine 2000; Van den Bosch and Teelken 2000).

Conclusion

This chapter has drawn on data from a recent study of new managerialism and management in UK universities and particularly on interviews with senior and middle-level manager-academics in 16 universities. Although the evidence for the permeation of these universities by new managerial ideas was somewhat mixed, much of what was found appears to have initially been introduced from outside, principally by government policy agendas and funding regimes and sometimes explicitly borrowed from elsewhere. Some policy documents made explicit reference to higher education policy in other countries (National Committee of Inquiry into Higher Education 1997; Department for Education and Skills 2003) to the extent that external (if also often national rather than global) factors were crucial, and change in UK universities might be more accurately described as 'steering at a distance'. However, the accounts given by senior manager-academics appear consistent with the possibility that the new managerial agenda is drawn upon as a legitimation for introducing changes, especially organizational re-ordering and the development of new forms of financial discipline and performance monitoring. At the middle levels of management, deans and HoDs appear to have less scope for introducing radical organizational change but can and do work hard at changing individuals, research and teaching activities and introducing 'team spirit' to their departments. Though the values and aims of manager-academics at this lower level vary a great deal, many of the technologies used to steer change are the same. Of course, some manager-academics have always had an eye to change; this much is not new. But what is new is that current UK higher education policies (and indeed wider public policy agendas), as elsewhere, increasingly privilege the modernization of public services and the sweeping away of old ways of doing things. This external legitimation of the manager-academic's role is relatively new. And it has the potential, not yet at all fully realized, to overturn what some researchers have seen as so far only slightly reworked academic values and identities. This potential for radical change in higher education certainly exists not just in the UK but in many other countries too.

Notes

1 The academic team consisted of the author (project director), Rachel Johnson and Sam Hillyard (now both at Nottingham University, Sam in the Sociology Department and Rachel in the School of Education), Mike Reed and Oliver Fulton (respectively in the Department of Behaviour in Organizations and Department of Educational Research at Lancaster University) and Stephen Watson (now Principal of Henley Management College). Heidi Edmundson of Lancaster provided administrative support for the team.

2 The term manager-academic is used to indicate academics who have taken on a management role, either permanently or temporarily, rather than referring to career administrators such as registrars or finance directors.

3 Premature Retirement Compensation which gives added pensionable years to those retiring early.

5

Major trends impacting faculty roles and rewards: an international perspective

Ann I. Morey

Introduction

The academic profession is at the heart of the development and transmission of the intellectual heritage of the world. Over the centuries, the expectations, challenges and opportunities of many national and social settings have shaped its character. While symbolically held together by its traditions, the academic profession today is diverse and complex. In recent decades, the accelerating pace of change has pressured higher education institutions in many countries to re-examine their missions, structures and modes of operation. The academic profession may be altered significantly as a result.

The purpose of this chapter is to examine the changing roles and rewards of the professoriate from an international perspective within the context of the complex and converging larger forces that are reshaping, even transforming, higher education as we know it. Given the nature of the paper, it will, of necessity, use a broad perspective that will have varying degrees of applicability to specific contexts. In order to narrow this perspective, the paper focuses only on faculty rewards and roles in universities, including polytechnic and comprehensive universities.

The academic profession

Through their teaching, research and other activities, academics define the nature and quality of an institution. Seen from afar, the academic profession can appear to be held together by some overarching beliefs and values that explain the meaning and value of their work to themselves and others (Austin 1990). Primary among these is the idea that the purpose of the university and its professors is to preserve, create/discover and transmit knowledge and understanding through teaching and research. Additional beliefs and values encompass the commitment to serve society, the commitment to intellectual integrity and fairness, and the necessity of academic freedom and autonomy in doing academic work (Clark 1987a, 1987b; Austin 1990).

Upon closer inspection, however, the 'academic profession' appears highly fragmented and differentiated by discipline, institutional mission, organizational structures and national systems. For faculty members, their academic discipline provides their primary identification and constitutes the basic building block of the organization (Clark 1987b). Each discipline has its distinct culture and traditions, its methods of inquiry, body of knowledge, orientations to research and teaching, criteria for status and rewards (Clark 1985; Becher 1987; Austin 1990). Disciplines have been classified along a number of dimensions that serve to highlight disciplinary differences and underscore the diverse cultures and subcultures in which academic work occurs (see, for example, Snow 1959; Biglan 1973). These combined disciplinary forces also link faculty members across institutions and national boundaries as 'invisible colleges' form by discipline and specialties.

Any attempt to describe the academic profession must also take into account the types of institutions in which academics work. Within any given country, institutions may differ by a variety of factors, such as mission, size, type of organizational control, professional authority, student characteristics and faculty expectations and roles. Additionally, status and prestige hierarchies exist, with research and inquiry being the key determinant of an institution's standing. For an individual faculty member, research is also a key factor along with the perceived prestige of a discipline.

The UK, Japan and the USA provide examples of this diversity. Higher education in the USA is perhaps the most diverse, with its public and private sectors, community colleges, liberal arts colleges, and comprehensive and research universities. Faculty members within these institutions have different research expectations, teaching loads and curricular emphases, and the reward structures generally reflect these institutional priorities. Japan has a hierarchy of national research universities with heavy research expectations and an extensive and varied private sector where teaching is often the primary emphasis.

Prior to 1992, higher education in the UK had a binary system comprised of universities and the polytechnics. These two types of institutions differed not only in terms of function, but also in terms of work conditions, resources and status (Perkin 1987). The polytechnics were primarily teaching institutions and as such, not funded for research. Academics in these two types of institutions constituted two distinct cultures with differing reward systems, and mobility between these sectors was quite limited (Fulton 1996b). While the binary line was ended by the Further and Higher Education Acts of 1992, and the research function now has a place in the newly designated universities (erstwhile polytechnics), two distinct faculty cultures persist.

In addition to differentiation by discipline and type of institution, national systems influence faculty roles and rewards (Clark 1983, 1987b; Clark and Neave 1990; Altbach 1991). Significant variation exists among countries regarding roles and functions of higher education, the role of government, the availability of resources and relationships with business and industry. Differences also occur in characteristics of students, curricular emphasis, organization and structure of faculty, and horizontal and vertical differentiation among institutions. In noting national variation in the professoriate, Altbach (1991) writes that faculty roles and functions vary from one country to another. Just as academic systems are defined by their national circumstances and history, so too is the academic profession. While academic freedom in some countries is well established with few constraints on professoriate research, in others, it is not. Differences also exist regarding remuneration, academic support facilities, teaching and research responsibilities, arrangement of the academic career and other matters. For example, in Latin America, the research function is weak; faculty salaries are low and the use of part-time faculty extensive. With regard to traditional curricular emphases, the USA values general education during the undergraduate experience, France is more oriented toward specialized training; and Germany stresses the sciences (Clark 1983).

Thus, disciplinary, institutional and national forces influence and shape the professoriate into a diffuse and diverse profession. This situation makes it difficult to generalize about faculty roles and rewards. At the same time the disparate parts are symbolically linked together by common beliefs about independence to pursue the truth, epistemic rules of inquiry and, especially, the role and value of higher education in knowledge preservation, generation and transmission (Clark 1983; Henkel 2000). Rewards include intrinsic satisfaction, status in the discipline and expert authority. Academics are also motivated by desire for increased monetary rewards that come in the forms of salary, consulting fees, royalties from books and patents, service on prestigious boards and other sources of income. In her insightful book on academic identities, Henkel (2000) observes that a central dynamic of academic life in the Western world has been that academic work has provided the conditions for strong identities, especially building individual identities embedded in defined communities.

However, dramatic changes are occurring worldwide that are altering higher education as an institution and may bring about unprecedented changes in academic staff as its labour force. Most of these forces are external to higher education. While these changes will impact on specific disciplines, institutions and national systems differentially, the general direction of those impacts can be discerned.

Trends

To meet the demands of the 21st century, higher education institutions around the world are undergoing reforms regarding their missions and better use of their intellectual resources. The convergence of such external factors as globalization, the increasing economic role of knowledge, information technology and reduced public funding of higher education place enormous pressure on institutions to change. Other forces include:

- changes in governmental structures,
- increasing rate of knowledge creation,
- demographic shifts in student populations,
- changes in societal expectations for higher education,
- the market model as applied to higher education, and
- the emergence of other providers of post-secondary education.

These factors and their interactions are driving the transformation of universities and impacting on the nature and quality of academic work.

One major force for change is the globalization of economic, cultural, political and intellectual institutions, along with the increasing interdependence of nations. The revolution in technological communications has accelerated this transformation by bringing about a real time, globally connected world. As markets become more global, economic development is linked to a nation's ability to acquire and utilize scientific, technical and socio-economic knowledge, and medium to high levels of technology content now characterizes over half of international trade (Salmi 2000). Business and industry increasingly are entering into partnerships with academic researchers and institutions of higher education for the development of new products and processes to bring about these applications (Salmi 2000). Furthermore, in these and other areas, governments are attaching greater importance to knowledge-based production as a source of national wealth, and are providing incentives to increase innovation in order to compete in world markets.

However, concurrent with these changes, governments in many countries have reduced their support of higher education. The overall expenditure per student decreased from 1980 to 2000 (Clark 1998; Coaldrake and Stedman 1999; Henkel 2000; Varghese 2000). At the same time, many institutions are expected to increase enrolments in order to widen student access and meet employer demands for a trained workforce. Governments have urged institutions to seek private forms of funding to compensate for the decline in public funding for higher education. In many countries this situation is accompanied by government incentives for specific initiatives, especially to form and strengthen relationships between corporations, government and higher education to increase product development and innovation.

Thus, in recent decades, we have witnessed a rise in the market forces in higher education, mainly due to the convergence of the corporate quest for new products and higher education's search for increased funding. This situation has resulted in policy frameworks that are built on market-driven phenomena. While problems exist with over-reliance on the market model to shape higher education policy, the acceptance of market forces and orientations as part of the higher education discourse represents a fundamental shift in conceptualization of higher education in many nations (Mortimer 1999).

In their insightful analysis of political and economic changes in Australia, Canada, the United Kingdom and the United States, Slaughter and Leslie

(1997: 1) documented the relationship between the growth of the global political economy and higher education policies which seeks 'to enhance national competitiveness by linking postsecondary education to business innovation'. As Slaughter and Leslie point out, this movement towards academic capitalism is developing at varying rates in the four countries they studied. Based on their findings, they concluded that these changes had significant implications for the academic profession:

> As the industrial revolution at the end of the nineteenth century created the wealth that provided the base for postsecondary education and attendant professionalization, so the globalization of the political economy at the end of the twentieth century is destabilizing patterns of university professional work developed over the past hundred years. Globalization is creating new structures, incentives, and rewards for some aspects of academic careers and is simultaneously instituting constraints and disincentives for other aspects of careers.
>
> (Slaughter and Leslie 1997: 1)

Some alliances between corporations and faculty members in the sciences first formed in the 1980s. This shift towards increased market activity occurred because institutional efforts to acquire increased funding converged with corporate needs for new products (Slaughter and Leslie 1997). This link between diminished government funding and 'marketization' has been well documented in the United Kingdom (Henkel 2000), Australia (Marginson 1995) and the United States (Massy and Zemsky 1994) and cross-national studies have underscored the pervasiveness of this trend (Clark 1993, 1998a; Slaughter and Leslie 1997). Universities themselves have entered into types of agreements that would have been unthinkable two decades ago.

Related to this trend, Clark (1998a) studied the growth of entrepreneurial activities in five European universities. He documents the 'demand overload' on these universities and their limited capability to respond to these expectations. Clark (p. 4) defines an entrepreneurial university as one that on its own 'seeks to innovate ... to work out a substantial shift in organizational character so as to arrive at a more promising posture for the future'. He identified faculty involvement and ownership of entrepreneurial activities as one of the five elements necessary for institutional transformation.

Marginson and Considine (2000: 5) use the term 'enterprise university' to symbolize an emergent institutional type in Australia. Enterprise universities have both academic and economic dimensions. Their fundamental mission is to 'advance the prestige and competitiveness of the university as an end in itself'. Enterprise universities are characterized by strong executive control, the corporate character of their missions and governing bodies, diminished authority of traditional academic governance structures and running of research as a system of measured performance.

In Europe, the confluence of mass access, the increasing complexity of higher education due to market forces and the changing view of knowledge as commodity has resulted in universities which are more 'distributed' than 'core' (Scott 1997a). These institutions are becoming more complex places of work for academic staff, causing academics some uncertainty about institutional priorities, core values and stability. Scott (1997a) observed that for universities to survive in a 'knowledge society', they will have to transgress the once-fixed institutional boundaries and traditional organizational forms, as well as the former social base and the old academic culture with its inflexible approach to truth seeking.

Williams (1998a) believes it remains unclear whether diversified funding diminishes or increases academic freedom and institutional autonomy. Somewhat related, the increased bureaucratization of universities, in part due to massification and the desire to maximize the value of public expenditures for higher education, has implications for faculty authority. In the UK, for example, the development of a more corporate model as outlined in the 1985 Jarratt Report has resulted in changes in academic power. Those academics who have become senior academic administrators have more influence over their institutions. However, most academics report some loss of autonomy mostly due to increased scrutiny of some areas of their work by senior management and other groups (Henkel 2000).

Along with increased managerial structures, many governments in the 1980s began to hold higher education more accountable. Tighter scrutiny of academic work has taken various forms in different countries. The assessment movement in the USA, for example, focuses on the measurement of student outcomes, and has resulted in accrediting associations holding institutions accountable for planning and implementing assessment systems. By and large, assessment results have not been linked to resource funding. The situation is the reverse in the UK and Australia, where assessments of faculty research productivity are linked to resource allocations.

Trends impacting teaching and learning

Before the last quarter of the 20th century, new knowledge was created and disseminated at a rate that assumed people accumulated knowledge before they contributed to it. This is no longer true. The incredible rate of knowledge creation coupled with the information technology revolution has resulted in our being in a 'much more chaotic environment when the very concept of established knowledge even in the rigorous hard sciences is open to question' (Williams 1998a: 91).

As Clark (2000: 12) notes: 'The globalization of knowledge propels its growth at an accelerating pace, rattling universities to their very foundations.' The literature in chemistry, for example, increases by over a million articles every two years. Since 1980, historians have made more new contributions to their field than in all prior recorded time. It is no wonder that the disciplines have fractured into multiple specialties that increasingly distance faculty within a discipline from one another (Clark 2000). Within this context of proliferation of knowledge, faculty members seek to master a meaningful sphere of knowledge and make meaningful curricular choices to guide the education of students. This situation adds stress to faculty jobs and can leave them feeling less than empowered within their own disciplines. In addition, as institutions face the inevitable reality of making choices regarding what specializations and disciplines they will include, faculty may face decisions about the nature and place of their careers.

The challenge for faculty members and universities is to diversify and specialize. Williams (1998a: 91) believes '. . . the dispersal of knowledge, and its relatively easy access from almost anywhere, means that institutions which depend on being knowledge specialists must themselves expand and diversify if they are to retain their market share'. Gibbons (1998) argues that universities have to fundamentally restructure their approaches to teaching and research if they want a role as problem solvers and purveyors of knowledge. To accomplish this universities must adopt an approach that places emphasis on teams, networks, connectivity and other characteristics that are counter to the current dominant culture, which emphasizes individual personal autonomy and discipline based research.

Response to the fragmentation of knowledge

Transdisciplinary patterns of new knowledge is a growing area. These arrangements reconfigure faculty into units that reorganize research and training around the search for solutions to complex problems. Such groups often develop their own theoretical structures and research methods (Salmi 2000). Faculty members may be permanently reassigned to such groups or split their identification between their 'home' discipline and these new configurations. Transdisciplinary groups also give rise to new academic degree specializations.

Another type of new configuration is represented by Fathom, a company whose founding partners include Columbia University, The London School of Economics, Cambridge University Press, The New York Public Library and the Smithsonian Institution's National Museum of Natural History. Through these partnerships with world-renowned academic and cultural institutions, Fathom is a for-profit portal that brings high-quality knowledge to global users (Rynearson 2000; www.fathom.com). Faculty expertise becomes just one source of expertise in this partnership. The central notions of the venture are 'knowledge as a commodity' and connectivity between participating institutions and their customers.

Technology and learning

In some respects, we are just beginning to perceive and understand the full impact of information technology on the nature and future of the university.

As these technologies emerge as new mediums, not just new ways to engage in old modes of communication, their impact on the nature and status of knowledge itself as well as teaching and learning becomes clearer (Brown 2000). For example, Moore (1998) maintains that there is an emerging global awareness of a dramatic shift in the ways in which individuals can connect to knowledge and learning environments. Within this context, she views 'both individuals and organizations as dynamic and complex open systems marked by a high degree of interdependency' (p. 3).

In an insightful article, Brown (2000) explores the Internet as a transformative learning technology. Acknowledging that it is still too early to fully understand its potential as a new medium, Brown observes that the 'new literacy' goes beyond text and image and is characterized by information navigation, discovery-based learning, judgement, discernment and synthesis. Based on his observations of children using the Internet, Brown (p. 14) believes that learning occurs from learning with and from each other. The Internet becomes 'a *learning medium* where understandings are socially constructed and shared. In that medium, learning becomes a part of action and knowledge creation'. Brown posits that the Internet will move us to a new learning ecology that is an open and adaptive system comprised of elements that are dynamic and complex. In this interactive world, then, the boundaries between producing and consuming knowledge are fluid. University faculty, the traditional producers of knowledge, will continue to be a rich intellectual and educational resource, but they will increasingly also be consumers of knowledge produced by their traditional consumers (students, alumni, business and industry, government agencies and so on) (Brown 2000).

The implications for faculty roles of Brown's glimpse into a possible future are conceptual and pragmatic. Faculty members will be more active in forming cross linkages. Faculty culture will change from focusing on producing and transmitting knowledge to one that also will honour and facilitate fluid boundaries among knowledge producers from other organizations and settings. For example, academics as facilitators will bring about face-to-face connections between their students and individuals who are producing knowledge by addressing serious problems in business and industry. They might also foster mentorships through the use of technology with experts in public and private agencies and organizations.

Changing demographics

Another trend influencing faculty roles and rewards is changing demographics of students. Many countries have experienced dramatic changes in the cultural, ethnic and racial diversity and gender mix of their students. These changes present challenges to academic staff regarding curriculum, instructional strategies and their personal attitudes and orientations. To be sure, the context of these challenges varies by region and even continent.

Some societies within the Asian and African contexts are in the process of constituting their national identities, whereas the European and American discourses take place in societies that assume they are integrated states.

Furthermore, as more students from underrepresented groups enter higher education, there is increasing pressure in some countries for academic staff to better reflect the diversity of students on their campus. Progress has been slow for racial and ethnic minorities and for women to enter the professoriate and the call to alter the 'traditional ranks' has met with some resistance (Glazer-Raymo 1999; McInnis 1999).

In addition to increasing diversity, in Europe and Australia, massification of higher education has stretched institutional capacity and challenged faculty to teach students who are less prepared for college work. Universal higher education has presented similar problems. Further, the need for lifelong education has increased and post-secondary education is required for entry into more jobs than ever before.

Adding to this environment is the growing numbers of students who are adults. For these students, many of whom work, higher education is just one of many activities in which they engage every day and they value convenience, quality, service and cost (Levine 1997). As noted earlier, many students prefer active modes of learning and concrete or practical methods. This contrasts sharply with the prevalence of the lecture mode of teaching and faculty orientation toward concepts, ideas and theory.

The types of students academics serve influence faculty identities. The changing student body is welcomed by some academics and unsettling to others, as it represents a less elite student clientele and a shift in society's vision of the mission of higher education. Distance education is often seen as part of the solution to serving increasing numbers of students. It frees education from being time- and place-bound, making it more flexible and attractive to some students, especially adult learners. Changes in modes of instruction and delivery mechanisms have increased dramatically over the last decade. This evolution is slower at higher education's traditional centres and faster on its perimeters (Green 1999).

This general context of the changing college student also makes a ready market for institutions that are 'no frills' and offer programmes with active instructional strategies and at times and locations convenient to students. Thus, a diversified market of knowledge providers and learners is emerging at the perimeters of traditional higher education. Rapidly expanding among them in the USA are for-profit, degree granting institutions. Fueled by venture capital, the needs of adult learners and technology, these for-profit higher education institutions have the potential of providing real competition and altering some segments of non-profit higher education. The Education Commission of the States (2000) has identified 622 degree granting, for-profit organizations in the USA alone.

The University of Phoenix (UOP) is the foremost example of these new breeds of higher education providers. It serves 113,500 students at 116 sites in the US and Canada. It also serves students via the Internet, with the

University of Phoenix Online enrolling 37,000 students worldwide. The university has no tenured faculty, and employs about 250 full-time faculty members and over 11,000 adjunct (part-time) faculty. Like most for-profit institutions, courses and instructional materials are designed at the corporate level by a group of experts hired specifically for the task. As such, it removes individual faculty from their important role of control over the curriculum, and diminishes the need for their subject matter expertise

The emerging professoriate

The convergence of these trends has placed enormous pressures on higher education structures to change, even transform, in order to respond to the new realities. They are the major forces with the potential to redefine the professoriate. Their impact continues to vary across and among higher education sectors and within national contexts. During this period of complexity and rapid change, we cannot predict with certainty what the outcomes/affects on faculty roles and rewards will be, but we can discern some general directions and turning points.

Core tasks of academic work: teaching and research

Academic work involves a complexity of tasks, which can include service on university committees, advisement of students, coordination and management of academic units, and participation in various civic and professional groups and matters. The core of academic work is teaching and research.

Teaching

How academics teach has changed little over the decades. Professors and students in classrooms today behave very much the way they did 30–40 years ago. Many scholars and administrators acknowledge the difficulty of changing academic behaviours and cultures. Nevertheless, while perhaps not leading to the widespread transformation of teaching, today's environment may significantly alter teaching in many institutions and disciplines. As noted earlier, the knowledge explosion has challenged academics to decide what content to include, how to organize it and for what purposes. Moreover, technology alone has introduced new learning modalities that challenge our assumptions about how students learn. Technologists and other specialists often work in collaboration with professors as they learn to use technology as part of the teaching/learning process.

Moore (1998) believes that in the emerging learning environments, individuals must do more than merely understand a certain knowledge domain, they must develop advanced conceptual abilities, complex problem-solving skills and a high degree of creativity. Many others share her view and call for academics in the disciplines to place greater emphasis on these learning outcomes.

In the USA, a movement to improve teaching has been underway for several decades that has sought to restructure the teaching role of faculty. Guskin (1994: 18–19) observes that the fundamental problem and challenge in this effort is to shift one's thinking from how faculty members teach to how students learn:

> ... to create learning environments focused directly on the activities that enhance student learning, we must restructure the role of faculty to maximize essential faculty-student interaction, integrate new technologies fully into the student learning process, and enhance student learning through peer interaction.

The emphasis on student outcomes is furthered by calls for accountability, which have resulted in professors assuming broader roles as assessors of student learning.

The focus on student learning requires a fundamental shift away from the core focus on faculty members' disciplinary and research interests. A change of this magnitude is certainly difficult (Clark 1987a). Indeed, the American experience bears this out. Efforts to reward teaching and learning did result in innovations, but little has changed the research prominence in the reward system. In their review of the major American reform movements, Lazerson, Wagener and Shumanis (2000: 13) conclude:

> ... there is little evidence that the changes add up to a systemic reconsideration of how and why students learn or of how institutions, rather than individual professors, can revise their approaches to teaching. With few exceptions, teaching changes have not been tied to higher education's incentive and reward system. Research remains the primary avenue to individual and institutional prestige.

Perhaps the real revolution regarding teaching is yet to come. New pedagogical approaches involving active and interactive learning, in synchronous and asynchronous formats, are emerging from the concurrent use of multimedia and computers. Salmi (2000) cites examples of such innovations in Brazil, Australia, Denmark, Scotland and elsewhere.

Many faculty members in the future professoriate will need to learn more about how teaching and learning occurs, and institutional and external incentives and rewards hopefully will support this challenge. Coaldrake (Coaldrake and Stedman 1999) projects that a more professional approach to university teaching will emerge. For example, he reports that Australian academics are being asked to respond to the needs of diverse student groups, design curriculum across disciplines and around learning outcomes, employ new theories of learning, gain expertise in technology, teach at flexible times and places, and conduct assessments and make improvements.

Research

Research remains preeminent in Western universities and is the major source of prestige for professors and institutions. Faculty rewards for research are tangible and are reflected in upward career mobility, increased prestige and salary. Changing the culture that rewards research, even at teaching institutions is unlikely to occur (Clark 1987a; Lazerson *et al.* 2000). But changing the nature of research and the patterns of research work is possible, and evidence abounds that university research is itself changing in orientation, rewards structures and organizational relationships.

Governments are exerting influence by their funding patterns and research priorities. For example, academic research in the UK is formally evaluated and organized. The Research Assessment Exercise is used in determining the flow of research funds from the government's Funding Council to the universities. The research ratings have made the research outputs of individuals, departments and universities more transparent and public and have resulted in a growing power of universities to frame the activities of academics (Williams 1998a; Henkel 2000).

In Australia, the binary system ended in 1989, and all universities were eligible to receive research funding. Institutions can seek to increase their share of the Research Quantum that is allocated by the government on the basis of certain performance measures. Even though it is a relatively small proportion of total university funding, the Research Quantum is influential in shaping university research priorities (Coaldrake and Stedman 1999).

As noted earlier, faculty efforts are increasingly directed towards programmes and research that intersect with the market. In their four-country study, Slaughter and Leslie (1997) found that national policies promoted a shift from basic or curiosity-driven research to commercial or targeted or strategic research. Their interviews with faculty in units heavily engaged in academic capitalism provide us with a glimpse of the possible effect of the convergence of globalization, diminished national funding of higher education and faculty/institutional entrepreneurism on academic research:

> At the unit level . . . conceptions of knowledge were changing markedly. With regard to altruism, professors engaged in academic capitalism were ambivalent. Although they still hoped their research would benefit humankind, they began to speak about research paying its own way . . . They still considered basic research the bedrock of science, but they saw entrepreneurial research as folded into that stratum, forming a new composite. Merit was no longer defined as being acquired primarily through publication; rather it encompassed at least in part success with market and marketlike activities.
>
> (Slaughter and Leslie 1997: 21)

Organizational imperatives influence the balance between the teaching and research functions. As one goes down the status hierarchy of institutions, teaching becomes more prominent and careers are defined more locally. At the uppermost levels of the institutional hierarchy, the central interest of the university is supportive of the research accomplishments of its faculty members. Nevertheless, academics in all settings understand the value of research as it links them to the central system of higher education's rewards (Clark 1987b).

National policies can also have powerful impacts in this regard. Research policies in the UK have strengthened the separation of research from teaching, and the distribution of rewards and reputations has become more explicit. Henkel (2000) believes that the research policies have contributed to the restratification of the profession with those who are categorized as 'non-research active' experiencing a drastic loss of identity and acquiring an undesirable status.

Other aspects of faculty life

Fundamental to university faculty is the personal autonomy faculty members enjoy in their teaching and research. It contributes to their sense of identity and is a primary source of work motivation and satisfaction. But this notion that faculty have control over all aspects of their teaching and research is being challenged by the new realities. For example, academic work in traditional and for-profit higher education is being unbundled with groups of specialists and other providers assuming specific tasks, such as curriculum design, teaching, instructional materials development and assessment (Morey 1999; Cunningham *et al.* 2000). McInnis (2000a) documents the 'unbundling' in traditional universities in Australia and its impact on academic identity. In particular, the application of complex technologies is blurring the roles of creator, provider and distributor of knowledge between faculty and other professionals, and collaboration becomes the prerequisite for success. As universities move to more flexible modes of delivery of teaching and learning, this trend will continue as more non-academics assume part of the traditional instructional tasks.

Several studies in Europe document the growth of management and other non-academic professionals and their increasing power (Rhoades and Sporn 2002a; Kogan 1999). The changing models of management are most often related to the reforms of devolution, massification and entrepreneurialism. These increases in managers and new professionals are associated with such factors as new modes of producing instruction that require specialized technical skills, the management of research and transdisciplinary centres, fundraising and academic capitalism, the development of new organizational forms, and the decentralization and unbundling of management. This growth in management and non-faculty academic professionals has shifted power away from academics and made their work more interrelated and less a function of 'isolated' professors (Rhoades and Sporn 2002a).

Diminished faculty authority is particularly likely in consortial arrangements when university administrators can often bypass faculty governance mechanisms. In this case, administrators claim that such curricular decisions are made by the consortium, further removing faculty from their central duty of knowledge organization and transmission through programmatic development. Furthermore, as systems of higher education become more interconnected both across and among sectors, some faculty will cross the lines between private, public and for-profit. As these and the boundaries between academics and business and industry are permeated, institutional and departmental identities may be weakened.

Along with differentiation and the unbundling of roles will come a diversification of employment arrangements. Complex functions will give rise to specialized staff, who probably will not enjoy lifetime employment or the same traditional intrinsic rewards as traditional faculty members. In their case study of 12 institutions from developed and developing nations, Hernes and Martin (2000) found that universities often hired staff for university-industry linkages on fixed term contracts. In the USA, the private, for-profit higher education sector's reliance on part-time and non-permanent staff is creating a different group of academic instructors (Morey 1999).

Thus, the capacity to respond quickly to labour market needs, the emergence of new disciplines and transdisciplines, new technologies, and other changing environmental conditions may require more flexible arrangements regarding traditional academics, including performance evaluation and the abandonment of tenure and civil service appointments. There is already evidence of such changes within traditional faculty ranks as higher education seeks to become more flexible, responsive and cost-effective. Based on the results of a collaborative study involving six countries (China, Germany, Japan, Singapore, Switzerland and the United States of America), Teichler (1998a) observed that protection for lifetime employment is lessening while merit-based salary increases are advocated. Henkel (2000) reports that in the UK academic careers have become less structured and more differentiated. Institutions are offering fixed-term contracts, employing different salary schedules, offering different working conditions and formalizing specialized roles. Academic salaries not only differ by rank but also by discipline and the perceived value of specific individuals to their institutions.

The proportion of part-time, non-tenure track instructors is also increasing. In the USA, for example, the percentage of full-time, tenure track faculty members has declined from approximately 80 to approximately 60 per cent during the last decade. Massification in European countries has given rise to a new part-time sub-group of teachers (Enders and Teichler 1997).

With regard to evaluation, post-tenure review is now required in 60 per cent of USA campuses (North, 1999). As noted earlier, national quality assurance mechanisms were implemented in the UK and Australia, and student evaluation of teaching is becoming the norm in several countries (Coaldrake and Stedman 1999). Some observers believe that permanent status, so essential to academic freedom, is going to be abolished. A more likely scenario, however, is that the core 'tenured' faculty will constitute a smaller proportion of the university workforce.

Academic salaries vary greatly by country, academic rank, institution and even discipline. Faculty members in Japanese universities are not well compensated by USA standards. In their study of six countries, Enders and Teichler (1997) reported that academics in the lower ranks are generally less satisfied with their salaries than are their senior counterparts. McInnis (1999) documented that the overall level of job satisfaction among Australian academics had declined, reflecting opinions about salary and key working conditions.

Academics also generate personal income from work outside the university, such as consultancies and book and patent royalties. The increasing collaboration of faculty members with private companies in developing courses and instructional materials is making the working relationship between faculty and their universities more complex, and policies regarding intellectual property rights are being scrutinized, revised and challenged. The lack of clarity about ownership of educational materials, even when developed by an academic's home institution, is a potential source of difficulty. As faculty members in entrepreneurial universities become successful, rewards, status and resources will flow unevenly throughout the institution (Coaldrake and Stedman 1999). Some faculty members will enjoy better working conditions and more authority and freedom over their work dependent on their perceived value to the institution. In such organizations, academic contributions are likely to be measured in more diverse ways than by strict disciplinary measures.

Even so, many rewards in academic life are of intrinsic value and academics consistently report that they are more motivated by intrinsic interests than by material ones. Certainly, for most faculty members the central system of rewards is recognition from their disciplines for their research and scholarly accomplishments (Clark 1987a). These rewards can be both social and intellectual, primarily centred in the invisible colleges of disciplines and subdisciplines that transcend regional and increasingly national boundaries. The prestige faculty accrue can have powerful effects on the recognition and opportunities they receive during their careers.

As Tierney (1999) observed, academics can no longer assume that they will be doing similar things in similar ways. Certainly, in this age of instant communication and globalization, faculty will become more global in their disciplinary perspectives and some faculty will even become citizens of time rather than place. Invisible colleges in those disciplines now mostly confined to national boundaries will likely expand, resulting in the measurement of prestige and status by one's colleagues worldwide.

In terms of faculty career options, some faculty might emphasize their involvement in course development that serves students via distance education. Other faculty members will choose to work on entrepreneurial activities, and may develop their own set of values and intrinsic rewards systems that honour their contributions and orientations.

While the members of the prestigious upper level of the profession have been more independent of clientele demands and related market forces than other academics, the new entrepreneurialism will bend elite faculty perspective towards the market. Nevertheless, entrepreneurialism will generally continue to create tensions for academic work, especially between entrepreneurial centres and traditional departments

Faculty identity

Many of the potential changes in academic life may impact on faculty identity. Norms of independence, integrity, commitment to discipline and intellectual standards are powerful determinants of the core role and identity of faculty. Yet, some of the changes in higher education bring into question whether higher education can still maintain, and not undermine, the underlying values that support academic life. As Henkel (2000) stated with regard to the UK situation: 'Traditional values now had to compete with a multitude of values and objectives – economy, efficiency, utility, public accountability, enterprise and various definitions of quality . . .'.

When control over the curriculum is curtailed, academics feel that their normative space has been invaded and their sense of self-esteem shaken (Henkel 2000). In a recent study, it was found that the dramatic changes in UK higher education have had a noticeable impact on academic identities. Nevertheless, one of the persistent themes is that academics continue to be centred in their disciplines. Henkel (2000: 265) concludes that the overall picture is one of a relatively adaptive profession.

> Those coming in were prepared to maintain individual and collective academic identities, in terms of chosen values, commitment to their own development as researchers and teachers embedded in their disciplines, and focused on acquiring a recognised place in it. At the same time, they were making their own analyses of the context in which they were operating and influencing their colleagues, as well as drawing on long-held values and traditions.

The changes in academic authority go beyond the curriculum and relate to shared governance in general and the role of disciplines as central to organizational structure and functioning. Marginson and Considine (2000) in their case studies of 17 Australian universities document the new executive leadership and the structural innovations in governance that are remaking or replacing collegial forms of governance. They report the discernible decline in the role of academic disciplines and collegial cultures in decision-making processes of universities. These changes in governance structure are observable in other countries and are occurring more through the addition of decision-making groups and the formation of other academic structures than from direct assault on collegial traditions.

Conclusions

The convergence of the forces of change presses against traditional higher education and the work of many academics and their institutions in unprecedented ways. The capacity to respond requires increasing flexibility and diversification of higher education, as well as the establishment of new resource streams. But the cultures, operational structures and missions of universities do not adapt easily to meet new external expectations and internal realities. Institutions will need to develop new organizational arrangements that can move individuals and institutions in desired directions. Among the arrangements are linkages with other entities, incentives, support systems, performance measures as well as new structures to accommodate the knowledge explosion, the applications of communications technologies and entrepreneurial activities. The need for flexibility especially impacts traditional patterns of academic appointments, rewards and careers. In many cases, needed changes will require renegotiating the balance between institutional objectives and individual academic work and autonomy. Increased differentiation and stratification of faculty roles and status within and across sectors of higher education will occur.

Within this context, some academics will become more integrated with their local region and institutions, other academics will undoubtedly be pulled by global forces and the development of disciplines across national and continental boundaries. All will be influenced by the revolution in communication and information technologies and the ever-increasing pace of knowledge generation. Even so, the 'transformation' of the academic profession will surely differ within disciplines and across institutions and national borders. While these changes may seem dramatic, and well they might be, the academic profession at its core has been resilient and stable over the centuries. Traditional and symbolic values of the profession will endure and allow it to adapt to higher education in the 21st century.

6

Using the performance dimension: converging paths for external accountability?

Adrianna Kezar and Elaine El-Khawas

> A palpable tension exists within the academy between the twin purposes of assessment – external accountability and internal improvement of programs and services.
>
> (Peter Ewell 1994)

Introduction

Over the last few decades, several countries have made systematic efforts to measure the performance of universities. A variety of performance-monitoring mechanisms have been introduced, from research and teaching assessments to quality audits and publication of quantitative performance indicators for all UK universities and colleges (THES 3 December 1999: I–XII; Brennan *et al.* 1996; Brennan 1997a; Stanley and Patrick 1998). Other countries have also adopted a performance focus, either nationally or on the state or province level (Commission of the European Communities 1993).

In the United States, experience with performance measures has developed primarily at the state level, beginning with Tennessee's pioneering plan in the late 1970s. By now, most other states have adopted procedures for monitoring institutional performance. Many American accrediting associations have decided to focus on assessing the actual performance, rather than the resources and capabilities, of universities. All of these efforts build on long traditions in the United States of external review, including peer review of research proposals, state monitoring of university expenditures, the use of external examiners and visiting committees and a century-long tradition of voluntary accreditation. Accreditation, the oldest process for examining performance in the United States (El-Khawas 2001), combines internal review by universities (i.e. self-study) with an element of accountability to the public.

Monitoring that is based on a performance dimension is nevertheless distinctive. As performance-based procedures have developed over recent decades, they have departed from earlier practice by their strong focus on outcomes and results, often with a quantitative emphasis, and by their commitment to wide public reporting of information on university performance. This new style of external review has been much debated and analysed. Project designs have been criticized, implementation strategies have been called weak or inconsistent, and negative side effects have been lamented. All too often, however, the debate has been burdened with rhetorical phrasings that thinly mask the biases of various proponents. The quotation cited above from Peter Ewell, a highly regarded analyst of assessment and evaluation methods in the United States, directs attention to the tensions that exist between two key purposes of performance monitoring systems, but it also reflects a widely held but somewhat simplistic view that the two are mutually exclusive. Hard evidence of either the strengths or weaknesses of using a performance dimension remains quite rare. This is an area in need of future research.

In this chapter, we examine recent experience with using the performance dimension in several states and accrediting agencies in the United States. Following a clarification about how we define performance, we review the efforts of US accrediting agencies to make performance more central to accrediting reviews as well as recent state initiatives to use performance indicators linked to budgetary decisions. Our purposes are to show the ways in which performance is currently being used as a tool for external review of universities and to identify some emerging points of convergence among the different approaches. We believe that the two processes we describe – those found in accreditation processes and those found in the use of performance indicators by state governments – represent different but complimentary lenses for thinking about performance. Furthermore, as the two processes have addressed weaknesses in their approaches to monitoring performance, some elements of convergence between them can be seen.

Defining performance in recent context

Performance in simple terms means the relationship of outcomes to goals. More nuanced definitions have emerged in the debate around accreditation's recent attention to performance, as complex issues have been raised about measuring student achievement or the overall educational effectiveness of a university. Still other definitions have emerged from state government policies to use performance indicators to evaluate both administrative and academic aspects of university performance.

Differences in language and assumptions are important, as they have led to different practices and to lengthy disputes when performance-based approaches have been introduced. Fully articulated performance systems typically include the following components: 1) identifying goals or standards; 2) developing methods for measuring relationships between goals and existing practice (for example through assessment, benchmarks, or performance indicators); and 3) analysing actual results. Performance is the more inclusive term used for these different concepts.

Strictly speaking, performance is a neutral term, describing a continuum in which no judgement is made about any specific points on the continuum. Actual systems of performance measurement, however, are not necessarily neutral about the goals of performance measurement. The quality assurance systems of many countries have been designed to ensure that basic, or minimum, levels of performance are achieved. In contrast, the quality improvement or 'outcomes' movements that have recently had wide influence on US higher education generally insist that universities attain more than minimum standards. Indeed, the underlying premise of total quality management (TQM) is that institutions should continuously improve and strive to reach the higher levels on a performance continuum.

Some background about the emergence of performance monitoring systems will help place our analysis in context. In the United States, several overlapping approaches can be found, from national rankings to regional and specialized accreditation, from state-mandated programme review or state use of performance indicators to university-level outcomes assessment tied to overall planning (El-Khawas 1993). This varied attention to evaluating performance is reflective of the general pressures towards accountability evident in most countries, as well as the pressures felt by US accrediting and state agencies to provide better information about university performance to legislatures and to the public, especially by answering basic questions about student achievement.

Although approaches vary, a common set of issues can be observed in the performance-based systems of states and accreditors alike. Continuing debate has centred on questions affecting the structure and design of approaches to using performance. Especially contentious have been issues of whether accountability or improvement is to be sought, as well as issues of whether self-regulation can accomplish more than external regulation. Concerns have also been raised about the level of flexibility a system offers for internal groups to define performance measures, especially to recognize institutional diversity and difference in mission.

On most of these issues, states and accreditors have taken different stances. Most state-based performance systems assume that objective criteria for performance can be applied to all institutions, regardless of institutional differences. State approaches are primarily externally driven, and emphasize accountability over improvement. In contrast, accreditation generally assumes that performance must be defined within each institutional context and, therefore, no definition or measure can be utilized in all situations. Accrediting procedures also give priority to self-regulatory review, increasingly focusing on improving educational practices. As the following sections show, however, both states and accreditors have gradually moved closer together in their approaches, based on a more complex view of the issues in measuring the performance of universities.

Recent reforms in accrediting approaches

Accreditation is a voluntary structure, created and maintained by the collective actions of colleges and universities, that publicly attests to the quality of
academic institutions in the United States. A century in existence, accreditation has achieved such general legitimacy that several formal linkages have
developed between accrediting and the oversight roles of federal and state
governments. Because the US has no national ministry of education or
other official body setting academic standards, for example, the US Department of Education, a federal agency, provides oversight of the standards and
actions of accrediting bodies, but not of individual institutions. While
accreditation is unusual, it has been said to have contributed to the long-
term success of American higher education by its decentralized approach to
change and improvement, where each institution is expected to gauge its
own performance and problems.

There are two distinct types of accreditation: regional (also called institutional) and specialized. Regional accrediting agencies certify that institutions meet basic resource and performance criteria and assure the public
that these institutions meet certain minimum standards (Dill *et al.* 1996;
Stanley and Patrick 1998; El-Khawas 2001). Accreditation also works to
strengthen educational quality by encouraging institutional self-study and
improvement. This chapter focuses on the six regional accreditation agencies that, together, have the broadest responsibility for certifying the integrity
and quality of universities and colleges in the US. Short names are used in
the text, with a full listing of their formal names at the end of the chapter. It
should be noted, however, that reforms are also being undertaken by other
agencies, including the eight national associations and approximately 75
specialized and programmatic accreditors that evaluate specific disciplines
such as journalism, business, law, nursing or chemistry.

Regional accreditation takes several forms, but the following are typical
processes: 1) the agency establishes a set of standards; 2) it develops a regular
schedule in which each institution performs a self-study comparing itself to
those standards; 3) the agency selects a team to visit the institution to determine if the standards are being met; and 4) if the accrediting agency is
satisfied, it grants accreditation to the institution, effective for time periods
varying from one to ten years (Crosson 1987; Cohen 1998). A gradation of
'sanctions' are employed when problems are found: programmes that do not
meet standards are put on probation until they come into compliance; where
limited problems are identified, institutions are given a specific time in
which to make corrections. Because each agency establishes standards for
the institutions in its region, standards vary among the agencies.

The strengths of accreditation in comparison to other systems of understanding performance have been said to include the following: 1) it is a
context-based review process, sensitive to local institutional circumstances; 2)
its review is conducted by outside evaluators who have professional experiences in settings comparable to those they evaluate; 3) multiple definitions

of performance are used, tied to the specific mission and goals articulated by the institution; and 4) the focus is on understanding how institutions perform and the relationship of goals, processes and outcomes.

In the last decade, several forces have led to fundamental changes in accreditation and to dramatically new efforts in how they define and evaluate performance. First, federal legislation and the US Department of Education have focused greater attention on the regulatory function of accreditation. Federal requirements imposed on accrediting agencies, especially to address issues of institutional integrity and good performance, have increased. Recent concerns over the cost of higher education and the long-term prospect of decreased public funding have also generated pressures to examine effectiveness and efficiency as important goals. The National Commission on College Costs and Cost Containment stated, for example, that accreditation processes should focus more on student outcomes and less on resource acquisition as the hallmark of quality.

For much of its history, accreditation was a largely private process, turned inward to provide universities with information on educational quality but with little emphasis on programme improvement (Cohen 1998). Today, accrediting associations increasingly look outward, to federal and state governments and to the general public. The major purposes of accreditation today are to help assure the consumers of higher education – parents, students, employers and government agencies that provide student financial aid – that an institution or programme is meeting minimum standards and to stimulate those institutions to move beyond minimum standards. The improvement aspect of the accrediting role, although relatively new, has become a dominant concern (Eaton 2001; WASC 2001, 2002).

The standards adopted by the New England association illustrate the multi-layered approach that is typical to regional agencies (NEASC 2002). The general standards have multiple components, covering such areas as institutional mission and purposes, planning and evaluation; undergraduate and graduate programmes of instruction; resources related to student services; library and information resources; physical resources or facilities; and financial capability. For each of these standards, the institution must describe its goals and give evidence to assess its performance, which is later reviewed by a visiting team. This is an extensive, detailed process of assessing performance, but one that organizes relevant data at the local level so that it can provide guidance for institutional improvement.

In recent years, all regional agencies have embarked on a systematic revision of their accrediting standards. Rather than having a laundry list of structures and processes in place, agencies are streamlining their processes to better address issues of effectiveness, outcomes and integrity. The New England association, for example, is conducting a review of its standards for accreditation, examining ways they could be changed or modified for today's circumstances. The Western association, working to develop a more effective review process, plans to consolidate a lengthy set of standards around a few broadly comprehensive standards. Thematic self-studies are another technique to provide greater focus; rather than reviewing all institutional processes, new areas or special issues become the focus of accreditation review.

A related trend is the development of Internet-based data portfolios that separate data reporting into two forms: data in electronic portfolios designed to show that the university meets basic compliance standards; and the data needed for self-study and team visits, more aligned with the developmental, improvement function of accrediting. Internet data portfolios, and recent suggestions for web-based reviews, capitalize on existing data capabilities, streamline the reporting process and allow for timely and inexpensive compliance monitoring. Some associations are implementing yearly reports or other frequent updates; others have mandated data portfolios after four years, to be used to frame the full ten-year self-study.

Several of the regional accreditation associations are trying to develop benchmarks for examining levels of performance, rather than simply labeling institutions as in or out of compliance. Such efforts involve the development of rubrics that define levels of performance. Once in place, such rubrics could help self-study teams to view institutional practices on a continuum of development rather than as a single snapshot of institutional functioning. In initiating such new approaches, regional accreditors are trying to move from a mostly penalty-oriented system to one that spurs change by allowing institutions to understand more accurately the ways they need to improve.

A focus on results, especially on student outcomes, is another major direction of accreditation reform. The New England association, in its effort to focus on outcomes, has surveyed its members to identify processes that would allow better collection and use of student outcomes assessment data. The Middle States association now has a process called 'accreditation for growth' that allows institutions to shift their evaluation procedures toward outputs. Institutions will now obtain accreditation on the basis of continuous growth in student performance. This new process serves two purposes at once: meeting accrediting needs and offering greater support for university improvement initiatives.

Increasingly, accrediting agencies are emphasizing the improvement aspect of their objectives, pressing for reforms that promise to make institutions more effective. The focus on effectiveness goes beyond traditional questions of whether universities have good procedures in place, raising new questions about how procedures work together and, more importantly, whether they work together effectively. The New England association now has a policy on institutional effectiveness. It calls for the use of outcomes assessment and for a detailed review of institutional planning so that a university can understand and evaluate its own effectiveness. Under this approach, each institution determines the way it will measure and demonstrate effectiveness. The Western association has called for institutional experimentation with new ways to assess the effectiveness of educational programmes. Thus, for example, California State University, Sacramento organized its self-study around assessment while California State University,

Fullerton utilized a model of student and faculty learning for its accreditation review. Each model focused not on procedures but on outcomes; the broad objective being to identify more effective models for accreditation review.

Tied to the new focus on results and effectiveness is a renewed emphasis on value added. This involves a shift in emphasis towards finding ways to improve or offer more effective programmes; such a focus could engage faculty in asking questions, collecting information and discussing strategies for implementing improvements. This has a very different emphasis than accreditation's traditional compliance model where, for many well-established institutions, self-study reports were put on a shelf and little used. Among the proposed models to support a value-added review is the use by the Middle States association of a 'reflective institutional portfolio' that would review and comment on evidence of teaching effectiveness, student learning and programme quality. Another approach is to share good practices within the region through websites and periodic meetings.

Several foundations have funded accreditation associations to support their new directions. Under its project called Restructuring Expectations: Accreditation 2004, the North Central association is redefining the priorities, goals and stakeholders of its association (NCA 2002; Crow 2002). Through a survey, a working team and an action committee, the North Central association will examine the place of quality assurance, outcomes assessment and cost containment, among other issues, in its activities. In another project, the North Central association will help its member institutions build an internal culture of quality, able to monitor and improve institutional practices on an ongoing basis. The Western association has grant support from the Irvine Foundation and Pew Charitable Trusts to examine effectiveness within the accreditation process. Its objectives are to create a functional accreditation model organized around educational effectiveness and to build institutional capacity to communicate, educate and evaluate educational effectiveness more efficiently (WASC 2001, 2002).

As this review of recent initiatives indicates, regional accrediting agencies are involved in significant self-assessment and reform. Their adoption of student outcomes requirements and their emphasis on results and effectiveness has given them a new, more publicly responsive direction. Yet, it is also clear that their reforms are tempered by accreditation's tradition of honouring the importance of institutional context and experience. The reforms set new directions, but they are consistent with the long-term reliance on detailed, context-specific review procedures that allow complex educational processes to be examined.

Recent state approaches

Over the past two decades, many states began to use performance indicators to establish new systems of accountability to assure the public that tax dollars were being well spent. Most of these states mounted ambitious plans and models that would affect all institutions of higher education within their state. By 2002, however, most state governments faced severe budgetary pressures, a dramatic reversal of budgetary gains made just a few years earlier (Selingo 2003); the result has been a major slowing down of activity related to performance funding. Some states have entirely shut down their performance-focused programmes. Others have slowed the pace of implementation (Schmidt 2002b). Even so, for our purposes, there is much to learn. The following discussion focuses on an analysis of four elements that have emerged as distinctive to state accountability programmes that are performance-focused. The four elements include: selection of a discrete number of performance goals that can be assessed by quantitative measures; the use of financial incentives, or sanctions, tied to the performance results obtained by each university; public reporting of performance results, often through wide media coverage; and the release of information in such a way that each university or college can be compared with others (Banta *et al.* 1996; Layzell and Caruthers 1995). These four elements, major aspects of most state approaches to performance, are generally not found in accrediting practice.

By the late 1990s, a majority of state governments in the US had made some use of performance measures in their oversight of universities and colleges (Christal 1998; Schmidt 2002b). Terminology differed, as did the specific approaches found among these states. Some states used performance-funding, defined as systems in which a specified amount of additional funds is awarded to those higher education institutions that meet certain performance criteria. Other states assessed and examined universities on the basis of certain performance indicators, but did not tie performance results directly to funding amounts. Several recent publications (Christal 1998; Burke and Serban 1998) offer capsule descriptions of the systems adopted by individual states.

Although states differed in their approaches to performance, their actions can be distinguished analytically as either self-regulating, externally regulated, or a combination of the two – mixed or hybrid models. State use of performance indicators most often has followed the externally regulated model, where the government sets the terms and administers the entire process. Some systems are mixed, where state governments mandate that a performance measurement process be conducted, but allow each institution to develop its own criteria or procedures. Tennessee followed this approach, especially in its first decade of operations. Minnesota built flexibility into its approach by allowing institutions to decide how to achieve statewide objectives while requiring them to submit plans and progress reports. Such hybrid approaches allowed for some decentralization of procedure, yet require that the same criteria be imposed on all institutions, thus setting limits on local initiative (Schmidt 2002b).

Missouri experimented with a more decentralized approach. Under its Funding for Results programme, now ended, it included an option for rewarding universities that designed their own campus-based projects for improving teaching and learning (Albright 1998; Schmidt 2002a). Kentucky allowed flexibility in its performance-based system by mandating institutional use of five common indicators, counting towards half of an overall score, while allowing institutional choices from among six other indicators to make up the remaining half of the institution's score on performance.

Performance-based systems also differ in the extent to which they emphasize compliance or improvement. Most state systems using performance indicators have tilted strongly towards accountability, in contrast to the way that accreditation has tried to balance both compliance and improvement. Tennessee, which has the longest history with performance indicators, began with a compliance emphasis but, over time, shifted towards improvement (Banta 1996). As Tennessee's programme evolved, several indicators were introduced that evaluated an institution's improvement over several years, rather than focusing solely on the absolute scores achieved in a single year. Missouri had also sought a balance, rewarding improvement as well as attainment of goals.

Some models emphasize performance monitoring by institutions themselves. This approach typically supported improvement initiatives, because universities were expected to document the changes they made based on their own review of assessment results. Under Kentucky's plan, institutions were rewarded for the first two rounds of the plan's operation if they took steps towards use of performance indicators; actual results counted only during the third round. This approach allowed institutions to work on improvement before facing direct accountability judgements. South Carolina, which established a performance-based system only in 1996, constructed performance-funding criteria that required continuous improvement by its universities (Schmidt 1999; Schmidt 2002b; South Carolina Commission on Higher Education 2001).

States also differ in the goals they have chosen to include in performance monitoring. Most state systems included attention to student retention and graduation rates among their indicators. Missouri chose to be more specific, however, calling for data on the number of graduates each university produced in 'critical disciplines' that served overall state needs. Other states have introduced related goals, such as improved graduation rates for low-income and minority students. South Carolina's plan calls for performance data on employment rates for graduates and employer feedback on their satisfaction with graduates (Schmidt 1999).

Other goals extend beyond the traditional university focus on teaching and learning. Several states called on universities to show evidence that they contribute to workforce training or are engaged in service to the state or to their communities. Ohio expected its two-year colleges to report on their business partnerships, community involvement, job training and links with secondary school systems. Colorado's system required performance reporting in what the state legislature identified as five high-priority policy areas: workforce training; the use of new technology; improving undergraduate education; linkages with the school systems; and productivity increases.

An important but often unacknowledged tendency was for states to mix efficiency goals with goals that are directed to performance. Arkansas, for example, included goals related to teaching load, faculty and staff diversity and administrative costs in its performance system. Florida pressed for information on faculty productivity, requiring data on five different components of workload. Colorado set goals for space utilization and course availability in its performance-based system. In Ohio, two-year colleges could earn a performance reward for holding back on increases in tuition and other fees. Performance reporting often mixed performance and efficiency, especially in those states that developed a long list of goals, resulting in mutually inconsistent indicators.

At the same time, some state governments moved towards performance budgeting, a more flexible approach than performance funding in that state officials take performance scores into account as they make funding decisions but are not constrained to blindly allocate funds according to a formula (Burke and Serban 1998). Also noticeable was a softening of the impact of performance scores on institutional budgets, especially when certain universities report low scores; many states now give developmental funds to those with low scores. This reflects an awareness that the state's interest is served not only by rewarding the 'winners' but also by assisting those who currently do not meet performance goals (Schmidt 2002b).

Most states changed aspects of their designs over time, partly due to changing political conditions (for example, a new governor, changing legislative leadership, different university actions and so on) but often also in response to what was learned from earlier experience. There has been continuing difficulty with developing measures to fit targeted goals. Substantial problems have been encountered, for example, with attempts to document that graduates have acquired the skills and knowledge needed by employers. In the early 1990s, New Jersey conducted an intensive effort to test students on key skills and competencies (Jemmott and Morante 1993). Complex technical issues arose, and the financial investment needed to establish a full-scale testing system eventually undercut the programme's political support. Most states that sought to develop measures on the quality of undergraduate education have resorted to the use of graduation rates, even though such rates are widely acknowledged to offer limited measures of a programme's effectiveness. Even in states that have had stable performance systems for many years, most measures continue to be, at best, weak proxies for the goals they are intended to represent.

Despite their mixed experience and current budget constraints, most states remain committed to the use of performance indicators as part of the overall surveillance of their systems of higher education. While states have revised their measures for assessing specific goals and have changed their implementation processes, the overall objectives remain consistent: universities today are to be assessed on their current performance, not their past achievements or reputation, and they are to be assessed on matters related to student learning. State experience with using a performance dimension has also given state officials a new appreciation that universities themselves must be active in improving educational practice and, too, that such engagement is supported by flexibility in a state's directives (Newman and Couturier 2002).

Summary and conclusion

From the developments we have reviewed, it is evident that substantial experience has accumulated among both state and accrediting officials on approaches to measuring the performance of universities. Especially noteworthy are three general tendencies in their evolving practice: 1) the convergence of accreditation and performance monitoring systems on certain lessons learned in common; 2) the important ways that the two systems mutually reinforce one another; and 3) the synergy achieved by combining both systems, creating a more powerful system than the two separately. Following comments on each of these points, the chapter ends with recommendations for continuing to refine performance-monitoring systems.

Viewed in broad perspective, it appears that both states and accreditors have moved towards common ground in how they use the performance dimension. From initially contrasting positions, some convergence can be seen towards a broadly similar strategy, which blends flexibility of methods with a focus on results. Common to both agencies today is the explicit focus on goals or results, and the conviction that external bodies can properly set those goals.

Accrediting agencies are strengthening the accountability components of their generally flexible review processes while also pressing universities to document their results. Despite variations in terminology, a strong and consistent focus has emerged among accrediting agencies, one that insists on directing attention towards educational effectiveness, programme quality and student achievement. Yet, while their procedures have become more results-oriented, they remain flexible. The Western association, for example, now allows universities to choose a specific focus for the evaluation visit along with very general data reporting on other matters (Eaton 2001).

State governments began by focusing almost exclusively on results, with quantitative systems based on performance indicators, weights and institutional scores. Over time, they became more flexible, allowing universities more options on how they assess performance. Both states and accreditors have backed up their strong emphasis on goals with equally strong expectations that universities assess their results and report their degree of success with improvement efforts.

With both states and accrediting agencies, a results-oriented stance is accompanied by a conviction that better results occur if institutions have some flexibility on the means by which they meet external mandates. This has resulted in the adoption of what has been called a 'steering' approach, in which agencies set specific goals but allow universities considerable discretion in how those goals are met (Van Vught 1989). Such flexibility stands in sharp contrast to the approaches of state policies in the past, where details of administrative procedures and strict rules about allowable expenditures had dominated the relationship between higher education and the state. Under performance-based systems most states avoid spelling out how goals are to be met. Certain score levels – or an improvement in scores – are required, but there is no prescribed way to produce acceptable scores. In this sense, state approaches are moving closer to those of accrediting agencies, which have typically granted much greater leeway in what procedures are followed.

Some other clues suggest that the two separate paths – accreditation and state use of performance indicators – may have their best effect when they work together. Formal cooperation between accreditors and states has grown over the last decade, for example. Many accrediting groups have worked with state agencies to develop joint protocols that serve as the basis for joint visits and formal reports (El-Khawas 1993: 118–19; El-Khawas 2001: 113–16). Some states have specified that certain accrediting actions will serve as evidence that a university has met performance standards in that area. As another approach, South Carolina established a performance standard that its institutions must achieve accreditation in certain programmes. In other instances, collaborative agreements have been reached to allow an institution's accreditation status to be recognized as a basis for meeting certain state requirements. This has occurred, for example, with teacher preparation programmes, which have long been subject to detailed oversight by both states and by the agency that accredits teacher preparation.

One of the most significant ways that accreditation and state performance systems have reinforced each other is through a form of synergy, in which pressure from both agencies, each combining flexibility and specific direction, brings about a good result. Recent studies have found that the institutions most successfully using outcomes assessment operated under both an accrediting and a state requirement for outcomes assessment; however, both requirements were flexible: the state did not mandate the type of assessment to be used and the accrediting requirement was flexible but provided clear guidance on suggested measures and processes of assessment (Peterson and Augustine 2000). As the authors suggest, accreditation guidance on assessment was taken more seriously in states that mandated outcomes assessment. Conversely, states found that richer assessment data were collected and were more likely to be used if their mandates allowed flexibility but were backed up by accrediting guidelines. So too, with accrediting guidelines alone or with highly specific state performance requirements alone, universities may make little progress because of the inertia against change or because 'compliance behaviour' takes precedence. State mandates and accrediting guidelines, together, seem to have the power to overcome this inertia.

Several recommendations for performance systems can be drawn from this analysis of recent experience among US accrediting agencies and states. First, state performance-based systems may operate best if they move from primarily external regulatory models to mixed systems – combining both external regulation and internal or self-regulation. For performance systems to be effective, they must draw on expertise at the various levels of the system. External stakeholders, especially those with national or state-wide responsibilities, are well positioned to be aware of changing public pressures with respect to effectiveness, efficiency or outcomes. Internal university stakeholders – both faculty and administrative officials – may misjudge or not be sufficiently attentive to such external trends. At the same time, internal stakeholders have their special strengths; they can offer invaluable specific knowledge and 'local expertise' about institutional context and feasible improvement processes, about the way that complex and multiple goals might all be pursued and, especially, about what is needed to develop meaningful standards for evaluating performance.

States and accreditors should work with higher education institutions to identify broad goals for higher education institutions. However, they should maintain this macro-level emphasis and not get distracted by technical points of administrative procedure. In turn, universities should accept that the state, and accrediting agencies, have the right to identify publicly-valued goals, even as all parties should work together to specify goals and the measures and definitions that are to be used.

Another recommendation, useful for anyone seeking insights into the potential value of performance indicators as a policy tool, is to recognize the fundamental shift in orientation that performance indicator systems have achieved. As one US analyst has commented, the use of performance indicators has introduced a paradigm shift in how states think about the role of higher education (Albright 1997). Performance indicators helped states to refocus their policy decisions, away from the traditional focus on institutional structures and processes, and towards greater attention to results, especially to student outcomes and student learning. The introduction of performance indicators thus served to drive new notions about performance and accountability as legitimate outcomes. This is an important long-term change in understanding and defining university performance (El-Khawas 2001).

A second insight relates to the vital need to achieve balance between outcomes and processes. One of the weaknesses of early systems of performance indicators is that they pressed for a focus on results without paying attention to how such results were achieved. Constructing scores is but one step; knowing how to improve practice is just as important to the ultimate goals of improving student learning and achievement. Similarly, both states and accrediting agencies also benefit from a balanced approach to imposing efficiency goals within performance monitoring systems; here too, high performance requires that sound decisions be made to 'invest' in improved practices.

With respect to the evidence of a gradual convergence towards a steering approach, another recommendation can be offered. State government officials and accrediting agencies should discuss further ways to coordinate and reinforce each other's activities. Along with the examples of cooperation that have been cited, numerous situations exist in which the requirements of states and accreditors are still duplicative or work at cross purposes.

Finally, universities should engage in discussions among themselves about the relative gains of the flexible but goal-directed processes that have emerged under this 'steering' model of policy direction. If a consensus emerges that steering models have their benefits, universities should develop an agenda of their own that would support and build upon the steering model. Universities might develop a joint statement that outlines the resources and strategic steps needed to better measure key outcomes. Universities might also take the initiative to highlight and share information on emerging best practice on ways to achieve important goals.

The focus on performance – on the results or outcomes of university operations – is here to stay. Evolving practice may be moving towards processes that will be genuinely effective in measuring university performance. Much remains to be done.

Appendix

List of Six Regional Accrediting Agencies
   New England Association of Schools and Colleges
   Western Association of Schools and Colleges
   North Central Association of Schools and Colleges
   Middle States Association of Schools and Colleges
   Southern Association of Schools and Colleges
   Northwestern Association of Schools and Colleges

7

Convergence and divergence: differing approaches to quality and accreditation in Europe

Elisabeth Lillie

Contextual factors

As Europe works increasingly towards the creation of a European Higher Education Area, implementing the process first given impetus by the Sorbonne Declaration of 1998 and the Bologna Agreement of 1999, so the concern with processes of quality, evaluation and accreditation has grown both at European and national levels. Since Bologna, further activity and meetings (most notably that of Ministers of Higher Education in Prague 2001, with another meeting in Berlin in September 2003) have continued to feed into the process of educational development within the countries of Europe, maintaining the momentum towards enhanced mutual understanding and, ultimately, a fuller harmonization of systems (a harmonization that nonetheless seeks to respect key national specificities within the multivariate European mosaic).

Within the various debates in this arena, the interrelated themes of quality, evaluation and accreditation are ones that concern educators across a range of institutions and subjects throughout Europe. If the desired goals of educational interchange and professional mobility are to be achieved, then all those concerned (educators, students and employers) must be satisfied as to the validity, content and levels of the qualifications offered in educational institutions throughout the Higher Education Area. With increasing mobility within Europe and the force of globalization, there is a strong sense of the importance of transparency and the adherence to generally understood national norms, which can have validity at a European as well as at a more local level.

An enhanced move towards quality and accreditation responds also to the need to evaluate standards and the quality of the student experience at a time of mass higher education expansion, on the one hand, and to monitor the use to which public funds are put, on the other. This is particularly pertinent in countries of Central and Eastern Europe where, in response to the widespread demand for higher education, there has also been the emergence of a wide range of private institutions alongside the long-established state ones, making it important for these countries to ensure the quality of the work of these new establishments. In certain instances, too, there has been a concern to effect changes in the nature of the curriculum offered, whether in older or more recent institutions, coupled with a desire to establish a generally understood and recognized system for ensuring quality within a new situation.

European countries offer different traditions of the role of the state and its relationship with higher education. Inevitably, these traditions condition the nature of the control and monitoring process to which universities in particular countries are subject: on the one hand, ministries of education in highly centralized states will prescribe in considerable detail the regulations to which institutions of higher education are subject (France, for instance, which, despite moves in the direction of devolution, has long had a tradition of centralization), whereas in other countries such as the United Kingdom, universities have enjoyed higher degrees of autonomy.

This chapter will consider areas of quality monitoring, evaluation and accreditation in the countries of Europe. By its very nature, this is an evolving field as countries seek to set in place mechanisms for assurance that respect long-standing traditions as well as taking account of new educational developments. Countries look inwards at their own educators who must respect and accept the procedures; they look outwards too towards European institutions, companion European states; and they look towards the future of a more co-operative, interactive Europe and an increasingly mobile student and professional body able to cross boundaries and work transnationally.

One locus of educational development in Europe is found in the political heart of the European Union as it works and influences governments and their national administrations. Another type of forum for discussion and action may be seen in those associations that bring together educators at very many diverse levels to discuss and work or common interests. Such associations range from the top levels of institutional management (European University Association) to those concerned specifically with quality (European Network for Quality Assurance in Higher Education – ENQUA – open to quality assurance agencies, public authorities responsible for quality assurance in higher education and associations of higher education institutions in the member states of the European Union). At the level of teaching, higher education lecturers may work through a variety of subject and professional groupings on a European level. One such type of interaction may be found in the thematic networks of subject specialists that bring together staff in a particular specialist area from different countries to work on specific subjects or themes and which receive financial support from the European Union's SOCRATES programme (ERASMUS). The author of this chapter has participated in the work of the Thematic Network Project in the Area of Languages as a member of the Scientific Committee on Quality Enhancement in Language Studies. In addition to matters specific to languages, this has also involved some consideration of quality and accreditation systems in a variety of European countries through work on national reports written by participants in the committee.[1] The analysis undertaken here is largely based on these reports.

In Europe different processes may be distinguished (although, as will be seen, there is sometimes a certain fluidity and overlap between them). When new institutions or programmes are first approved, they undergo a process of accreditation. The institution, if newly established, may be subject to processes of approval to ascertain its fitness to undertake higher education, which will constitute a first accreditation of the institution. Where the curriculum is concerned, there is, for it as for institutions, the first authorization to mount a subject or programme.

Once institutions and programmes are in operation, they are then subject to a process of monitoring and evaluation at specific intervals. Depending on the country concerned, the nature of these processes varies. For instance, there may be regular inspections at the level of the institution, looking at institutional systems as a whole, which may or may not be complemented by a consideration of subject delivery. Institutions in some countries will operate a process of regular annual monitoring of their subject delivery, complemented by a periodic in-depth review at less regular intervals. Some countries may require the courses to be resubmitted to a national body for renewed accreditation after a certain number of years or the review may be based within the institution. This renewal may occasionally take the form of a new accreditation request or there may be a re-submission of programmes for approval to the ministry or body concerned.

National accreditation or evaluation bodies

While the characteristics of the approach may differ somewhat, many countries have now established a body or national agency which is generally charged with institutional review as a whole, as well as the accreditation and evaluation of courses and programmes (in some countries, however, there are a number of different bodies exercising slightly different functions but, as will be seen, there is often a move towards a national body with overall oversight or responsibility).

The nature of the monitoring or validating agency and its relationship with the state will reflect the political ethos of the country concerned. Thus in countries where the state has traditionally played a major role in determining the content and nature of higher education structures and curricula, much of the evaluation or accreditation will be undertaken by the ministry of education or by a body very directly responsible to it. Universities have traditionally enjoyed a greater degree of autonomy, although a recent movement towards greater uniformity may be discerned.

The United Kingdom and France may be considered as exemplars of different approaches to accreditation and evaluation. In France, for instance, most tertiary education (as indeed most primary and secondary education) is subject to the control of the ministry of education (Ministère de l'Education Nationale), whereas in the United Kingdom, there has been a tradition of much greater autonomy for universities. Education in France is considered to be a public service, a right to which all citizens must have equal access, irrespective of social or geographical origins and the provision is also expected to be of equal quality throughout the country. University qualifications are thus for the most part national ones awarded within frameworks defined by the ministry and all new courses leading to these national qualifications have to be approved by the ministry (Toudic 2002). Yet even in this highly centralized country, the role of the ministry is complemented by a further body, the Comité national d'évaluation (national evaluation committee), a development that was triggered by a perceived need for more rigorous assessment of performance and results. This is an independent but state-funded body composed of appointed representatives of the academic community and senior civil servants that conducts regular audits of HE institutions, looking at areas such as financial management, academic organization, human resources and buildings (Toudic 2002). Research, on the other hand, is subject to annual assessment by ministry experts on the submission of reports by research groups or teams (Toudic 2002). In France there is thus an approach where ministerial control remains strong in the different areas, even when a slightly more devolved system is operated.

The United Kingdom may be considered to sit at the other end of the spectrum from France, with universities that in the past had considerable independence and that also have the right to establish and validate their own degrees. Here it is interesting to chart the movement towards higher levels of control in view of the growth and spread of institutions, the need to diversify and offer access to higher education to a larger proportion of young people as well as the concern to ensure greater accountability and transparency, given the levels of public funding involved. After the establishment of new institutions, then known as polytechnics, in the public sector (as distinct from universities that had a more autonomous status) in the late 1960s and early 1970s a dual system of accreditation and review was set in place with a specific body (the Council for National Academic Awards – CNAA) overseeing their work. The older universities continued to enjoy considerable discretion in the ordering of their affairs, although they were increasingly subject to a number of codes and controls. This duality lasted until 1992 when the UK moved in favour of a more uniform system for the whole of the sector.

Within the longer-established university system, the United Kingdom gradually began the shift from a position in which the institutions were largely self-regulating, with the first codes of practice being established by the sector itself. By the 1980s, the older university sector had responded to pressure from government for greater accountability and transparency in procedures by the development of a certain number of codes of practice (in relation, for instance, to the role of the external examiner and to appeal procedures at postgraduate research level). These codes were developed by a working group of the Committee of Vice-Chancellors and Principals (CVCP) – now UniversitiesUK – the umbrella body bringing together the Heads of Universities. Essentially, these codes were based on current procedures and sought to develop and share best practice throughout the sector but compliance with them remained voluntary.

In 1990, a further step was taken in the direction of national assessment with the establishment by the CVCP of the Academic Audit Unit to undertake reviews of quality assurance systems in place in universities. Universities thus recognized mounting external pressure for control but sought to meet this through self-regulation. The Audit Unit was thus owned by the CVCP, its audits were undertaken by teams drawn from throughout the sector and were based around aims and objectives formulated by universities themselves, which were considered in relation to the codes and guidelines for good practice already drawn up by the CVCP.

The principle of extending quality assurance and accountability was included in the Further and Higher Education Act of 1992, which entrusted the Higher Education Quality Council with the task of undertaking audits at the institutional level in all parts of the sector; thus replacing, on the one hand, the work of the Academic Audit Unit and, on the other, the Council for National Academic Awards (which, in addition to its validation role at course and subject level, also had responsibilities in this respect for certain institutions). While still self-regulatory and owned by the sector, the Higher Education Quality Council represented a clear stage in the creation of a more unitary system of quality assurance within higher education in relation to institutional governance and organization.

Monitoring and evaluation of universities has, since 1997, been undertaken by the Quality Assurance Agency, which has responsibility both for the auditing of institutions as a whole and for subject delivery. (The monitoring of subject provision had previously been undertaken under the auspices of the Higher Education Funding Councils for the various areas of the United Kingdom.[2]) Assessment of research within the UK is undertaken separately from that of subject provision and this continues to be the case. Although established through government initiative, the Quality Assurance Agency is not part of the civil service but is established as an independent company, limited by guarantee with representation on the board of directors from the universities, commerce, industry and the professions. Noteworthy in this connection is the recognition implied in board membership of the responsibilities of higher education towards society, its economic needs and the future employability of students.

In the United Kingdom, accreditation of courses continues to be the responsibility of the University, although the conditions under which this is conducted have been increasingly standardized and subject to processes of audit and evaluation undertaken by the Quality Assurance Agency (which works largely through panels and teams composed of members of academic institutions). The United Kingdom has in effect, through its various evaluative methods and modes of implementation, obtained a standardization of processes by persuasion, publication of reports and judgements ('name and shame' – and ability to create a negative image, which might effect recruitment) that has continued to apparently respect the autonomy of institutions to order their own affairs but which has, equally, seen movement towards increased harmonization of process.

Between these two countries, considered in some detail as representing different approaches, there is in the countries of Europe (whether they be long standing members of the European Union or countries from Central and Eastern Europe) a wide range of practice but at the same time certain common features. The European Union has also been concerned to promote criteria of quality and a qualitative approach to evaluation, and is giving encouragement in a variety of ways to initiatives in the field of quality, evaluation and accreditation.

In addition to the events that stem from the Bologna process through the meetings of ministers with responsibility for higher education in the European continent as a whole, specific initiatives emanating from the European Commission have also given impetus in this direction, such as the European memorandum on Higher Education of 1991 and the 1993 study *Quality management and Quality Assurance in European Higher Education: Methods and Mechanisms* (Brussels: European Commission, Education, Training and Youth, Studies No. 1). In fact, this study represented the recommendations of the Confederation of European Union Rectors' Conferences presented to the European Commission, which led in 1994 to a European pilot project for 'Evaluating Quality in Higher Education'. Then in 1998 came the 'Council Recommendation on Quality in Higher Education', promoting the concept of quality among higher education institutions in Europe.[3]

It is striking how many countries now have some sort of national body or bodies dealing with accreditation and evaluation. There have also been relatively recent Education Acts in certain countries establishing a clearer system of accreditation and evaluation. In Finland there is, for instance, the Finnish Higher Education Evaluation Council, established in 1996 that assists institutions of higher education and the ministry of education in matters relating to evaluation and also initiates and undertakes a range of evaluation projects in higher education, as well as promoting research in the area of evaluation. By 2000, all Finnish universities had undergone evaluation in one form or another. In should, however, be noted that while the evaluations in Finland are undertaken by the Evaluation Council, each higher education institution makes its own decisions as to the principles to be taken into account in its evaluations (Sajavaara 2003). In Slovakia proposals from 2002 cover the establishment of a national coordinating body coupled, however, with considerable measures of self-regulation and external evaluation by academic peers (Blašková 2003). In Hungary the national system of accreditation is carried out by the National Accreditation Board (NAB) with validation at both institutional and subject/curriculum levels (Szabó 2002).

In certain countries too, there is an emerging movement from self-regulation in the sector to a somewhat greater measure of national control and conformity. In Poland, for instance, in addition to the University Accreditation Commission established by the Conference of Rectors of Polish Universities, there is now also a State Accreditation Commission established in 2001 (Urbanikowa 2002). Interestingly, this is in tune with developments in countries such as the UK, where initial self-regulation by the sector seems to have paved the way for an enhanced degree of state involvement.

Sometimes rather than a single agency, there may be different players involved. In Lithuania, for instance, there is one body with strategic oversight and responsibility (Council for Assessment of Scientific and Study) and another charged with the implementation of the processes (Study Quality Centre) (Skurvydiene and Juceviciute 2002). In Norway there is close cooperation between the ministry and the agency concerned, since, as a result of a recent report on education, universities have undergone evaluations that have been initiated by the ministry although administered by the Norway Network Council, the latter being financed and established by the Ministry of Education and Research (Swan 2002).

Initial accreditation for institutions and programmes

This may be given directly by the ministry of education in the country concerned, which may indeed be the body that largely establishes new institutions, particularly any that are within the public domain (for example in France, Toudic 2002). Elsewhere, this responsibility may be devolved by government to an agency (as in the case of the UK where existing institutions applying for university status and degree awarding powers are subject to validation undertaken by the Quality Assurance Agency, which advises government in relation to such applications). In Slovakia too, there is a body that accredits new institutions on behalf of the state (Blašková 2002). In Norway, when the most recent education law takes effect, new institutions will be accredited by a state-appointed accreditation agency (Swan 2002).

Where accreditation or the first authorization to mount a programme is concerned, the more centralized countries will have established a general framework at ministerial level for particular categories of programme (after consultation with relevant stakeholders). Depending on the country, such frameworks will be more or less tightly prescribed. However, even if there is a firm level of prescription (as for example in France), the individual institution will still have some latitude within the given framework to evolve its own course to reflect local needs, conditions and specialisms. France is, however, not alone in indicating that ministerial approval must be given for new courses (for instance, Denmark and Finland may be mentioned; Lauridson 2002; Sajavaara 2003).

In other systems universities may have the right to mount new programmes without ministerial approval but, in general, such freedom is hedged about (and increasingly so) with conditions. This is the case in the United Kingdom, for instance, where national guidelines indicate that course approval should be undertaken by a university evaluation panel that includes representation from outside the institution and where there are also a range of guidelines and principles to be taken into account. In the United Kingdom compliance with such practices would be checked when the university as a whole is audited.

Some countries where newer institutions have grown up alongside long-established universities operate a dual system of accreditation for curricula (as was previously the case in the United Kingdom). While more autonomy is given to older universities, there is a validating body for the new sector. Ireland is a case in point with its Higher Education and Training Authority from which the more recent institutions must seek accreditation (Broderick 2003).

Processes of evaluation and monitoring

Whatever the arrangements for accreditation, there will also normally be a process of evaluation for existing institutions as well as for subjects or courses. While there are many different permutations, such processes may be said to relate, on the one hand, to the institution and its overall procedures for management and maintaining the quality and standards of its provision, which are likely be scrutinized at stated intervals. On the other hand, there will be consideration of the curriculum itself and the course provision offered to students. Typically, there will be a mixture of monitoring internal to the institution as well as external control, monitoring or auditing with the precise nature and relative weighting depending on the country and its traditions. A lighter form of monitoring of subjects may, for instance, take place regularly (often annually) within institutions, but this may be coupled with a periodic form of revalidation or re-accreditation of the subject or course, in greater depth, undertaken either by the institution itself or by an outside agency and operating on a regular pattern. The following discussion attempts (inevitably somewhat arbitrarily) to discuss such systems from the point of view of interaction with external bodies or agencies and then moves on to focus more fully on the processes within institutions.

Interaction with external bodies

There are varying procedures in the conduct of evaluation where a body outside the university is involved and, while not all stages may happen in every country concerned, a general pattern does emerge.

It is customary for a self-evaluation or assessment report to be prepared by the institution, in relation to the aspect of the institution being examined, whether it be the overall institutional processes, or subject provision or a mixture of the two spheres. This report will then be considered by a committee of the agency, which may be variously constituted. Sometimes the report will be sent to a specially constituted panel of experts either nominated by the agency or (occasionally) by the university.

After receipt of the self-evaluation report, there may well be an on-site visit (although this does not happen in every case). During the visit, discussions may take place with those concerned – usually managers (heads of department, heads of centres), teaching staff and students. The visit also enables the accuracy of the self-evaluation report to be checked. Visits may last for one or two days, although they may occasionally be of slightly longer duration.

More freedom is sometimes allowed, as for instance, in Finland where institutions are responsible for their own evaluations although they are supported by the Finnish Evaluation Council Finland (Sajavaara 2003).

On the basis of the panel's deliberations, there will be a report containing conclusions and recommendations. This will be sent to the institution and to the national agency concerned. In the best cases, the institution or department (depending on the aspect of the institution's work under scrutiny) comments on a draft for accuracy.

The period of time between external evaluations varies with periods ranging from eight (Hungary, Szabó 2002)) and four years being common. Compulsion is becoming widespread and where a system is voluntary the take-up is not necessarily very high. (6 per cent of departments participated in a voluntary scheme in Greece; Tocatlidou 2003: 8.)

Criteria for evaluation vary from country to country. There is also some overlap between criteria for external evaluation and those used in internal procedures. This being the case, the criteria for both internal and external evaluation will be considered together in the following section.

Sanctions would normally include the power to end or suspend degree programmes (Portugal, Sequeira 2002). In Portugal funding may be reduced or withdrawn. In Denmark finance is conditional on the good conduct of quality assurance mechanisms and students are only eligible for loans and grants when attending programmes approved by the ministry of education (Lauridson 2002).

Panels of evaluators, at least in Western Europe, most frequently would be staff from other institutions in the same country nominated by the national agency, and would sometimes also include members from outside the university sector. In Central and Eastern Europe there are instances of panels being supplemented by or, indeed, largely composed of international experts from outside the country (a practice no doubt motivated by a wish to secure greater international credibility for the graduates from within what is essentially a relatively new state). In the Czech Republic, for instance, evaluation teams would have both internal and external members (Voskova 2002). However, the authority of such panels varies. In Estonia, for instance, international panels of experts make recommendations but the final decision rests with the Estonian Centre for Higher Education Evaluation which has commissioned them (Vogelberg 2002). The practice of international panels may be found too in Western Europe, and in Norway evaluations of subject areas have been undertaken by panels that are international in their composition (although initiated by a national body) (Swan 2002).

In cases of good practice, evaluation, particularly at course/subject level, will take note of the views of existing and former students and employers as shown in Belgium (Tudor 2002) or the United Kingdom (Lillie 2003). Also a needs analysis for new courses will also be undertaken, for example in Denmark where it is also considered important that the views of the professional area are taken into consideration (Lauridson 2002).

Where subject provision or curricula are concerned, it would be the norm for general guidelines to be given at subject level, with the department having freedom to work out the details of the curricula, which would not be expected to be standardized throughout the various universities in that country (Tudor 2002). (See, for example, Lithuania; Skurvydiene and Juceviciute 2002, or the United Kingdom; Lillie 2003). In Denmark there are no subject benchmarks as such but programmes must be designed in accordance with the relevant ministerial regulation specifying the general content and structure of the programme. In Finland ministerial approval is conditional on consultations (Lauridson 2002).

Internal evaluation

A consideration of internal evaluation reveals once more a range of practice, with different degrees of autonomy and types of quality procedures being found. Yet again, however, while there is some variation in nomenclature and in the levels and extent of review that may be found in different countries and universities (reflecting in part existing structures and hierarchy), certain patterns and stages may be discerned.

Internal and external procedures are often closely intertwined in that prior to external evaluation there will be an internal procedure preparing the curriculum or institutional evaluation report that has to be sent outside (whether to the ministry or national evaluation agency).

In some countries, however, institutions will effect their own evaluation or accreditation procedures internally (although as has been seen these will normally be constrained by national guidelines or benchmarks where these exist, as in the United Kingdom or also in Switzerland, Lüdi 2002) or these procedures will be checked checked on audit or other evaluations of the institution (as in the United Kingdom). Elsewhere, there may be a requirement that a review, particularly of subject provision, be conducted by the university every so many years. As well as larger scale in-depth reviews, internal procedures may also cover annual reconsideration or updating of curricula at the level of the department or teaching group.

If the review relates principally to university processes rather than to course provision, it is likely to follow a slightly different route to documentation relating to course provision and be considered principally by those areas of management concerned and related committees. Good practice would suggest, however, that there should be as wide a sharing and dissemination of such reports as possible.

Where course provision is concerned, the most basic level is no doubt that of teaching delivery, where individuals themselves undertake regular evaluation and reflection on their own work, a process that has always been part of individual teaching practice. However, this is essentially a personal exercise and interactive institutional processes and evaluation usually start with the subject or department, however variously this may be defined. The evaluation material or request for accreditation will be put together at this level. Good practice would suggest that this assessment would be undertaken through consultation so that the teaching team themselves effect an evaluation of their practice, rather than there being a report written up by solely managers or professors. Such material may include evidence of student assessment on teaching and feedback on a range of course related issues.

Above the level of delivery there is often what may be termed local oversight from a body to whom the teaching team may be said to be responsible but who may be considered to be at a certain remove from them, so there is also an element of distance and somewhat greater objectivity. This is frequently the level of the faculty, although it may be some other unit. At this stage, there may be consultation with the department and suggestions or amendments made before the report is sent on by the faculty to a wider university body charged with academic affairs or more specifically with quality matters. If the evaluation has been driven by the need to send a report relating to a subject on to a ministerial body or quality agency, it will leave the university at this stage (although ideally there will be feedback from the external agency into the university system).

If, on the other hand, the process has been a review conducted by the university itself to evaluate its own curricula, programmes or courses, the process will generally involve a report back from the university body to the other levels within the university. In the United Kingdom institutions are expected to develop formalized procedures for internal review of subject provision and there is also evidence of this from the reports of internal procedures in countries such as Switzerland, Finland, Hungary and Austria (Lüdi 2002; Sajavaara 2003; Szabó 2002; Besters-Dilger 2002). Different countries allow universities more or less potential to develop their own criteria for review, sometimes within a framework of national guidelines. In Denmark institutions may choose to have their own evaluations on certain themes as well as on the required national ones (Lauridson 2002). In Hungary, in addition to the more periodic national reports, there is an annual self-evaluation held in the institution (Szabó 2002).

The criteria that may be employed in external and internal evaluations include the following, itemized below, which, it must be stressed, do not necessarily all appear in any one country or report nor are they all necessary for particular areas or types of evaluation. They represent, however, the various criteria that may be found. It is obvious that some (such as the assessment of staff capacity) are particularly appropriate to external evaluations.

- Staff (number; qualifications; publications)
- Curriculum (content; structure; appropriateness; currency; teaching and learning methods; conformity to national guidelines; benchmarks)
- Resources (teaching areas; specialist language provision; new technology; staff facilities)
- Students (feedback; mechanisms; issues; progression and achievement; profile)
- Staff evaluation in relation to performance (evidence from course committees; study councils)
- External comment (for example from external examiner(s) where this system exists)
- Employment (destinations; employer feedback; alumni feedback)

Thinking of criteria such as the ones above and taking into account the overall systems that exist or are gradually emerging, it seems appropriate to ask what they tell us about the main objectives of the quality procedures, beyond the promotion of mobility and transparency, already discussed. These emerge as being most obviously a concern with the maintenance of standards in the sector (seen, for instance, in the focus on the curriculum or the quality of the teaching staff). Then – at both national and intra-university levels – there is a recognition of the need for regular review and updating of the curriculum (something which, of course, is likely to happen more frequently within the university than within the context of an in-depth review conducted by a national body). As well as considering the curriculum, it is also the case that some quality procedures may also focus on the identification of areas where there is a risk of deficient performance. To do this the evaluators may consult statistical material on student performance or more qualitative sources of student comment. Finally, the principle of peer review may be seen as a key element in the system. In addition to ensuring the input of evaluators with specialist knowledge and a genuine understanding of the area, this also serves the purpose of introducing a comparison with national (and sometimes international) trends and a greater awareness of subject developments. The comparison with national trends may also be effected through the use of national statistical information in addition to that supplied by the institution.

Monitoring and enhancement

It is clear that a prime function of the various evaluation activities which take place is, therefore, one of validation or assurance of fitness for purpose. However, it is also clear that such exercises are concerned, in a range of countries, with enabling the university or subject to effect improvements and a general enhancement of delivery in areas of practice (c.f. El-Khawas who in chapter 6 discusses differing functions of evaluation). The diverse elements in evaluation are well illustrated by recent (and changing) practices in the United Kingdom with regard to subject evaluation, where the movement from just pronouncing a judgement to a greater concern to foster improvement emerges.

In the United Kingdom the subject assessment of areas of study was previously centred on categories relating to the student learning experience. From the early 1990s, each subject was reviewed in turn over a period of approximately two years during which time each subject provider was assessed in a visit lasting some 3–4 days. Each of the six aspects of provision (Curriculum Design, Content and Organization; Teaching, Learning and Assessment; Student Progression and Achievement; Student Support and Guidance; Learning Resources; Quality Management and Enhancement) was the subject of a judgement made on the basis of the aims and objectives stated by the subject in question. For each of the six areas a score ranging from 1 to 4 was given (1 being the lowest grade and indicating a failure in provision and 4 being the highest grade indicating that the provider's objectives were fully met). (C.f. for instance, *Subject Review Handbook: England and Northern Ireland*, Quality Assurance Agency.) Slightly different arrangements were made for Scotland but the basic principles were similar.

The first cycle of subject reviews of the student learning experience concluded in the academic year 2001/02 and proposed alterations to the process had undoubtedly been conditioned by the establishment in August 1997 of a single Quality Assurance Agency for higher education (QAA) covering both the audit functions and subject-based assessment in relation to course provision (see above). From 2001, activities in higher education have been informed by new guidelines and codes of practice for provision, which have been (or are being) elaborated by the agency. These include national subject benchmark statements, which are, in effect, guidelines for subject provision and broad specifications in the different subjects taught in universities. There is also a template for course specification, indicating areas that should be included in course descriptions. There is also a variety of codes of practice for the different aspects and types of provision that are crucial to the student experience. These outline key elements in good practice (there are, for instance, codes on matters such as assessment; distance learning; placement learning; academic appeals and student complaints). In addition, the *Framework for Higher Education Qualifications in England, Wales and Northern Ireland* and *The Scottish Credit and Qualifications Framework*,[4] published in 2001, indicate the levels and qualifications to be attained at the various stages of study with a view to effecting greater uniformity and transparency among the qualifications offered. They also contain brief descriptors for the different qualifications (qualification descriptors being defined as generic statements of the outcomes of study).[5] In 2000–2001 a revised review process for subjects was proposed for England and was piloted in Scotland for subjects scheduled for review. In the late Spring and Summer of 2001, however, universities continued to exert pressure on government regarding the system of university review, with a view to obtaining a significantly lighter and less cumbersome system of quality control. Wide-ranging discussions were held and a system based on audit has evolved.

The new system, now being implemented, charges institutions with the responsibility for ensuring quality and standards within their own provision. Audit visits allow a national check on how this is done in relation to their overall structure and various functions and procedures. Auditors also look at the way in which the university's systems deliver quality and standards in selected disciplines through discipline audit trails.

As not all institutions will be audited in the immediate future, there is provision for a number of full subject reviews in some institutions but in the main institutions not scheduled for audit for some time will, in the interim period, have a small number of interactions at subject level, called developmental engagements, which will normally be in those subjects that, under the previous system, would have been scheduled for subject review. This process is particularly interesting in that it is conceived certainly at one level as a health check on the provision, since reviewers have to indicate that they have confidence in the quality and standards of the provision under consideration. However, there is also a learning element to this as reviewers look specifically at the ways in which the institutional processes contribute to ensuring the proper delivery of the subject in tune with national requirements. The report that ensues from the visit is a confidential one and (in contrast to reports for former subject reviews) is not openly published. It may also be argued that other elements of the United Kingdom system now in existence such as national subject benchmark statements, course specification template and codes of practice, while ensuring certain standards and a measure of uniformity, perform a further purpose by also fostering an enhancement of practice through models and advice.

Financial constraints

Evaluation and quality enhancement systems come at a price. The compilation of reports, the recruitment of experts and visits to institutions demand resources. So too does the provision of electronic management information systems that facilitate the measuring of performance and quality. These information systems would generally be available electronically in Western European countries, although the level of provision and implementation may vary. However, while a number of Central and Eastern European countries report extensive use of statistics (for example Hungary, Szabó 2002), there are also indications in some instances that electronic versions of these are not developed due to the poor provision of information technology tools in the universities and the countries concerned.

The expense implied in quality systems is thus an aspect of quality. Financial problems may be worse in certain Central and Eastern European countries where, for instance, one country report indicates that teachers have many ideas but lack the wherewithal to implement them. This is also the country where despite measures for validation, courses remain unvalidated (Lithuania; Skurvydiene and Juceviciute 2002). Elsewhere (Romania; Bakonsky 2002) posts remain unfilled to save money with the result that staff have less time to devote to their students as well as less time available for research and the necessary support staff – both secretarial and technical – cannot be appointed. Lack of finance may impact on the capacity of the university and the department to provide training for staff. In the Czech Republic, for instance, there are said to be no staff development courses (Voskova 2002). Linked to the financial position of the university sector are the worsening conditions for staff, their lower remuneration and decline in social status, again a theme reiterated in numerous reports. (Slovakia, Blašková 2003; Lithuania, Skurvydiene and Jucevicinte 2002; and elsewhere).

While financial constraints are for historical reasons sometimes more in evidence in Central and Eastern Europe, Western European countries too point to the detrimental effect of financial considerations on the ability to manage and to offer quality in their provision. On the negative side, it is argued by some that at a time of funding constraints and restrictive staff recruitment policies, the system has created an additional administrative and bureaucratic burden for academic staff. There are cost implications both at national and institutional levels. Within the United Kingdom, university unhappiness with the system has been strongly voiced and continuing lobbying has led to the most recent rethinking of the approach to quality assurance and procedures, outlined above.

A quality straitjacket?

Within the higher education sector some fear that the codification implied in systems of monitoring, guidelines and benchmarks may act as a brake, stifling the innovation and creativity that may arise from university and staff autonomy. At least in the United Kingdom there is some stress within the current system on the recognition of innovatory or exemplary practice and in other countries too, the system should not be such as to hinder inventiveness or promote uninspiring uniformity. There is, however, no doubt that the process of review may lead to greater transparency and an enhancement of standards of delivery, as well as a sharing of good practice between different institutions. Within the United Kingdom, this academic discussion and interchange of ideas between staff has been facilitated by the establishment of a number of bodies such as the Learning and Teaching Support Network (LTSN), a network of centres for the different academic subjects, supported by the Funding Councils with the aim of disseminating and increasing good practice. The recourse to codes and guidelines in the United Kingdom should also play a role in permitting the spread of the more satisfactory aspects of provision across the sector as a whole.

Monies devoted to quality monitoring are certainly monies that cannot be used for delivery of teaching, yet in the current situation, a number of governmental and user stakeholders are demanding the transparency and enhancement that quality procedures can effect.

Convergence or divergence?

Common elements have been observed in the processes observed above, as well as continuing differences conditioned by time-honoured practice and a desire in many countries to protect at least something of their university traditions. Nonetheless, with greater interaction between the different parts of Europe, a degree of harmonization is being effected as Europeans engage in a process of interaction and inter-learning.

In certain instances, the realization of this vision and the rolling out of harmonization to third level teachers and their institutions owes much to European support, initiation of pilot projects and dedicated funding. This may be seen clearly through the project 'Tuning Educational Structures in Europe'[6] in which national, institutional and subject interests come together with European aspirations. This has as its focus the generic and subject specific competences of first and second cycle graduates in a number of subjects with specific reference to educational structures and curriculum content. The 'Tuning' project is financed by the European Commission as well as by the participating universities and covers all EU and EFTA countries. In addition, the European University Association (EUA) and a number of national Rectors' Conferences (most particularly Italy, Portugal and Spain) play an active role in 'Tuning'. The fields concerned in the first stages of the project were Business Administration, Educational Sciences, Geology, History, Mathematics, supplemented by the thematic networks for Physics and Chemistry, and involves 105 institutions. In addition, the above inner circle was supplemented by synergy groups in Languages, Humanitarian Development, Law, Medicine, Mechanical Engineering and Veterinary Sciences. This project started officially in December 2000 with preparatory work and was formally launched in May 2001 and held the closing conference for phase 1 in May 2002, with its second phase running in 2003–04. The stated aim of the project is not to effect some sort of uniformity but rather to 'tune', namely to enhance understanding and transparency by opening a debate that will lead to the identification of common points of reference, learning outcomes and professional profiles.

Interaction of this type between staff and institutions in a variety of countries working at the curriculum level must point forward to enhanced European interchange as well as to a certain convergence coupled with an understanding of divergence in tradition and practice. Such projects serve to underpin and spread the development of a common European understanding at the level of delivery. They also provide a practical example of the extensive, multi-faceted outreach of Europe and the way in which its endeavours serve to underpin the political will.

Yet, there are also other signs that different discipline areas and institutions are themselves looking beyond the national arena. This may be seen in instances where accreditation is sought from a European or international body rather than just the national authority. A case in point is EQUIS (European Quality Improvement System, the quality assurance scheme run by the European Foundation for Management Development). Thus, for example, in Switzerland, St. Gallen had its management school evaluated on a European level to gain EQUIS (Lüdi 2002) and it is not alone in Switzerland to have done so. The Swiss schools are joined by an impressive number of management schools throughout Europe, largely but not only in Western Europe, with schools from the following countries having successfully undergone EQUIS validation – Denmark, UK, France, Finland, Poland, Sweden, Netherlands, Ireland and Germany. Again in Switzerland it is reported that medical schools are going through a process of international recognition (Lüdi 2002). It is noteworthy that these evaluations are in professional areas where there is likely to be an element of competition across Europe (business schools) or where there is a strong need to ensure professional recognition and standing to enable European movement.

Subject specialists and institutions are looking outwards to Europe and are taking account of the needs and potential career aspirations of their students, in a world in which national recognition may no longer be viewed as an adequate assurance of quality for a mobile workforce where some element, at least, of working outside their country of origin may become the norm. Perhaps too they are also trying to secure the future of their institution and of their subject field within it, as well as their own prospects and those of their successors, by gaining recognition as European and global players, able to hold their own beyond the purely local and national spheres.

The process currently taking place within Europe is certainly a diffuse one with many players and it is responsive to different influences and drivers. What is striking, despite deep-rooted heritages and retention of national specificities, is the recognition at various levels throughout the continent of the imperatives imposed by a future that demands a vision beyond the purely local level of the institution or even the nation state.

Notes

1 These reports are available on the Internet at www.uni-koeln.de/phil-pak/aspla/tnp2/reports.html
2 The Higher Education Funding Council for England (which also has responsibility for Northern Ireland, consulting as necessary with the appropriate Northern Irish department); the Scottish Higher Education Funding Council (SHEFC); there is also a funding council for Wales (Higher Education Funding Council for Wales

(HEFCW) but review of finding provision was undertaken in conjunction with the English funding council.

3 This recommendation was formally adopted by the Council on 24 September 1998 – n° 98/561/CE – O.J. L 270, 7 October 1998.

4 Publications by the Quality Assurance Agency may be viewed on their website: http://www.qaa.ac.uk

5 It should be noted that the *Framework for England* is a qualifications framework and not a credit framework, nor does it depend on the use of credit (while universities are expected to organize and structure teaching clearly to ensure progression, they are not obliged to use a credit system, although credit systems are now very widespread in the UK).

6 See, for instance, the European Union website for *Tuning Educational Structures in Europe.* http://europe.eu.int/comm/education/tuning.html or Wagenaar, R. *Tuning Educational Structures in Europe.* Presentation for the pre-Berlin Conference, Working on the European Dimension of Quality, Amsterdam, 12–13 March. http://www.jointquality.org/content/nederland/Tuning_Presentation.doc, *Tuning Educational Structures in Europe: Background.* http://odur.let.rug.nl/ TuningProject/background.asp

8

Trends relating to higher education reform in Europe: an overview

Barbara Sporn

Introduction

European higher education has been facing fundamental changes. Triggered by a new relationship between the market, the state and the institution, post-secondary education has been moving towards diversification, decentralization and deregulation (Gumport and Sporn 1999; Rhoades and Sporn 2002a; Sporn 1999c). At the same time, principles of public accountability, evaluation, quality control and the use of management instruments have been designed to provide necessary surveillance and supervision. Academic performances in teaching, research and service have become publicly scrutinized. Universities are expected to respond to the demands from the labour market for highly qualified graduates (Clark 1998a).

Looking at some trends across Europe, a general shift towards increased market-orientation of higher education systems is apparent (Brennan, Fedrowitz, Huber and Shah 1999; Scott 1998b). In the UK the binary system has been abolished and universities now have to compete for students and research money (Kogan and Hanney 2000). In the Netherlands institutions of higher education have gained more autonomy in managing themselves and in working with external constituencies (De Boer 2001). In Germany and Austria universities have found themselves confronted with performance-based funding (Sporn 1999b). In Sweden and Denmark institutions have become self-regulated and quality oriented, and they are regularly evaluated by a group of external peers (Askling 2001).

Another overall trend in Europe has been the new role of the state (Henkel and Little 1999). With increased economic and social pressures, state ministries have been changing their relationship with universities and colleges. Mostly dominated by public (and rather large) institutions, the state used to control most issues from budgets to personnel. Starting in the early 1990s, the state has been moving away from control to supervision. As a means to secure external control of academic outcomes, buffer organizations like boards and councils have been created and evaluative measures have been introduced. Universities have been given more autonomy and now take decisions upon matters such as resource allocation and faculty hiring. These changes have been occurring all over continental Europe but have been especially prominent in the Netherlands, Scandinavian countries, Germany and Austria (Müller-Böling, Mayer, MacLachlan and Fedrowitz 1998; Rhoades and Sporn 2002a).

These two major trends – the introduction of the market and the withdrawal of the state – have led to responses on the institutional side (Clark 1998a; Sporn 2001). Universities in many European countries discovered that their structures and processes were not adequate for these new challenges. Dominated by a state bureaucracy, universities had often kept the same organization for many decades with only minor changes. The 1990s called for restructuring in countries like Austria and Germany on a larger scale, extending from administrative functions to the organization of teaching and research. The goal of most of these efforts has been to reach a satisfactory level of efficiency and effectiveness, which usually implies increasing quality and improving productivity. A further aim is to regain public legitimacy, credibility and trust by producing well-prepared graduates for the job market, research publications and involvement in technology transfer.

In this chapter, major patterns of higher education reform in Europe are described, with the focus on organizational restructuring. In order to understand the key issues involved, it is necessary to review the substantial environmental changes that have engendered these reforms. Factors inside the institutions that influence the process of adaptation to these external pressures will also be considered. Reference is made to several empirical studies of European universities, which give some indication of the future character of European higher education.

Environmental changes

The changes within Europe relating to its higher education systems stem from four major areas in society: economy, demography, globalization and telecommunication. Countries need to develop competitive advantage in response to the effects of globalization. The new knowledge-based economy emphasizes modern technology, lifelong learning and graduate training, and calls for flexible institutions and companies. The demand for education comes from people of all age groups and ethnic backgrounds. Modern day research places its emphasis on an interdisciplinary approach to problems, enhanced through industry partnerships. These trends place colleges and universities in a new and uncomfortable situation, necessitating them to reform their structures and processes.

1. Economy

In many countries in Europe economic pressures, mainly arising from new patterns of public spending and the creation of the European Union (EU), are affecting the traditional role of universities. Public spending and the allocation of state money to higher education institutions has been changing dramatically. From World War II to the 1980s European universities had experienced continued incremental growth in public financial support. In the 1990s, however, reductions in expenditure for higher education occurred in most European countries. For example in France, Germany, the United Kingdom and Austria, public expenditure stagnated over the last decade while student numbers rose significantly (Rhoades and Sporn 2002a). The share of higher education funds from non-public sources increased (Slaughter and Leslie 1997).

The EU with its fifteen member states, soon to be 25, has evolved into an important factor in national economic restructuring (Neave 2002; Teichler 1998b). The introduction of a common currency, the E, has accelerated the need for standards. Accordingly, state budgets have to meet certain requirements regarding deficits and spending, unemployment and inflation. With these economic imperatives in Europe, individual countries have had to sacrifice some long held traditions and in response often employed neo-liberal policies (Ferlie, Ashburner, Fitzgerald and Pettigrew 1996). State budgets have had to be cut to reduce national debt and spending restructured, based on EU-standards. As a consequence, public expenditure for research and teaching has been either reduced or held at the same level. At the same time, there have been greater demands by industry for research, and teaching has had to take place in a more diversified post-secondary educational system. In short, universities are confronted with a situation of doing more with less (Gumport 2000).

2. Demography

The composition of the national populations in Europe has been changing with regard to age and ethnic background. The traditional pyramid of a large number of young people and fewer elderly people has been turned upside down and now consists of a majority of old people and a relatively small group of young people. Additionally, through increased immigration from the South and the East, European countries have grown more diverse, containing a variety of ethnic groups with diverging skills and needs. The challenge for higher education arises from a job market calling for flexible and 'technologically literate' graduates and a more diverse student group.

Additionally, with the lifetime of knowledge continuously decreasing, continuing education and relearning have become important factors of economic productivity. A new market for postgraduate education and training has developed in Europe that offers new programmes customized to specific needs ranging from computer courses to management training. As a result, the number of continuing, post-secondary and professional education courses has been steadily increasing. While students as new entrants to the workforce need 'hands-on' programmes to increase their chances of finding a job, companies need to update the skills of their employees on a more regular basis. Higher education systems have to react by diversifying and offering innovative post-secondary courses (Gellert 1999).

3. Globalization

International competition, the importance of strategic alliances and mergers, and the development of know-how and comparative advantage are dominating policies of national economies. Products and services have to be improved for multiple markets and customers (Peterson and Dill 1997; Prahalad and Hamel 1990). Globalization in general has pushed states to devote more resources to the enhancement and management of innovation, so that corporations and the nations in which they are based can compete more successfully in world markets. For higher education systems, more funds have to be devoted to support corporate partnerships between universities and businesses. Trends show an increased demand for technology transfer, for a combination of basic and applied research, and for professors contributing to spin-off or start-up companies (Etzkowitz and Leydesdorff 1997a; Sadlak 1998; Slaughter 1998).

Globalization has also caused markets to move closer and to concentrate. Mergers and takeovers in many industries like banking, entertainment and media, and pharmaceutical companies demonstrate this trend. In higher education, strategic alliances between US and European universities have become popular. Increasingly, renowned US universities are entering the European market for business training and distance education. Examples are the University of Phoenix offering programmes in the Netherlands; the University of Chicago with its International Executive MBA in Barcelona; or the International MBA jointly offered by the Vienna University of Economics and Business Administration and the University of South Carolina. Many European universities look for solutions in the US to solve their problems relating to university management and governance. Hence, a trend towards the 'Americanization' of European higher education can be observed (Rhoades and Sporn 2002a, 2002b).

4. Telecommunication

The expansion of interactive telecommunication networks and the availability of relatively cheap computers and software has led to the widespread use of technology in higher education (Peterson and Dill 1997). The impact on how students learn, how professors teach and conduct research, and how administrators manage the institution are multi-faceted. Virtual classrooms, Internet-based research collaboration between international scholars, and administrative information systems using intranets are a few examples (Adelman 2001; Guri-Rosenblit 1999).

Changes and improvements in teaching through modern technologies include new forms of communication and collaboration between teachers and students. Online services like e mail, teleconferencing and Internet browsers enhance the exchange of content and ideas independent of time and location. Internet-based distance education offering complete academic programmes increase the diversity of the student population. Universities can thus expand and serve different groups by 'mass customizing' courses to individual needs through information technology (Bull 1994; Müller-Böling 1997a; Sporn and Miksch 1996).

Research activities have been influenced by the Internet as well (Epelboin 1994). A new form of international and transdisciplinary collaboration links industry, universities and government agencies around the world to tackle problems such us global warming, social mobility or international competitiveness (Etzkowitz and Leydesdorff 1997b; Gibbons 1995; Nowotny 1995). Access to information and data is facilitated through CD-ROMs and library servers enhancing literature searches and analysis. Electronic publishing makes access to the findings of research considerably easier.

From an institutional perspective, technological changes have the potential of providing much improved performance data for universities (Senge 2000). Sophisticated information systems enable academic organizations to learn about internal processes, markets and customers. The feedback can be used for programme development, marketing and decision making. A new form of 'Management by Information' can make structures and processes more transparent and help increase efficiency and effectiveness (Müller-Böling 1997a).

These broad social changes in the environment of universities have caused an imbalance between external demands and internal (academic) responses (Clark 1998b), as exemplified in the summary of an OECD study on redefining tertiary education:

> Tertiary education is changing to address client and stakeholder expectations, to respond more actively to social and economic change, to provide for more flexible forms of teaching and learning, to focus more strongly on competencies and skills across the curriculum. Decision-makers, managers and educational leaders have major responsibilities in fostering such developments and in taking actions to overcome dichotomies, status differences and other barriers that stand in the way of intelligent decision-making by individual students and strategic resource allocation.
>
> (OECD 1998: 10)

Accordingly, universities slowly started to adapt to reach a new level of balance between inside and outside. In Europe, converging patterns of institutional reforms emerged. They can be summarized under issues of organizational restructuring and are described in the next section. Following that, factors positively influencing these adaptations are discussed.

Issues of restructuring

The reform of higher education in Europe has been characterized by a certain drift towards the market. Formerly dominated by state control and drawing on public funding, as well as offering open and free access, higher education systems in many countries have now become more client-oriented and more accountable and work closely with industry and commerce. This development has affected almost all areas concerning higher education institutions: access and diversity, state control and self-regulation, finance, governance, external relationships, research and development, and evaluation and assessment.

1. Access and diversity

The trend towards a knowledge-based economy stresses the importance of education and lifelong learning. Countries aim at achieving high percentages of post-secondary education graduates. Additionally, aging populations and longer lifetime work require employees to update their skills and knowledge regularly. Recent public policies, as in Austria, call for wider access to higher education, a more diversified set of degree programmes and an emphasis on continuing education (Pechar 2002). As a consequence, student numbers are rising all over Europe and universities are having to restructure in order to accommodate these new groups (Teichler 2001).

Traditionally designed for uniform education with free access for everybody with secondary school matriculation, European universities have had to learn to serve a wide range of students with varied employment aims and to provide a range of short-cycle courses to update knowledge. Universities in Europe have also focused on internationalization and exchange in order to provide experiences to students with different ethnic backgrounds, regional interests and an interest in international careers (Scott 1998a; Teichler 1999). In general, this expansion requires professional university management and a diverse faculty who can serve and respond to many different external needs.

2. State control and institutional self-regulation

Europe has a long tradition of state control in higher education. In recent years and with new economic imperatives the state has re-interpreted its role (Henkel and Little 1999). In countries like Germany, Austria, Sweden,

Denmark and the Netherlands state control has been shifting to state supervision. With this, institutional self-regulation has been strengthened and many decisions have been decentralized from the state to the institutional level. The stronger leadership now required of university managers has enabled them to take over the responsibility of establishing a wide range of relationships with external constituencies. State ministries have set up buffer organizations or created external evaluation schemes to guarantee quality (see Lillie) and to increase the accountability of universities.

This supervisory and self-regulation model (Van Vught 1994) calls for professional management. Organizational restructuring often puts emphasis on the 'administrative estate' of universities and their procedures to increase efficiency and effectiveness. Through transferring decision-making power from the ministries to the institutions, universities are increasingly able to manage their own budget and personnel. Under these circumstances, individual contracts, resource allocation based on performance indicators or priorities and incentives for additional services can be implemented. This arrangement requires more administrative capacity, leading to shifting governance structures within the institution and rising numbers of administrators (Gornitzka, Kyvik and Larson 1998; Maassen 2000). This tendency has been criticized as university 'managerialism' (see Deem), as faculty becoming 'managed professionals' or as a new interface between the academic and the administrative side of the institution (Gumport 2000; Gumport and Sporn 1999; Kogan 1999; Rhoades and Sporn 2002b).

3. Finances

Shifts in financial resources and public spending for higher education have caused restructuring at colleges and universities. In Europe, where public funding dominates, state budgets have been less able to accommodate growing student numbers (Schmidtlein 1999). For example, performance-based budgeting using fixed and flexible budget items has been proposed in countries like Germany and Austria (Fedrowitz, Krasny and Ziegele 1999). Universities started to build innovative and entrepreneurial structures in order to meet this challenge. Fundraising activities, technology transfer units, research centres and alumni clubs have been founded to increase private giving and endowments, and to attract research grants.

The source of funding is a key factor in defining the structure of an institution (Slaughter and Leslie 1997; Tolbert 1985). More diversified university budgets (from fundraising, research grants, extracurricular activities and so on) can help to subsidize new initiatives. Universities can thus develop management structures to create a budget, to introduce cost accounting, to align budget planning with institutional expenditure, to control spending and to attract additional funds outside the state budget. In many cases, universities created vice rectors for finance with a staff responsible for those areas. Although the intention has been to provide a better split of tasks between the faculty and the administration (and thereby moving away from the European tradition of faculty-managed institutions) it needs to be kept in mind that those in control of the finances also have the power to control the institution as a whole (Gumport and Sporn 1999).

4. Governance

With increased market-orientation and less state control, new forms of governance have emerged. As has been described earlier, the state – in a continental European context, the owner of higher education – still maintains substantial influence over public universities, while in the new circumstances internal management requires more freedom to implement adaptive strategies. The consequence has been the establishment of external boards to represent the public interest, and a shift in the roles of university committees towards more advisory functions (De Boer 1998; Müller-Böling 1998). Boards often have a vote in selecting the rector or president, putting together the budget or in other critical decisions regarding academic programmes (Mignot Gerard 2003; Morgan 2000).

Generally, governance structures at European universities have been changing from a traditionally collegial to a more monocratic style of decision making. The power of rectors, vice rectors, deans, chancellors and other members of the administration has thereby increased. As the example of the Netherlands demonstrates, faculty senates have turned into advisory boards whereas the rector makes all the critical decisions (De Boer 2001). Governance structures are also becoming leaner, that is fewer committees with more responsibilities and the leadership of the institution holding the most decision-making power. Problems could arise from this trend towards 'managerialism' when the bureaucrats or administrators start to dominate the academy, and the faculty who provide core academic services lose authority to act for the institution (Brennan and Shah 2000a; Newton 2002; Rhoades and Sporn 2002a). At many European universities administrators and leaders are drawn from faculty positions and return to the faculty after their period of office. This practice has enhanced faculty support and collegiality within universities (Sporn, 1999a). Of course the question remains whether, with more environmental demands, 'faculty administrators' will be able to maintain their ability to stay as academics and still manage the institution professionally.

5. Differentiation and periphery

European universities have traditionally been divided along disciplinary lines and organized in institutes or departments responsible for teaching and research (Clark 1983). The Humboldtian principle of freedom and unity of teaching and research has been under jeopardy in recent years. As a response to conditions of scarce resources and public accountability, universities in many European countries have been starting to differentiate and to strengthen their periphery (Clark 1998b; Sporn 1999a).

A differentiated structure divides research and teaching into separate areas and makes several – sometimes opposing – market strategies possible. Hence, structures can differ for undergraduate, graduate and postgraduate education, as well as basic and applied research. As the examples of the University of Twente, the University of Warwick and Universita Bocconi demonstrate (Clark 1998b; Sporn 1999a), universities in Europe can be divided into undergraduate schools, research centres or graduate and continuing education schools. Basic research is often done at the department level but the same faculty is also involved in research centres for applied and contracted research. Because these universities are still steered by their faculty, conflict emerges only occasionally. The academic community worries more about integration mechanisms to hold the whole institution together. The examples show how academic staff can be entrepreneurs, academic managers, teachers and researchers at the same time.

The periphery refers to structural arrangements at universities which mainly deal with the boundary spanning and bridging activities. As external demands accelerate, universities have to create a strengthened periphery to translate external demands into adequate internal responses. This enhanced developmental periphery could include units for technology transfer, fundraising or external relations. Outreach activities then include contract research, contract education and consultancy. Together with a differentiated structure this periphery can form a matrix-like dual structure at universities (Müller-Böling 1997b). This matrix structure can be a new tool for handling the growing service function of universities through specialist groups of academics in departments, complemented by project groups defining 'practical' research problems and identifying additional training needs. Centres are often interdisciplinary, linked to departments and carry the name of the university. Traditional departments are supplemented by centres linked to the outside world. Groups working on the periphery then cross old lines of authority, promote environmental linkages and create a potential source for additional funding for the university (Clark 1998b; Van Vught 1999).

6. Research and development

Closely related to these processes of differentiation and strengthening the periphery is the importance of research and development at universities (Etzkowitz and Leydesdorff 1997a). Research has become increasingly interdisciplinary and problem-oriented (Gibbons *et al.* 1994). New sources of funding and of strategic direction can develop through new ways of knowledge production and dissemination. Society in general and the job market in particular require solutions to complex problems, which can be solved better by cooperation between universities, industry and government. If successful, universities gain enhanced status in the community. Success requires a willingness to cross disciplinary boundaries and to rethink institutional structures as well as reward systems (Clark 1996).

As a further step, development at universities involves the transformation of research results into application-oriented tools that enable higher education institutions to contribute to regional economic development (Goldstein, Maier and Luger 1995; Goldstein and Luger 1997). The matrix structure discussed earlier can thus enhance the coexistence of basic and applied research and benefit the whole university. Some US universities (for example Stanford University) have been supporting spin-offs or investing in start-ups by faculty as part of their development strategy. Additionally, joint projects or contracted research can strengthen the cooperation between universities and industry. From a long-term perspective all these activities help to diversify the funding base and improve institutional survival in times of resource constraint (Clark 1998b; Gumport and Pusser 1999; Sporn 1999a).

7. Evaluation and assessment

Universities in Europe have been criticized for the alleged lack of relevance of their teaching and research (Gellert 1999). Evaluation and assessment have developed to measure academic quality and gained importance in many European countries in the early 1990s (Jeliazkova and Westerheijden 2002; Rhoades and Sporn 2002b; Yorke 2000). Evaluation at European universities mainly concerns the academic side of teaching and research (Brennan and Shah 2000; Middlehurst 1999; Stensaker 2000). Here, quality is controlled through instruments to analyse classroom performance and measure the research productivity of faculty. For example, in Austria and Germany, newly created positions such as deans of study are now responsible for implementing tools for evaluation including questionnaires and feedback loops to improve faculty performance and student satisfaction.

Assessment of European universities is also becoming more oriented towards the administrative side (Bauer, Askling, Gerard-Marton and Marton 1999; Ewell 1997). External teams of experts (i.e. peer review) visit universities to check institutional structures, programmes and outcomes. The aim has been to assess the use of resources and the objectives of the universities in relation to their external context (for example, job market, public policy, industry structure). An additional method of assessment is that provided by professional bodies who can give accreditation to particular courses or entire institutions. A market is developing for a 'label' of quality – not unlike US institutions. Examples include EQUIS (European Quality Improvement System), which mainly focuses on institutional accreditation, or FIBAA (Foundation for International Business Administration Accreditation), which specializes in accrediting business-oriented programmes mainly in Germany. In addition, AACSB (the Association to Advance

Collegiate Schools of Business) is quite active in the European market, which is of particular interest to those universities seeking to be globally competitive.

Institutional success factors

Two recent studies can serve as a basis of evidence that indicates the process of transformation of universities in Europe. Both are based on extensive case studies of institutions in the late 1990s; one study has been conducted by Burton Clark (Clark 1998b) and the second by the author of this chapter (Sporn 1999a).

In his work, Clark analysed five innovative universities in Europe with reference to their entrepreneurial activities: University of Warwick in England, University of Strathclyde in Scotland, Chalmers University of Technology in Sweden, University of Twente in the Netherlands and University of Joensuu in Finland. He found five elements of organizational transformation, which he claimed created entrepreneurial universities: a strengthened steering core, an expanded developmental periphery, a diversified funding base, a stimulated academic heartland, and an integrated entrepreneurial culture. These elements enabled the institution to adapt to environmental demands by bringing about organizational development:

> The entrepreneurial response offers a formula for institutional developments that puts autonomy on a self-defined basis: diversify income to increase financial resources, provide discretionary money, and reduce governmental dependency; develop new units outside traditional departments to introduce new environmental relationships and new modes of thought and training; convince heartland departments that they too can look out for themselves, raise money, actively choose among specialties, and otherwise take on an entrepreneurial outlook; evolve a set of overarching beliefs that guide and rationalize the structural changes that provide stronger response capabilities; and build a central steering capacity to make large choices that help focus the institution.
>
> (Clark 1998a: 147)

My study included Universita Bocconi (a private business school in Milan, Italy), Universität St. Gallen (a public business school in Switzerland) and the Vienna University of Economics and Business Administration. These institutions had been facing major external changes to which they had to adapt. The study showed that the response to environmental change can be played out quite differently. Depending on the history of the institution, its past experience with changes and its current situation regarding resources, environmental demands get translated into either a crisis or a strategic opportunity. In the process of adaptation six factors were most influential: a clear mission and goals, an entrepreneurial culture, differentiated structure, professional management, shared governance and committed leadership. A clear mission and goals served as important sources of identity and integration for the members of a decentralized and loosely coupled academic community. Academic entrepreneurs created a structure of profit centres next to the basic academic units (departments) thereby linking the institution with its environment. A differentiated structure included units with diverse functions reaching from undergraduate to graduate education and basic as well as applied research. They were accountable for their activities and had the freedom to design and adjust their services to external expectations and needs. The university management consisted of full-time professional employees using modern management tools, and the leaders of the institutions had sufficient power to make decisions for the institution. Shared governance extended to the democratic participation of interest groups in decision making to reach consensus about activities in response to environmental demands. Those in leadership positions like rectors and presidents had to demonstrate their commitment through financial support of projects and activities.

Two additional critical factors emerged from my study, namely institutional autonomy and diversified funding. Public universities in Europe have increasingly gained autonomy through deregulation and decentralization. This autonomy enables self-regulation and independent strategies to be established. A diversified funding base decreases the vulnerability of institutions. Universities that are totally dependent on one source of income are less able to adapt proactively to environmental demands. As this brief outline shows, these two studies provide similar findings. The successful adaptation and transformation of universities in Europe is characterized by an entrepreneurial culture, professional management, diversified funding, strong academic identity and shared governance. With these success factors in place, higher education reform in Europe might lead to successful redefinition and redesign of its institutions in the future.

Outlook

Higher education reform in Europe is an ongoing process. Organizational restructuring in universities is still under way. Particular trends that are driving this process include: privatization, diversity of provision, state supervision and the effects of information technology.

In many European countries, private universities already exist or are now being accredited. Additionally, many US-based universities have entered the European market for higher education offering educational goods for market prices. Teaching and research is also being offered by other bodies, such as consultancies, the media or IT companies. As a consequence, competition among institutions, the discussion of the relevance and accountability of academic services, and the need for strategic positioning of traditional public universities in Europe will increase.

A second trend points to a multiple sector and multiple tier system. European higher education will increasingly consist of private and public, vocational and continuing education institutions offering different degrees at the undergraduate and postgraduate level to a multi-faceted and multi-ethnic student group. Examples are the creation of Fachhochschulen in Austria and the importance of vocational colleges (HMO) in the Netherlands. Additionally, European systems have started to harmonize curricula. The Bologna declaration signed by 29 European ministers of education in 1999 is based on these objectives: comparable degrees, two main cycles (undergraduate and postgraduate), a system of credits, promotion of mobility, quality assurance and common patterns of higher education. As a consequence, bachelor/master degree programmes have been introduced in many European countries such as Denmark, Germany and Austria for which there is increasing demand. For traditional universities this has triggered a rethinking of the split between research versus application-oriented education.

State supervision will prevail as the general principle for the relationship between the owner of higher education and its institutions. Eventually, universities in most European countries are likely to gain sufficient autonomy for them to manage themselves. Control will either be delegated to buffer institutions or regulations will be established to prescribe quality assessment through peer review, external audits and self scrutiny. Although the state will still be responsible for financing higher education, budgeting will be based on performance contracts. The policy will be to create entrepreneurial, market-oriented, publicly accountable institutions.

Information technology and the Internet have been impacting on higher education for the last decade. Virtual universities and Internet-based programmes have brought innovations to teaching and research. Distance education has gained market value and for-profit companies have established their own universities. Research will be further internationalized through the ease of connecting geographically dispersed scholars through the Internet. Publishing will be revolutionized through reduced costs for journal production and delivery, as well as faster and easily accessible articles being available on the Internet. Taken together, competition from other providers will increase for traditional universities and scholars.

As this chapter has outlined, environmental dynamics have changed the face of higher education in Europe. Economic, demographic, technological and global shifts have triggered higher education reform in Europe. The whole academy is affected – administration, teaching, research. Certain factors can help to ease the problem of adaptation ranging from structural remedies like differentiation to behavioural factors like committed leadership. European higher education is in the process of reform and difficult times are still ahead. The result, hopefully, will be a more competitive system, but one that remains uniquely European, one that combines the values of the market with that of a social institution devoted to individual learning, the preservation of knowledge and the socialization of citizens.

Part 2

Case studies

9

Higher education reform in Australia – an evaluation

Simon Marginson

Introduction: national reform and global convergence

Guy Neave remarks that after 1985 there was a 'fundamental revision' in the relations between the university on one hand, and government, society and economy on the other. The purpose of higher education altered. The formation of elite citizens was subsumed in the creation of private and public economic returns. The change was attended by 'massive internal reforms to governance, management and academic productivity' (Neave 2000: 10 and 17). Another point can be added to Neave's observation – increasingly, higher education was shaped by the compression of space-time (Harvey 1989) that characterized the emerging global era. There was a new synchrony in the reform of the different national systems of higher education.

Before the mid-1980s, policy everywhere was implicated in cross-national themes such as 'investment in human capital' and 'equality of opportunity'. Nevertheless, these remained broad policy abstractions. They did not signify common methods of government. 'Mass education' was associated with a wide range of national participation rates; and the national triangulations of government, university and academic profession diverged: consider university self-government in the UK, American universities grounded in civil society, state cultures of the disciplines in France, and higher education as a department of government in Germany. There was much variance in the substance and the timing of reforms, mediated by national traditions and polities. But after 1985 or thereabouts, there was a change. Everywhere the various national reform programmes begin to converge at a single point, both in the timing and the substance. Recognizably common methods and models of government and management emerged. The nation was still the context in which policy was played out; but there was a new level of precision in the common global elements; and a new haste and simultaneity about the execution of reform, as if no nation wanted to fall behind.

The new policy globalism had its roots in the deregulation and realignment of national financial systems and the associated tendency to convergence in all economic policies. It also coincided with the dominance of neo-liberalism in economic and social policy, and the emergence of techniques associated with that approach such as simulated markets in the public sector. Strongly supported in the finance sector and by the economics profession, the policy hold of neo-liberalism became everywhere apparent, especially in the English-speaking countries.[1]

In the 1980s the Australian government became an enthusiast for neo-liberal policy globalism in finance, where it risked a 'clean' float of the currency in 1983; in trade, where it cut agricultural protection and hoped the world would follow; in fiscal policy, where it ran surpluses from 1987–88 onwards; and in education. Previously, Australian higher education had been nationally idiosyncratic: determined by its British origins, and affected by British and American policy developments, while shaped by national cultural-political dynamics. Between 1987 and 1992 the Australian system underwent a major reconstruction along neo-liberal lines, modified in one respect by national social democracy. After 1992 the Australian system continued to evolve in the directions established in 1987–92.

The reform program is now 13 years old, and its effects can be interrogated. Did it achieve what it set out to achieve? What were the outcomes, expected and unexpected? In evaluating higher education reform in Australia, this chapter refers to government statistical data and also to studies conducted in the 1990s, including the first independent empirical study of governance, management and university strategy making since the reforms, published as *The Enterprise University* (Marginson and Considine 2000). From time to time, the chapter touches on parallel changes in other countries, highlighting the global character of reform while drawing out the national specifics of the Australian case.

Before the reforms

Although the first university in Sydney opened in 1851, the Australian higher education system was constructed in the twenty years between the mid 1950s and the mid 1970s, and almost entirely financed by government. The Murray report (1957) established the basis of national funding and policy leadership. The Martin committee (1964) doubled student numbers and created a second polytechnic-style sector, the colleges of advanced education (CAEs), which at first operated mostly at sub-degree level. The Whitlam government of 1972–75 completed national centralization and abolished tuition fees. The system expanded from nine universities in 1955 to 19 universities and 75 colleges of advanced education in 1980. Student numbers rose from 30,792 in 1955 to 273,137 in 1975. From 1969–70 to 1975–76 national government spending on higher education multiplied almost four times in constant price terms, and in 1974–75 reached 1.7 per cent of GDP (Marginson 1997b:

11–45). There were strong research programmes in Medicine and in areas drawing on the land and a southern hemisphere location, such as Agriculture and related plant and animal sciences, the Geo-Sciences, Astronomy and later, Ecology. Despite the key role of government, the universities were modelled as independent academic entities. Internal governance drew on the collegial tradition. Policy programmes were administered by 'arms-length' statutory commissions, a buffer zone between government and institutions.

Under the Fraser Liberal-National Party government of 1975–83 enrolment growth slowed, and both funding and policy were frozen. The election of the Hawke Labour government in 1983 was followed by the consolidation of neo-liberalism in economic policy. In 1985 commodity export prices fell, and the balance of trade and the deregulated Australian dollar both collapsed. The government began to focus closely on 'micro-economic reforms' that would facilitate 'structural adjustment' in the global environment (OECD 1987), especially reforms that would stimulate knowledge intensive exports in elaborately transformed manufacturing and services, and thus reduce Australia's long-standing dependence on agriculture and minerals. There was renewed policy interest in education, training and research. In contrast with the system-building period, policy was specifically focused on those aspects of education that facilitated the market economy; and was *prima facie* critical of public funding and public provision. While it was broadly agreed that participation should expand, the economic departments argued that government should bear only part of the cost, and growth should be joined to reforms that rendered higher education more outward looking, more responsive, more entrepreneurial and more efficient.

Following the introduction of full-fee international marketing in the UK, guidelines for Australian educational export were promulgated in 1985. The next year the Prime Minister's Department prepared a report supporting the return of tuition fees and advocating a subsidized private sector to carry part of the growth in participation (ASTEC 1987). Questions were also being raised about the continued viability of the binary division of labour between universities and colleges of advanced education. Of the 201,312 students in advanced education in 1987, 72.7 per cent were enrolled at three-year bachelor course level or above: 841 were in research higher degrees though CAEs were ineligible for research funding (DETYA 1995).

The Dawkins reforms of 1987–92

In July 1987 the government appointed a senior economic minister, John Dawkins, to an enhanced portfolio of Employment, Education and Training.[2] Dawkins abolished the Commonwealth Tertiary Education Commission and administered programmes directly via his restructured department. In December 1987 he released a Green Paper, *Higher Education: A Policy Discussion Paper*, which outlined a full reform program; and he also set up the Wran committee to investigate potential non-government sources of funding.

Arguing that higher education conferred substantial private benefits, in May 1988 the committee proposed an income-contingent tuition charge, with repayments through the tax system to begin when students' income reached average weekly earnings. The Higher Education Contribution Scheme (HECS), fixed at an average 25 per cent of course costs, began in 1989. In July 1988 Dawkins confirmed the Green Paper in his White Paper, *Higher Education: A Policy Statement*. The final report was *Higher Education: Quality and Diversity in the 1990s*, issued by Dawkins' junior minister Peter Baldwin in October 1991, focusing on quality assurance, teaching and new technologies (Dawkins 1987, 1988; Wran 1988; Baldwin 1991).

The specific reforms are set down in Table 9.1. Dawkins sought to increase the annual number of graduates by 50 per cent; and to expand the proportionate enrolment of students from groups under-represented in higher education. Baldwin added better access from sub-degree institutions in Technical and Further Education (TAFE). The government also wanted to increase the share of places in fields reckoned economically utilitarian.[3]

The map of public provision was fundamentally altered. In contrast with reforms in Chile, Argentina and parts of Eastern Europe, instead of creating a subsidized private sector, the government concentrated on the marketization and corporate reform of the existing institutions. The binary system was abolished and firm size limits were imposed. Institutions were expected to enrol at least the equivalent of 2000 full-time students to remain eligible for funding, and 8000 full-time students to be fully supported for research. In the unitary 'Unified National System', which replaced the binary system, all institutions were designated universities and conducted research and doctoral programmes. This forced a round of mergers, with the colleges of advanced education either joining existing universities or forming new universities.

The Unified National System was modelled as a set of financially autonomous institutions with defined products and markets, expected 'to compete for teaching and research resources on the basis of institutional merit and capacity' (Dawkins 1988: 28). Institutions were encouraged to raise money via the newly proclaimed international student market, the deregulation of vocational postgraduate tuition and short courses for industry, and consultancy and commercial research. At the same time, data and accountability requirements were tightened and the government began to emphasize outcome measures, and the relationship with employer and student 'stakeholders'. Each year institutions negotiated their funding and their profile of student enrolments on a one-to-one basis with the government. Institutions were expected to prepare plans in such areas as their future strategic development, performance measures, quality assurance, and steps to improve teaching and research management. Part of the research support that had previously been implicit in the operating grants received by each institution was centralized and subjected to competitive mechanisms and national priorities. Institutions were urged to professionalize management and to shift decisions from collegial governance to executive leaders.

In the Green Paper/White Paper structure of 'consultation' the Australian government followed the Thatcher government in the UK. There were other similarities between the two groups of policies, reflecting a common policy heritage and common neo-liberal orientation. Australia preceded the UK in the abolition of the binary divide, the creation of a unitary competitive system and the introduction of user charges. Australia followed the UK in international marketing, in the national centralization of research policy, and emphases on links to industry and cultural change inside the universities. Like the UK government, and to a lesser extent European governments as well, the Australian government was increasingly impressed by American models of education which valorized high levels of participation, mixed public and private funding, student fees leavened by scholarships, and relations with industry and a donor culture; and sustained the ideology of a competitive system-market. The Australian government's focus on broader social access, the facilitation of feeder relationships between higher education and the technical and further education sector, and also the careful structuring of the Higher Education Contribution Scheme, were more specific to Australian politics, reflecting the social democratic roots of the Labour Party. Free education, a Labour reform in 1974, had been strongly supported: the HECS was fashioned so as to minimize financial barriers to participation (Marginson 1997b: 224–31). The HECS was the one element in the Dawkins reforms that was technically original and nationally unique.

The Dawkins blueprint had a major and lasting effect on Australian universities. But before looking at the specific outcomes, it is important to consider what government was trying to achieve: the promotion of changes in society that lay behind the reform in the higher education sector (the meta-objectives of reform).

Meta-objectives of the reforms

The 1987 Green Paper recycled the 1960s rubric of investment in human capital but, like the Thatcher Green Paper, it focused more on private investment and less on social investment than did the Robbins (1963) and Martin (1964) reports. It was also permeated by a sense of economic globalization and international competition. It found that these pressures demanded 'changes in attitudes, practices and processes in all sectors and at all levels of the Australian community' and 'the education sector, and our higher education system in particular, must play a leading role in promoting these changes'. The transformation of higher education was meant to achieve three economic meta-objectives. First, the opening up and modernization of the Australian economy, by lifting skills, speed and responsiveness; generalizing information and communications technologies; and sensitivizing Australian companies to regional markets in East and Southeast Asia. 'What is important is the flexibility to capitalise on new opportunities as they arise' (Dawkins 1987: iii and 2). Second, the recreation of Australian manufacturing as a technology-intensive export sector, grounded in advanced production skills, science and technologies and a global vision. Third, by developing services exports in education itself and thereby shoring up the balance of trade.

It was assumed that by positioning the institutions of higher education as quasi-corporations in a competitive market, they would become more porous to business and industry, facilitating education-economy links; and would be colonized by the market virtues of entrepreneurialism, allocative efficiency, customer responsiveness and innovation. Also, quality would improve, especially if quality assurance procedures were established (Baldwin 1991: 9). The logic was as follows: with higher education now defined as a private good, the quasi-corporate universities, motivated by their own economic position, would tailor their courses to meet the needs of graduates and their employers. Courses would become more relevant, and teaching quality and graduate outcomes would improve continuously. The same logic entered research policy. It was expected that competition, and a newly-introduced product format, would drive efficiencies and a client-style culture. This would correct the perceived imbalance in favour of 'basic' (academically-controlled) research at the expense of applied research for industry. Thus the government would secure a more focused and useful higher education system, while reducing its share of funding.

The reforms of 1987–92 also set out to translate the government-institution relationship from bureaucratic policy direction and input controls, into indirect steering and output controls. The government liberalized the earlier constraints on local management of strategic directions, budget priorities and capital expenditures; while developing a range of new policy instruments. It used not just expenditures but austerity to manipulate institutions. It remade their internal life using funding formulae, targeted grants, competition games, output definition and incentive structures. Compliance with particular policies was often voluntary, yet it was clear that scarce government funding depended on that compliance:

> To achieve its aims the Government's approach will be to offer financial and other advantages to institutions willing to adopt those principles and practices considered to be for the general community good. Institutions may choose not to adopt those principles and practices, but will receive less support from the Government.
>
> (Dawkins 1987: 3)

Chevaillier (1998: 66) distinguishes between *decentralisation*, in which decision-making powers are transferred to a legally autonomous authority; and *deconcentration*, in which power is shifted in an authority that is located away from the centre but subordinated to it. Australian universities were modelled in terms of deconcentration.

> The Government will also ensure that institutions are free to manage their own resources without unnecessary intervention, while at the same

time remaining clearly accountable for their decisions and actions. The system of educational profiles will be an important instrument for this purpose. Institutions will be free to establish their own priorities and develop their strengths, to accredit their own courses, to develop a broader base of funding support and to introduce more flexible staffing arrangements . . . The Commonwealth will adopt new funding mechanisms that give maximum autonomy and flexibility to institutions in the management of their resources, within a framework of agreed institutional goals and objectives. The performance of institutions against these goals will be a key factor in determining their future levels of income from Commonwealth sources.

(Dawkins 1988: 10)

Control was exercised not through neo-liberal 'legislative formalism' but through techniques of public management (Kogan 1998: 124–33). As in Chile, government refashioned itself from 'resource provider' to 'purchaser of production' (Brunner 1997: 225). As in Finland, it focused more on 'the outputs and performance of universities instead of regulating the inputs' (Holtta 1998: 55).

Despite the abolition of the binary system and the new standardizations in place, the government 'sought to encourage diversity' in course mix, student mix, university mission including links with industry, and in institutions' 'philosophical approach to education'. It argued that larger, more broadly-based institutions were better placed to provide for a variety of needs (Baldwin 1991: 11 and 39). It believed that autonomy of mission, competition and client relations would together generate diverse responses to particular clients and needs; and this would translate into greater variation between and within institutions.[4]

Outcomes of the reforms: the specific policies

Table 9.1 summarizes the 1987–92 reform programme. The Dawkins policies were remarkable for the degree to which their proposals were pushed through, and for the extent of the change that followed. In that sense Australia was almost a model case of neo-liberal reform.

System size and structure

In terms of success/failure, the Dawkins era policies fall into three main groups: policies that were achieved in full; policies that were achieved in part; and policies where progress was limited or non-existent. The first is the largest group including policies such as the major structural changes to the size, shape and system dynamics of higher education. The government achieved its expansion of graduate numbers in half the expected time

Table 9.1 The 1987–92 Dawkins reforms in Australian higher education: outcomes

Proposed reform	Outcome	Summation
Growth in annual number of graduates from 86,850 (1988) to 125,000 (2001)	Annual number of non-international graduates reached 126,587 in 1994 and by 2001 was expected to exceed 143,000 (170,000 including international students)	Policy goal achieved in half the time expected
Improved access to social groups under-represented in higher education	Little change in share of participation held by bottom s.e.s. quintile. Decline in share held by students from rural areas. Participation of indigenous students rises from 3307 students in 1989 to 8001 in 1999. Increase in women in non-traditional areas, e.g. Engineering	Limited success in achieving goal
Improved articulation with vocational education and training (VET) sector	Fostering of formal credit transfer arrangements and other articulation between sectors. Significant university resistance. Proportion of undergraduates entering with prior VET qualifications reaches 11% in 1999	Policy goal partly achieved, mainly in Business and Engineering
Enrolment shift in favour of Computing, Electrical Engineering, Business Studies, Asian Studies	Enrolment share of all of these fields of study expanded, except for Asian studies. Students in Business, Economics, Management, Administration rose from 91,568 (21%) in 1989 to 178,771 (26%) in 1999. Main area of decline was in Education	Policy goal almost entirely achieved
Abolition of colleges of advanced education and installation of standard 'template' for universities	Existing colleges of advanced education merged with universities, or merged with each other or upgraded to form new universities. 65 funded institutions average size 6057 students (1987) replaced by 42 institutions average size 16,340 students (1999). In the new system all universities are comprehensive doctoral level institutions: small specialist institutions almost disappear	Policy goal achieved. 'New binarism' with Vocational Education and Training sector (VET)

Creation of corporate-economic competition between universities	Institutions compete directly for one dollar in four, including tuition fees, industry monies, all research funding, some competitive public money. In 1993–5 national quality assurance creates league table rankings	Policy goal achieved: culture of competition established
Mixed public/private funding to replace almost sole reliance on public funding (91% of institutional incomes in 1983)	Creation of income contingent Higher Education Contribution Scheme (HECS) at average 20% of course costs, rises later. Deregulation of tuition for international students, short courses, some postgraduates. In 1998 52% of income from public sources, HECS 17%, other fees and charges 16%, non-market private incomes 5%	Policy goal achieved, via the coupling of public austerity and deregulation of commercial work
Development of export sector in international education	Policy transition from aid-based approach to full-fee export approach completed by 1989. Fee paying international students grow from 3595 in 1988 to 83,111 in 1999. Tuition fee income totals $539 million in 1998	Policy goal achieved. Australia third biggest exporter
Internationalization	Bi-lateral relations with many international universities, especially in East and South East Asia, largely for commercial reasons. Growth of off-shore enrolments, twinning, campuses. Changes to curriculum are slower	Policy goal achieved
Stronger links with industry in training and research	Shift of part of research towards applied projects with economic spin-offs; fee-based upgrading courses; Cooperative Research Centres (CRCs) with industry	Policy goal partly achieved: university culture changes; industry take-up slow
Performance-based funding as the basis of national government grants	Too difficult to devise agreed set of performance indicators to cover teaching support ('operating grants') but c.6% of operating grant allocated on the basis of measured research performance, and other research monies subject to performance based assessments	Policy goal not achieved for teaching, but achieved for research
Establishment of national coordination and national priorities in research	Centralization of direct research funding under the Australian Research Council, and National Health and Medical Research Council.	Policy goal achieved

Proposed reform	Outcome	Summation
Focus on employability of graduates	Graduate employment/unemployment rates become seen as a significant indicator of institutional performance. Emphasis on generic work-related skills but government unable to secure competency-based approach. Some vocationalization of generalist courses (e.g. BA Tourism)	Greater emphasis on utitilitarian values suggests policy goal largely achieved
Increased emphasis on quality of teaching	National prizes for university teaching. Emphases on teaching quality and student evaluation of teaching in quality assurance. More policy focus on teaching but research and publications remain primary	Policy goal partly achieved
Encouragement of technological innovations in teaching and delivery	Funding for technological innovations via dedicated competitive funds. Australian universities have high micro-processor and Internet use. Recent innovations draw on technology and/or entrepreneurship, rather than academic change (Marginson and Considine 2000)	Policy goal achieved
Establishment of quality assurance systems	1993–5 Commonwealth Committee on Quality Assurance in Higher Education ranks institutions on the basis of (1) outcomes (2) internal quality assurance systems, and thereby installs culture of self-assessment	Policy goal achieved
Fostering of a corporate-style executive and professionalized managers	Major shift to corporate styles of organization, even in some academic units, and the augmentation and cultural transformation of senior leadership groups	Policy goal achieved
Fostering of transformation in internal governance: weakening of collegial forms	Uneven by institution, but traditional collegial bodies such as academic boards are increasingly by-passed. Power is resource power, resources are in the hands of managers	Policy goal largely achieved, despite academic opposition
Part deregulation in industrial relations in higher education	Changes to Australian industrial relations lead to 'enterprise bargaining' in higher education, albeit re-centralized by the pattern of union claims. Major shift to casual employment provides managerial 'safety valve'	Policy goal of greater manager flexibility achieved

Sources: Dawkins 1987; Dawkins 1988; Baldwin 1991; DETYA 1999b, 2000a; Marginson and Considine 2000; Meek and Wood 1997. US dollar values: 1 USD = 1.3016 AUD using 1997 Purchasing Power Parity

Table 9.2   Enrolments, Australian higher education, 1987 to 1999

	Total enrolments	*1987 = 100.0*
1987	393,734	100.0
1990	485,066	123.2
1993	575,616	146.2
1996	634,094	161.0
1999	686,267	174.3

* includes enrolments at funded private institutions (10,511 students in 1999, 1.5 per cent of the total)
Source: DETYA 2000a

(Tables 9.1 and 9.2). Between 1985 and 1996 the participation of 19 year olds in higher education was lifted from 15.5 to 24.8 per cent (DETYA 1999c). There was even more rapid growth at postgraduate level, where mass education emerged for the first time. Between 1987 and 1999 the number of higher degree research students rose from 14,567 to 37,739; while the number enrolled in coursework postgraduate programmes, mostly vocational in character, rose from 46,711 to 101,800 (DETYA 2000a).

Between the mid-1980s and the mid-1990s, the rate of growth of tertiary enrolments was high by historical standards in most of the world, though varying from nation to nation in the mix of university and non-university enrolments. In comparative terms the growth rate in Australia was at the upper end of the band. From 1985 to 1994 there was a 58.2 per cent increase in university-equivalent enrolments. In Europe growth rates were Norway 87.1, UK 56.4, Denmark 45.6, Spain 43.1, France 42.6, Italy 41.8, Finland 34.8, Austria 30.9, Switzerland 21.7, Belgium 19.3, Germany 15.2 and Netherlands 11.3[5] (Eicher 1998: 31).

Australian vocational education and training, the sector equivalent to UK further education, also expanded: the participation of 19 year olds in publicly-funded vocational education and training increased from 22.8 per cent in 1985 to 27.5 per cent in 1996. Total participation of 19 year olds in all tertiary education rose from 38.3 per cent to 52.2 per cent. Among women, tertiary participation increased from less than one third to more than half of 19 year olds, and achieved parity with male participation rates for the first time (DETYA 1999c).[6]

In universities the growth in student and graduate numbers was accompanied by a less than proportionate increase in academic staff, and a rising ratio of students to academic faculty; again corresponding with global trends. For example, Holtta notes that in Finland from 1990–96 teaching staff numbers were stable while the number of Masters degrees rose by 26 per cent and doctoral degrees by 73 per cent (Holtta 1998: 61). In Australia between 1990 and 1996 the number of Bachelor degrees rose by 67 per cent, Masters degrees by 240 per cent and doctorates by 110 per cent. Over the same time period, the number of full-time equivalent academic staff,

Table 9.3   Size and number of funded institutions, Australian higher education, 1987 and 1999

	Number of students	Number of funded institutions*	Average number of students	Largest institution	Institutions with less than 2000	Institutions with more than 20,000
1987	393,734	65	6057.4	17,855	18	0
1999	686,267	42	16,339.7	40,625	5	16

* excludes non-government institutions not receiving Commonwealth operating grant support. A government-instigated survey found in 1999 there were 86 accredited private providers in Australia, of which three received operating grants covering 729 effective full-time students. Of these 86 institutions, 79 responded to the survey: these institutions enrolled between them 31,212 students, translating into 18,877 effective full-time student units. The unfunded student load in private institutions was equivalent to just under 4.0 per cent of the student load in the funded institutions (Watson 2000)
Source: DETYA 2000a

excluding casual employees, increased by 18 per cent (DETYA 1999c).[7] The ratio of equivalent full-time students to equivalent full-time academic staff rose from 14.2 in 1990 to 15.6 in 1996 (DETYA 1998).[8]

The government also abolished the binary division between universities and CAEs; installed its standard template for university mission and size; and established national funding, administration and priorities in research. Average institutional size rose to the level of the largest universities in the pre–1987 system (Table 9.3). With three exceptions, small specialist institutions only survived, in a fashion, by merging with large universities.

In the old system *pro rata* funding distributions had been the norm. The new ideology was that of a 'level playing field' in which all universities competed freely while enjoying parity of role and status. In practice, vertical segmentation continued, with the older universities in each major city sustaining the dominant competitive position as before.

The installation of economic competition

Whereas universities had always jostled each other for prestige, high-scoring school leavers, research standing and industry research funding, competition was now installed as the political economy of the system and at the heart of university identity. Direct competition was extended to most forms of research funding, fee-based student places and work for industry, and from time to time was intensified by targeted government funds subject to competitive bidding, including monies for administrative and technological innovations.

Within the overall framework of government-steered competition, the government struck a balance between allocation by market demand and supply, and allocation by policy-based planning now reworked in contract mode. Four out of five student places, including all undergraduate places apart from international students, were financed not by direct tuition fees but by government subsidy plus deferred student charges under the HECS. The HECS was paid not to institutions but to government. The HECS-funded student load of each institution was determined not by the demand for places, but fixed in the annual negotiations between the government and each university. There was no immediate buyer-seller dynamic, and because it was a deferred income-contingent charge, the HECS generated relatively weak economic signals – so much so that it was almost neutral in socio-economic terms. Potential undergraduate students from poor backgrounds were not unduly deterred (Chapman and Smith 1994). This was important in the total mix of policy, as it retarded the tendency of competition to exacerbate inequalities. Despite recurring policy proposals (for example Fane 1984) Australia did not introduce vouchers, or follow Chile with differential funding for institutions that attracted high scoring school leavers.

At the same time, market-based steering had a wider reach than the strict economic mechanisms suggest. The ideology of the student as investor in private goods, becoming part of the policy language throughout the OECD (Daniel *et al.* 1999: 17–18), was asserted strongly in Australia. In this context, the government positioned itself as the collective agent of the student-consumer/investor, and in its negotiating position with each institution, as the totem 'spirit' of the market, rendering universities accountable for their economically defined outputs. It was able to do this because of its monopsonist power as the principal funding agent: a power it sustained regardless of whether universities were 80 or 50 per cent publicly funded. At the same time, and while using the HECS to sustain participation and equity, the government used its monopsony to intensify competition. The installation of competitive behaviours, even more than the installation of commodity production, was seen as the lynch-pin of higher education reform, *the* key to cultural change and incentives for better outcomes. The guiding theorist was not Adam Smith so much as Herbert Spencer (1884) and his idea of evolution as *laissez-faire* competition and the survival of the fittest.

Inter-university competition was also a control device, rendering institutions vulnerable to detailed policy manipulation and the subtle reworking of their market position, while negating their capacity for collective solidarity and pressure on the government. Competition reinforced state steering: state steering was used to intensify competitiveness. The significance of neo-liberal reform lay not only in the shiny new engine of commodification, competition and university enterprise, but in the creation of new forms of state control.

Again, the engineering of Australian institutions as economically-defined competitors was part of a larger global trend, extending even to erstwhile social democratic countries (Kogan 1998: 128). Nowhere did all government funding become competitively allocated. Everywhere market economics loomed larger and inter-institutional competitiveness stepped up, enabling the desired change in behaviours to be secured. In the continuum from

Table 9.4   Sources of funds for Australia higher education, 1986–98

	Governments %	Higher Education Contribution Scheme %	Student fees and charges for services %	Donations and investments %	Other sources %	Total %
1986	87	0	5	8	0	100
1990	68	12	8	7	4	100
1994	62	13	11	3	11	100
1998	52	17	16	5	10	100

Source: DETYA 1999b

social democratic collaboration to Hobbesian war of all against all, structured by a Hobbesian sovereign state, Australia fell towards the Hobbesian end. Marketization was not as dramatic as in Chile, where new private institutions were encouraged and over 40 per cent of the funding of public universities was subject to direct competition (Brunner 1997: 230–1). However, Australia went further than, say, Finland, where direct economic competition was largely confined to selected 'external' public monies (Holtta 1998: 59–60).

In 1986 87 per cent of the funding of higher education was from public sources (Dawkins 1987: 76). The HECS and international marketing, fee-based vocational postgraduate courses and short courses for industry; the removal of government financial penalties for private earnings; and the wavering and decline of per capita public funding (Table 9.6), saw the government share fall to 52 per cent by 1998 (Table 9.4). By then one dollar in four was subject to direct competition, and 'soft money' commercial income was routinely used to shore up core academic operations. In 1998 the Royal Melbourne Institute of Technology enrolled 6944 international students and received USD $49.3 million in fees. This was 23.6 per cent of total income (DETYA 1999b, 2000a).

All Australian universities began to market courses internationally (Tables 9.8 and 9.9) and there was concurrent growth in global communications and travel, staff and student exchange, and off-shore links. The rhetoric of internationalization fed the global self-conception of universities (Scott 1998a: 111). As in the UK (Williams 1998b: 78) Australian universities found it easier to export education than many had imagined. It was more difficult to create an American culture of alumni, corporate and philanthropic donations.

International fee income reached 8.3 per cent of all institutional income by 1998 (DETYA 1999b). The deregulation and commercialization of international education created a frankly capitalist dynamic at the margin of negotiated student load; in contrast with those European countries where the commercialization of international education did not occur (Dill and

Teixeira 2000: 115). In Australia international education was often handled by separate commercial companies attached to the university, controlled by executive leaders while separated from academic decision making (Marginson 2000a: 144–55). Marketing and corporate image-making began to shape institutional strategies, academic priorities and internal resource flows (Symes 1996; Marginson and Considine 2000); while strengthening the ideological hold of the competition/game that national policy had set in motion.

The culture of the corporation

As in most other countries the outcome was not a fully commercial market, but a government-steered quasi-market, in which the steering mechanisms themselves were modelled in market form. It was a market shaped by the 'visible hand' rather than the 'invisible hand' as Meek (2000: 23) states it. No doubt the government exercised more sway over public sector institutions remodelled as public enterprises than it would have exercised over the subsidized private sector under consideration in 1986 and 1987. Furthermore, the creation of mixed public-private funding in the public universities, rather than extending the notional market across both public and subsidized private sectors, also facilitated the cultural and organizational transformation of the public universities. This transformation closely followed the lines set down in the 1988 White Paper and later confirmed in a successor report (Hoare 1995). Again, up to a point the reform in Australia was part of common global trends. Everywhere income targets, accountability requirements and the pressures of competition strengthened centrifugal pressures inside institutions and brought administrators into conjunction with academic teaching and research (Coaldrake and Stedman 1999). Negotiations with government fostered chief executive officer-style leaders: for example Sjolund (1998) outlines the changing character of leadership in Sweden, Holtta (1998) in Finland, Chevaillier (1998) in France and Kogan (1998: 129) for Europe as a whole. Nevertheless, in Australia and in neighbouring and similar New Zealand (Peters and Roberts 1999), and in some British and Chilean institutions,[9] the cultural change was greater than in Western Europe. For example Kogan (1998: 127) notes that in Norway the professional academic mode of governance survived, though modified by state and market; whereas in Australia academic boards and faculty assemblies were largely sidelined (Marginson and Considine 2000). There was some variation. In the older Australian universities academic cultures were more independent than in the new universities, and academic entrepreneurs often exercised a good deal of market freedom. Nonetheless, everywhere power came to rest firmly with those in control of increasingly scarce resources: academic and non-academic managers, some of whom now led the new commercial operations. As in Chile the pronounced emphases on competition and income generation speeded the adoption of a 'business-like organisational culture' (Brunner 1997: 234) in public universities.

Though they were still more than half government-funded, and the old rationales for higher education as public good and citizen formation presumably still applied, Dawkins had re-positioned Australian universities as competitive companies responsible for their own economic fate. Extending Neave's logic, the ultimate objective of higher education was now the interests of the individual institutions as corporations – rather than knowledge, or the pastoral formation of students. In the minds of institutional managers, students ('customers') and research ('intellectual property') had become means to the true end rather than ends in themselves. Correspondingly, the values of administrators and leader-managers had been sharply set against traditional academic values, as empirical studies confirm (for example Sheehan and Welch 1994; Meek and Wood 1997; Marginson and Considine 2000). Academics in Business Studies were more comfortable in the post-Dawkins environment than were most of their colleagues in other disciplines (McInnis 2000c).

The conflict between money values and scholarly values was translated downwards. During the 1990s internal university budget systems were deconcentrated. Academic units became modelled as franchisees of the institution-corporation, while retaining much of the external income they generated. Consistent with Clark's (1998a) data on exemplary 'entrepreneurial universities' in the UK and Europe, those Australian institutions that succeeded in the new environment created a culture of 'academic enterprise' in which academic productivity was aligned with the maximization of financial returns. Compared to the cases analysed by Clark, the Australian institutions placed less importance on strengthening the 'academic heartland' (Marginson and Considine 2000).

The absorption of non-university higher education into an enlarged university sector, the growing distance between research funding and teaching, the inter-university market competition, the installation of monetary definitions of value: together they constituted a change in the 'Idea of a University' as Williams (1998b: 78) notes for the UK. The new 'idea' embodied a utilitarian emphasis on product and performance-based indicators of competitive market standing. The post-Dawkins system was more explicitly focused on graduate employability and services to industry, as in the former CAE sector. Even in the older universities there was a weakening of Newman's anti-utility and of the notion of advanced scholarship and research as *necessarily* inherent in academic labour (Marginson 2000a: 48–68). Consistent with this, there was a relative growth of enrolments in generalist-vocational departments in Business Studies and Computing, as in other countries. The government-supported annual survey of graduate employment/unemployment and satisfaction with courses (GCCA 1999), plus the official data on research income and publications, were used to compile unofficial university ratings, for example the annual *Good Universities Guide.*

Consistent with the corporate-consumerist ethos, the government also secured the generalization of quality assurance systems. The three successive Commonwealth-instigated national quality audits in 1993–95 led to official league tables and differential funding allocations (Harman 1998): each university was audited on the basis of both its performance and its quality assurance systems. As in other countries the process was potent in installing the dimensions of performance, external responsiveness and reflexivity in relation to institutional objectives. Running quality assurance as an institutional function rather than a discipline-controlled function meant that it encouraged consistency of minimum standards rather than maximum achievement, and overlapped with institutional marketing (Mollis and Marginson 2000). 'Excellence' became routinized as the signifier of university status, rather than the signifier of world-important insights or research. At the same time, quality assurance provided a data framework for judgements about competitive market position.

Institutions did not metamorphose into businesses pure and simple. They became an uneven, complex mix of commercial, bureaucratic-political, collegial and scholarly-pastoral behaviours; in which a performance culture had been firmly installed and the dominant ideological element was economic competition. There was continued scope for government policy intervention, provided that it used market codes. At the same time, the main policy debate was reduced to an impoverished binarism of government-controlled quasi-market versus commercial market. The leading universities and would-be commercial providers pushed for the free play of prices. In the second half of the 1990s, significant policy discussion was confined to the question of whether or not to introduce vouchers and/or direct tuition charges for undergraduates (West 1998), as if further marketization was the only imaginable means to educational improvement.

Less successful policies

A smaller group of Dawkins-era policy objectives were achieved in part but not in full. Performance-based funding was achieved in research, where inputs and outputs were readily quantified, but not in teaching where it proved impossible to develop agreed measures (Baldwin 1991: 4). The government distributed 6 per cent of its operating grants to universities through the 'research quantum'. This was a composite indicator, based principally on competitive income for research purposes, and to a lesser extent on the number of publications and higher degree research students: the formula favoured large projects in the applied sciences. The research quantum became a powerful influence on income and institutional prestige. Unlike the UK, there was no qualitative assessment of research standing or publications. The use of a solely quantitative definition of research activity enabled research to be imagined as a universal economy but eliminated its serendipity. The post-Dawkins system in Australia was remarkable in the extent to which research organization was centralized and subjected to one utilitarian formulae across all fields (Marginson 2000b). A smaller-scale version of the same regime was installed in research management within universities, weakening discipline-specific cultures (Marginson and Considine 2000) while advancing the partial transfer from 'Mode 1' to 'Mode 2' research sought by governments and managers world-wide (Sjolund 1998; Kogan 1998).

The opening of universities to industry also succeeded only partly. While universities became more closely attuned to the need for industry support, industry was slow to take up the new opportunities for product development and fee-based training. In the Cooperative Research Centre programme, intended as a joint programme of universities, government research laboratories and industry, the publicly-funded university component remained the dominant element. In 1998, ten years after the Dawkins policies were proclaimed, business enterprise expenditure on research and development in universities constituted USD $105 million, 5.2 per cent of all research and development activity in higher education. This was a modest return given the strenuous changes to research funding and management (not to mention the risk to basic research, especially in non-commercializable fields) in the drive for economic utilities.

The government was also less than fully successful in securing a focus on teaching in the shaping of academic careers (Baldwin 1991: 2). As in the USA (Fairweather 2000: 94), notwithstanding the increased policy and marketing emphases on teaching and learning, the quantity of research grants and publications remained the dominant element in appointment and promotion: not least because under the government's own funding formula it was performance in research and not teaching that fed directly into institutional funding levels.

Another area where there was relatively limited change was in course-based articulation and credit transfer between higher education and TAFE institutions (Baldwin 1991: 5). There was progress in Business Studies and Engineering but little in other fields. Though the government was hailed internationally for its national portfolio structure, which combined higher education and industry training within a single department (OECD 1989), the two parts of the department thought along different lines, and the state-funded character of TAFE was an obstacle to policy integration. For their part the universities were reluctant to make the structural and curricular changes that would facilitate cross-sectoral relations.[10]

Finally, there were policy objectives where progress was limited or non-existent. These related to the distributive social democratic aspects of Labour Party policy. Significantly, the nationally-specific reforms proved the most difficult to achieve. Even the HECS, which after student protests in 1988–9 was implemented and then successively increased with remarkable consensus, faced continuous political destabilization by the advocates of market-determined fees (see, for example, Kemp 1999b). Despite the benign socio-economic effects of the HECS, the expansion of enrolments was

Table 9.5 Access for students from social groups under-represented in Australian higher education, 1989 and 1999

| | Students from low socio-economic locations* | | Students from rural and isolated locations | | Indigenous students | | Women as proportion of all Engineering students |
	Number	% of total	Number	% of total	Number	% of total	%
1989	25,103	5.7	34,942	7.9	3307	0.7	8.9
1999	36,926	5.4	49,180	7.2	8001	1.2	14.8

* as defined by the socio-economic status of the postal district of residence
Source: DETYA 2000a

followed by some decline in the proportion of students from the bottom socio-economic status category and from rural and isolated locations; though there was growth in indigenous students, from a low base. There was some improvement in the number of women in fields such as Engineering (Table 9.5).

Other factors affecting the outcomes of reform

The longer term outcomes of policy reforms are inevitably contaminated by circumstances other than the reforms themselves: factors concurrent with policy implementation, and *post hoc* factors. It is necessary to isolate factors extraneous to the reforms and disentangle their effects from those of the reforms themselves. Such judgements are not precise.[11]

Certain trends in the larger environment worked in favour of Dawkins' policies: growth in the number of qualified school leavers, labour market demand patterns, feminism in the professions. Other partly endogenous elements included the professionalization of management and the growth of marketing and quality assurance, where some universities pre-dated Dawkins,[12] and the new technologies in delivery and administration. On the other hand, the major structural changes to the map and mission of institutions, the private/public mix of income, research funding arrangements, and the framework of government-institution relations can be attributed to the policy reforms themselves.

The policies pursued by the Labour government until 1996 sustained the 1987–92 reforms. Internationalization was more extensive and intensive than anticipated in 1987, but was consistent with Dawkins' recipe. There was one important shift, in 1995. The government abolished automatic funding compensation for cost increases, including salary movements, triggering a decisive downward trend in the value of government grants.

The Howard government and public funding

In 1996 the government changed and there was a larger break in continuity. The new Liberal-National Party budget under Prime Minister Howard was more enthusiastic for marketization and public austerity. Universities were permitted to charge direct fees to domestic undergraduates provided that no more than a quarter in any course paid fees. The HECS was increased and three levels based on course costs and graduate earning power were introduced. The HECS now constituted 25 to 80 per cent of actual costs, a relatively high tuition charge in world terms,[13] though modified in its impact by income contingent repayment. The government also followed the UK (Williams 1998b: 78) in funding some enrolments at marginal cost. Most significantly, it announced three years of reductions in public funding and the continued absence of salary supplementation, so that from 1996 to 1999 average government funding per student declined by 12.9 per cent (Table 9.6).

Table 9.6   National government funding of Australian higher education, 1985–99

	Commonwealth operating funds* $s million	*Effective full-time student units** thousands*	*Funding per student unit $s*
1985	2733.6	270.2	10,114
1986	2790.1	281.0	9929
1987	2857.7	289.2	9881
1988	2961.9	307.9	9620
1989	3110.7	322.9	9634
1990	3263.7	341.0	9571
1991	3355.2	370.8	9050
1992	3551.9	382.6	9285
1993	3617.0	385.8	9377
1994	3887.1	408.2	9524
1995	3902.9	419.1	9314
1996	4009.2	439.0	9132
1997	3891.5	451.5	8619
1998	3655.3	451.8	8090
1999	3636.8	457.2	7954

* net of receipts under the Higher Education Contribution Scheme. All dollar figures in year 2000 prices. US dollar values: 1 USD = 1.3016 AUD using 1997 Purchasing Power Parity
** refers to enrolments in government funded institutions only, of whom just over 1 per cent were in funded private institutions. The private sector plays a minor role in Australian higher education, constituting 5 per cent of total student load (Marginson 1997c; Watson 2000)
Source: Australian Vice-Chancellors' Committee (AVCC 2000), derived from DETYA data

No doubt this exacerbated the drive for private income, but this was insufficient to substitute for lost public funding. One sign was a fall in the number of academic staff, excluding casual employees. In the three years after 1996 equivalent full-time academic staff fell 1508 (4.8 per cent) and non-academic staff fell by 1943 (4.7 per cent), while at the same time student load units rose by 11.5 per cent (DETYA 1999a). Again excluding casual staff, the system-wide ratio of effective full-time students to effective full-time academic staff rose from 15.0 in 1995 and 15.6 in 1996, to 18.3 in 1999 (DETYA 1999a; 2000a).

In the 1970s Australia's direct public spending on tertiary education had been relatively high in international terms. By 1997 it was down to 1.0 per cent of GDP, the level of the OECD country mean and the average for the OECD region taken as a whole. Australian private expenditure was 0.7 per cent of GDP, higher than most OECD countries but below the average for the OECD region because of private inputs in the USA and Japan. Total Australian expenditure on tertiary education from private and public resources was 1.7 per cent of GDP compared to the OECD country mean of 1.3 per cent and OECD regional average of 1.7 per cent. However, in Australia participation in both university-equivalent programmes and other tertiary education was significantly higher than in most OECD countries. In 1997 17 year olds in Australia could expect an average of 3.7 years of tertiary education, the same level as the USA and well above the OECD country average of 2.4 years (OECD 2000: 56, 158 and 160). An average OECD level of expenditure was spread across a much larger than average student population. At the same time, the role of private spending was increasing faster than in most other countries, with effects still to be seen.

The part-shift from public to private funding sharpened resource disparities between fields with strong income raising potential, such as Business and Computing, and the older generalist courses in social sciences, humanities and natural sciences. As a result of the 1996 policy changes, universities experienced deeper problems of resource scarcity. It is likely that tendencies to corporate organization, marketing and fund-raising were enhanced. These developments did not change the trend line instigated by the 1987–1992 reforms, but they hastened the passage of universities along that trend line. The 1996 changes shifted the balance from public to private goods more than Dawkins had envisaged.

Outcomes of the reforms: the meta-objectives

When the Australian reforms are tested against the meta-objectives that they were designed to fulfil, the outcome is less clear-cut. On one hand, the government successfully reworked its relationship with the institutions, becoming more effective in shaping their inner life. On the other hand, the larger economic effects of reform in higher education are harder to trace.

First, were the changes to higher education and its relationship to industry

Table 9.7 Value of Australian exports by broad industry sector, change between 1987–88 and 1997–98: constant 1989–90 prices

	1987–88 $s million	1997–98 $s million	1997–98 1987–88 = 100
Elaborately transformed manufacturing	3503	13,871	395.9
Other manufacturing	3268	6063	185.5
Commodities	26,094	43,433	166.4
Services	7812	20,217	258.8
Total	40,677	83,584	205.5

US dollar values: 1 USD = 1.3016 AUD using 1997 Purchasing Power Parity
Source: Sheehan and Tikomirova (1998: 121), from unpublished Australian Bureau of Statistics data

associated with a more productive education-economy relationship, and the modernization of labour and management? The question cannot be directly tested, partly because (like the Dawkins policy) it turns on the one-dimensional assumption that the relationship between higher education and the economy is manifest primarily in the quality of labour. The economy-education relationship is also affected by work organization and the utilization of labour in production, not to mention business acumen and patterns of capital investment.[14] It *is* clear that the larger economic policy, of which higher education policy was part, was associated with the desired change in the pattern of exports. Between 1987–88 and 1997–98 elaborately transformed manufacturing exports from Australia grew by 14.8 per cent per annum in constant price terms. Services exports grew by 9.7 per cent per annum. Both forms of export increased faster than imports in the same category, and they increased their combined share of total exports from 32.4 to 40.4 per cent, though commodities remained the largest sector (Table 9.7). Unfortunately we lack data that would allow us to draw from this aggregate picture a judgement about the effects of higher education in technology-intensive industry.

While the proportion of higher education funding from private sources increased substantially during the 1990s (Table 9.4), this reflected an increased reliance on fees, especially from international students, more than an improved relationship between higher education and industry. In research, between 1988–89 and 1996–97 business sector expenditure on research and development increased from USD $1.9 to $3.4 billion (constant 1989–90 prices: ABS 2000a). The growth of business research and development was affected more by tax incentives than by policies on higher education; and spending fell after tax incentives were withdrawn. As noted, business sector investment in higher education research and development was disappointing overall.

Between 1990 and 1999 the proportion of the population aged 15 to 64 years with qualifications at Bachelor level and above rose from 8.4 to 15.4 per cent (ABS 2000c). The ratio between the unemployment rate for degree holders and the unemployment rate for all people showed little change: degree holders retained their advantage in selection for employment. The growth of graduates from Business Studies and Computing was matched by the growth in employment in property and business services, where the number of equivalent full-time jobs increased by 344,000 between 1985–86 and 1995–96 (ABS 2000b). These trends suggest that the growing number of graduates was absorbed vocationally. We do not know to what extent this outcome was a selection effect, with non-degree holders displaced by degree holders, and to what extent job contents were changing. There are no longitudinal data on the attributes graduates took into the workplace or on the take-up of those attributes.

There is no doubt that the government succeeded in developing an export sector in education. The government fostered that sector in the early stages by regulating tuition prices so as to ensure full cost recovery, and subsidizing and coordinating university marketing in the importer countries. The previous aid-based programme of international education was phased out after 1987. Between 1989 and 1999 the total number of international students in Australian universities grew from 21,112 to 83,111 (Table 9.8) and Australia became the third largest exporter of higher education in the world after the USA and the UK, with more than twice as many students as fourth placed Canada.[15] For Australia the fee-paying market was largely comprised of students from China's Southeast Asian diaspora, mostly with good English

Table 9.8 Growth of international marketing, Australian higher education, 1989 to 1999

	Number of international students	Increase in number of students from previous year %	Proportion of international student load located in fee-based places* %
1989	21,112		44.9
1990	24,998	18.4	66.8
1991	29,630	18.5	81.7
1992	34,076	15.0	91.7
1993	37,152	9.0	96.1
1994	40,494	9.0	97.8
1995	46,187	14.1	98.7
1996	53,188	15.2	98.9
1997	62,996	18.4	99.2
1998	72,183	14.6	100.0
1999	83,111	15.1	100.0

* includes students receiving scholarships from home countries, global agencies, the Australian government or higher education institutions. This column indicates the transition from the previous aid-based policy on international education, in which all places were underpinned by Australian government subsidy, to a fully-developed commercial regime with selective subsidized places
Source: DETYA 2000a

language skills. The main importer countries in 1999 were Singapore (16,603), Malaysia (13,739), Hong Kong (13,702) and Indonesia (8081). Many students from Malaysia and Indonesia were from Chinese families. Most international students were enrolled in Business Studies and related fields (42,021) or Science, mostly Computing (11,972). In contrast with the UK and USA, it was predominantly an undergraduate population (DETYA 2000a).

By 1998 international education was generating USD $539 million in university fees, and more again in student living costs. Extending also to vocational training and schools, education exports overshadowed the old Australian staples of wool and wheat. International education contributed to the balance of trade, and reduced the costs of higher education. Nevertheless, though it probably helped to strengthen Australian relationships in South East Asia, the economic benefits of fee-based international education were largely short-term. Unlike the education of domestic students, it did not contribute to longer-term national capacity in knowledge economy industries. The majority of international students were enrolled in undergraduate business and computing and made little input into Australian industry. This compared with the USA and the UK where international postgraduate research students made a significant contribution to technologically intensive industries.

Efficiency, responsiveness, quality, innovation, diversity?

Second, did the reshaping of higher education as a competitive market, and the re-engineering of universities as corporate organizations subject to quality assurance procedures generate greater efficiency and improved quality? It seems plausible that competition led to improvement in allocative efficiency. The unit cost of degrees certainly fell. However, it is not known whether the quality of teaching and learning was constant. If quality declined, this subtracts from efficiency gains. Unfortunately quality assurance processes do not produce longitudinal data on actual quality: their role is otherwise.[16] Similarly, while there were strong incentives to expand research outputs and the volume of research per unit of funding rose, for example as measured by the quantity of publications, this says nothing about research quality. Again, the question of efficiency is unresolved.

Although the reforms were followed by more professional marketing to prospective students, there is no clear evidence that they led to better teaching, or to a closer match between courses and student needs. In the leading universities, which tended to set the norms of good practice, the assumption that market competition would drive a closer orientation to the 'client' rested on a fiction. The 'positional power' of those universities allowed them to evade direct consumer pressures. As in elite institutions anywhere in the world, the demand for places was bound to exceed supply, regardless of the quality of the student experience (Marginson 1997a: 38–46 and 131–174; Marginson 1997d). If there was improvement in teaching quality, it owed itself not to competition *per se* but to professional academic and managerial commitments, and perhaps to technological innovations and quality assurance; and it was working against the deterioration in student–staff ratios.

The evidence regarding diversity[17] is more straightforward (Marginson 1999). The Dawkins reforms led to an increase in internal diversity of offerings within the much larger institutions; but diminished the degree of diversity between institutions in mission, discipline mix, and pedagogical and organizational cultures. The combination of a 'one-size-fits-all' institutional template with no segmentation by type of institution, an ageing academic profession and the pressures of market competition maximized the degree of uniformity between universities.[18] Far from encouraging educational innovations to build market share and attract niche consumers, market competition encouraged imitation and convergence between institutions. Instead of new universities outflanking their older competitors with novel approaches, they followed strategies of weak imitation that minimized risk. At the same time, the reductions in government funding further diminished universities' capacity for innovations with long lead-times. After Dawkins, major innovations were confined to commercial income earning, global links and distance education (Marginson and Considine 2000); all areas carried more by managers and administrators than by academic faculty.

In other countries that have moved to systemic competition, a similar outcome has occurred. Brunner (1997: 232) notes that in Chile 'imitation and not innovation has been the rule' despite many new private institutions. Meek (2000: 34) remarks that the pattern is particularly obvious in systems that move from binary to unitary. Fulton describes the post-binary UK as 'a single status hierarchy in which all of the main indicators point in the same direction. This is bad news for diversity: it gives great authority to the leading universities to impose their values and practices on the rest of the system'. The unitary structure underpins 'the robustness of the existing hierarchy' (Fulton 1996a, 174–9). UK universities have an apparent freedom to vary but more individualized missions have not developed (Meek *et al.* 2000: 2). Spencerian evolutionary competition has not led to Darwinian species diversity.

While the Dawkins reforms elevated a wider range of institutions to university status, they failed to provide the governmental support for difference that was necessary to counteract the tendencies to isomorphism generated by state-steered market competition. Market competition in Australia did sustain another kind of diversity: the vertical differentiation between universities in resources and status. After a period of modest discrimination in favour of the new universities in capital works and research infrastructure, all universities were placed on the same footing; and in the competitive environment, universities with the greatest capacity to compete tended to win. These were the pre–1987 universities, especially the Sandstone and Redbrick institutions founded before 1960, and to a lesser extent the large

Universities of Technology with established missions and clienteles. At the end of the 1990s there was significant differentiation between Australian universities in student composition and catchments, the level of research activity and income from research (where differentiation was very pronounced), the level of private income from non-commercial sources and the degree of financial independence. These were all areas of differentiation before the Dawkins reforms, and followed the historical segmentation of the system between Sandstones, Redbricks, the newer Gumtree[19] universities founded mostly between 1960 and 1975, the Unitechs, and the other New Universities founded out of the CAE sector after 1987 (Marginson and Considine 2000).

The distinction between universities with medical schools and those without remained important in determining relative institutional prestige and the capacity to conduct a full range of Modes 1 and 2 research. In 1995 the oldest eight universities received 59.8 per cent of the research quantum, while 40.2 per cent went to the other 28 universities. By 1999 there was a slight improvement in the research performance of the Unitechs and the New Universities, which had increased their small cohort of funded research students, but the top eight still received 56.0 per cent of the research quantum.[20] Some institutions received more than 20 per cent of their income for research purposes, others less than 2 per cent (Table 9.9).

It was expected that as competition bit deeper, and especially if public funding continued to decline, the Sandstones and Redbricks would further strengthen their edge. In 2000 the government announced that, in future, the expansion of publicly funded postgraduate research would be more tightly restricted (Kemp 1999a), blocking one of the few means whereby newer universities could use public funding to augment their capacity for innovation and their longer-term potential for upward institutional mobility.

Conclusion

After the mid-1980s Australian higher education shared the common global experience of reform, shaped by neo-liberal approaches to government and American educational models. The most nationally distinctive element was the policy of deferred charges through the HECS in place of the direct fee-charging of undergraduates, which modified the socially regressive effects of marketization. National policies implemented in 1987–92 largely achieved their specific objectives, especially the policies concerning the size, structure and economic character of higher education. Participation was substantially expanded, though there was limited success in improving socially defined access. The national system was re-ordered as a competitive market of institutions part responsible for their own funding, in which the competitive economic position of individual institutions (rather than knowledge, or the pastoral formation of students) became the principal *raison d'être*. At the same time the government used accountability requirements, output

Table 9.9 Market differentiation of Australian universities[1] 1996, 1998 and 1999

University and type of university[2]	Total students 1999	International students 1999	Externally enrolled students 1999 %	Total income 1998 AUD$ mill	Income for research: % total income 1996 %	Medical school or centre 1999
SANDSTONES						
U. Sydney	34,761	3162	2.9	482.9	15	YES
U. Melbourne	33,099	4043	2.5	433.8	23	YES
U. Queensland	29,305	2319	4.8	383.2	24	YES
U. Adelaide	13,429	1338	2.8	210.4	24	YES
U. Western Australia	13,333	1485	0	236.3	23	YES
U. Tasmania	12,078	1034	2.5	122.4	14	YES
REDBRICKS						
Monash U.	40,625	7648	17.3	409.9	14	YES
U. New South Wales	29,676	5543	11.6	434.8	20	YES
Australian National U.	9375	911	0	321.5	50	YES
GUMTREES						
Deakin U.	25,659	2088	40.1	186.9	2	NO
Griffith	22,601	2539	3.2	196.0	8	NO
La Trobe U.	20,873	1591	0.2	153.2	9	NO
Macquarie U.	20,212	2028	8.8	148.5	15	NO
U. Newcastle	18,415	1252	4.2	167.3	14	YES
U. New England	14,951	355	76.1	96.3	12	NO
U. Wollongong	12,335	2057	2.8	127.0	12	NO
Flinders U.	11,128	726	7.9	114.2	22	YES
Murdoch U.	10,660	1683	11.9	96.3	13	NO
James Cook U.	9871	535	11.6	99.7	10	NO[3]

University and type of university[2]	Total students 1999	International students 1999	Externally enrolled students 1999 %	Total income 1998 AUD$ mill	Income for research: % total income 1996 %	Medical school or centre 1999
UNITECHS						
Royal Melbourne IT U.	29,963	7849	3.0	209.0	6	NO
Queensland UT.	29,305	2458	8.3	224.3	5	NO
U. South Australia	24,480	3161	13.3	186.2	7	NO
Curtin UT.	24,005	6093	6.9	209.2	7	NO
U. Technology, Sydney	23,173	2335	0	170.6	5	NO
NEW UNIVERSITIES						
U. Western Sydney	29,107	2686	2.6	191.5	3	NO
Charles Sturt U.	24,398	2028	65.7	111.8	2	NO
Edith Cowan U.	19,259	1565	19.2	116.2	2	NO
Victoria U.	17,255	2479	0.3	115.9	4	NO
U. Southern Queensland	15,463	2781	69.9	78.4	3	NO
Central Queensland U.	12,320	2256	41.9	83.9	3	NO
Swinburne UT.	11,741	1504	0.1	81.0	5	NO
Australian Catholic U.	9,761	222	8.4	60.4	1	NO
Southern Cross U.	9,069	440	47.6	53.7	3	NO
U. Canberra	8,752	760	0	66.6	7	NO
U. Ballarat	4,573	327	0	37.6	3	NO
Northern Territory U.	4,145	149	15.6	43.3	10	NO
AUSTRALIA[4]	686,267	83,111	13.7	6496.4	14	11/35

[1] excludes unfunded private institutions, about 4 per cent of total enrolment in higher education

[2] for these categories see Marginson and Considine 2000; Marginson 1999

[3] commenced in 2000

[4] includes small funded institutions: Australian Maritime, Batchelor, Avondale, Marcus Oldham colleges, Austrailian Defence Forces Academy; National Institute of Dramatic Art; Australian Film, Television and Radio School, Notre Dame Aust. U., new U. Sunshine Coast

1 USD = 1.3016 AUD: 1997 PPP

Sources: DETYA 2000a [columns 2–4]; DETYA 1999b [column 5]; DETYA 1998 [column 6]

definition, annual negotiations over institutional 'profiles' and the centralization and standardization of research to shape the internal life of universities. This was not a deregulated market pure and simple, but a government-steered quasi-market. The state used its power to position itself as *de facto* universal consumer, transferring financial power over the 'product' from the universities to itself and the purchasers of private knowledge goods. As in other OECD countries the government increased its steering power while reducing unit fiscal costs.

It is difficult to assess conclusively whether the underlying meta-objectives of reform were achieved. The effects on the education-economy relationship are unclear. In the post-reform period the take-up of skilled labour appeared to expand in line with the growth in business services and the 'knowledge economy'; and the creation of an education export sector was certainly successful. However the expansion of private funding of universities was largely due to an increased dependence on student fees, especially from international students, rather than closer links with business and industry. Undergraduate international students made little contribution to Australian industry. Business research and development in higher education remained on a small scale. In the outcome, despite subsidization of the industry-university relationship (for example in the Cooperative Research Centres), universities focused more on the generation of short-term returns to commodified business and computing courses, than on longer-term building of 'knowledge economy' relationships with Australian industry. The log-jam here was probably the failure of business to invest. This could only have been corrected by a more active industry policy than neo-liberal norms permitted.

Educational diversity between institutions declined, while diversity within institutions increased. There is no conclusive evidence concerning the effects of market reform on producer efficiency, customer responsiveness or quality. However, in relation to quality there were worrying signs. A sharp rise in student–staff ratios indicates that in net terms resources for teaching and basic research declined. This was not evenly felt. Business Studies was relatively well placed, while the less utilitarian disciplines in the humanities, social and natural sciences began to experience a deep crisis of resources. In the last analysis, the main contributions made by private funding were an improved balance of trade and government fiscal relief, but at the price of corporate-academic bifurcation.

The change of government in 1996 accelerated the trends begun in 1987–92. It exacerbated resource problems, intensified economic competition and strengthened the relative position of leading institutions within the national hierarchy. It also augmented corporate-academic tensions, and problems of university identity. As Sjolund (1998: 116) notes in relation to Sweden, Australian universities were 'in danger of becoming reactive organisations instead of autonomous organisations governed by norms which they establish themselves'. As Holtta (1998: 61) notes in relation to Finland, corporate management and quality control tended to focus on minimum standards, rather than on creativity and the highest academic achievement. As

Brunner (1997: 234) notes in relation to Chile, problems of identity were acute in public universities, which had rested on notions of public good and social service that neo-liberal ideology sought to render obsolete. Because neo-liberal reform in Australian higher education was relatively large in its ambition and complete in its execution, these issues bit deeper in Australia than in most other OECD countries.

Notes

1 In its claims for the primacy of global economics over nationally specific politics, neo-liberalism was as universal in cast as the Marxist-Leninism that it set itself against (Hayek 1944; Cockett 1995; Marginson 1997a).
2 It was the first time in Australia that higher education and research had been conceived as part of an economic portfolio; and the first ministry to combine all of these functions. Dawkins was previously the minister for the public service where he ushered in corporatization reforms, and Minister for Trade where he had led the early development of full-fee international education (Marginson 2000a: 54–6).
3 The government wanted to increase enrolments in Asian Studies for trade-related reasons.
4 This tendentious expectation about diversity was consistently asserted. Meek and Wood remark that 'every official statement on higher education since the Green Paper has stressed the need for a more diverse and responsive set of higher education institutions'. The government saw 'competition in a deregulated environment' as key to this (Meek and Wood 1998: 4).
5 In Germany and the Netherlands, the major growth was in non-university higher education enrolments.
6 Three-fifths of men were enrolled in vocational education and training and almost three fifths of women in higher education (DETYA 1999c).
7 Casual staff are additional to these figures. Definitive data on casual staff were not collected until recently, so that no definitive data are available for trends in casual staffing; nor are the data on casual staff now collected disaggregated for academic duties. In 1998 there were 10,711 equivalent full-time casual staff out of a total staff complement of 80,285 staff both academic and non-academic (DETYA 1999c). As in some other countries such as France (Chevaillier 1998: 69), in Australian universities the role of casual staffing increased in the 1990s, facilitated by some decentralization of industrial relations and the greater managerial flexibility provided to universities. The student–staff ratio increased by less than the longitudinal data would otherwise suggest – albeit accompanied also by the downward pressures on academic quality that are implied by casualization – but these effects cannot be estimated with precision.
8 This compares to 12 to 1 in the early 1980s, and 13 to 1 at the beginning of Dawkins' Ministry in 1987.
9 Though significantly less so in the elite institutions of both countries than in the newer institutions.
10 For example, when the vocational education and training sector moved to adopt a competency-based approach to the shaping of specific standards in each field of occupational training, university courses in the professions did not follow,

although there was some commitment to the more ambiguous notion of generic work-related skills (Marginson 1993).

11 Except in the minds of those who believe that complex interactive contexts can be meaningfully represented by discrete variables that are subjected to regression analyses!

12 For example, several universities initiated internal quality audits in the late 1980s, following the introduction of policies on quality assurance in the UK, in advance of the first official discussion of quality issues in Australia in 1990–91.

13 For example, Eicher (1998: 35) notes that tuition was largely free in Germany, Austria, Denmark, Finland, Greece, the UK, Norway and Sweden, although fees were about to be introduced to the majority of students in the UK. Fees were low in France, and Ireland and Portugal were considering fee reduction or abolition. After the 1996 changes in Australia, the level of the HECS paid by Science students (the middle of the three levels of HECS) was similar to the average fees paid by in-state students in US public doctoral universities.

14 For example, a principal historic limitation faced by the Australian economy as a national economy has been a chronic shortage of capital (more so than a shortage of labour) and the dominance of key sectors by foreign business with little interest in skill investments or domestic research and development. Australia shares these problems with the economies of other nineteenth-century settler-states such as Canada, New Zealand, Argentina and Chile. By themselves, the Dawkins policies in higher education could do little to alter capital flows.

15 The growth of numbers was little affected by the 1998–99 recession in the source countries.

16 Arguably, where quality assurance intersects with marketing – as it will tend to do when both functions are managed centrally in universities, rather than quality assurance being controlled by the academic units (Mollis and Marginson 2000) – then it will tend to obscure trends in the conditions of student learning.

17 The term 'diversity' refers here to variety of type, with the main focus on diversity in type of institution, in institutional mission and in type of teaching and research programme. This is distinct from the American usage which refers to 'variations in student and faculty populations based on race/ethnicity, gender and age' (Fairweather 2000: 80).

18 This accords with Fairweather's findings in relation to US higher education. In America the segmentation into doctoral universities, four-year colleges and community colleges sustains diversity but within each segment, there are powerful isomorphistic pressures (Fairweather 2000: 84).

19 So named because of a distinctive use of Australian native plantings near-universal to the group, a characteristic the Gumtrees share with Redbricks Monash and the Australian National University. For the categories, see Marginson and Considine 2000; Marginson 1999.

20 These data exclude the Australian National University, which is subject to special funding arrangements. Inclusion of the ANU, a major research university, increases the extent of resource concentration.

10

Symbolism and substance: towards an understanding of change and continuity in South African higher education

George Subotzky

Introduction

The scale and significance of recent changes in South African higher education are profound and are probably unprecedented in recent times. This in itself constitutes an interesting case. However, what makes the South African case particularly informative is the way in which the pattern of this change has been shaped by two distinct and opposing discourses – the 'transformative-redistributive' and the 'global market-driven reform' discourses.

The first derives from the great expectations that arose after the demise of formal apartheid in the late 1980s to mid-1990s for the reconstruction of all sectors of South African society out of the ravages of apartheid. This strongly felt aspiration for democracy, social justice, human rights and the redistribution of wealth and opportunity was captured in the ill-defined, but symbolically significant discursive term 'transformation'. Indeed, amidst these widespread expectations for fundamental change, any perceived lack of transformation has been interpreted as a heresy and usually attributed to political recalcitrance (Muller 2003).

The nature and pace of this transformation process (and as part of this, the restructuring of higher education) has not met these expectations, for a number of inter-related reasons explored below. While the political transformation and the establishment of democratic organs of government have been successfully – indeed miraculously – achieved, the anticipated social and economic transformation has, for the majority of South Africans, not transpired. On the contrary, conditions for the poor have decidedly worsened (Terreblanche 2003). Unemployment remains rampant, with associated high crime levels and massive social dislocation, and South Africa has the highest HIV/AIDS rates in the world. While government consistently committed itself *symbolically* in all policy documents to reducing inequalities and addressing the socio-economic priority of the poor, it has not instituted the range of redistributive and social development measures required to achieve *substantive* structural changes that would widen opportunity and reduce poverty.

A number of recent analyses have attempted to track the trajectory of public policy and socio-economic change in South Africa (see Alexander 2002; Gerwel 2002). The key issue is explaining how the new government's progressive framework of redistributive transformation, which underpinned the anti-apartheid struggle and framed its first election manifesto in 1994, was subsumed in four short years into a basket of conservative macro-economic policies.[1] It is a deep irony that these have exacerbated, rather than reduced, social stratification and poverty in the new democracy.

The transformation process in South Africa has thus been increasingly shaped by the second discourse – the dominant neo-liberal 'global' discourse. This derives from the coincidence of two other significant inter-related developments: the intensification of globalized socio-economic and cultural relations, and the collapse of the Soviet Union with the concomitant ascendancy of market-driven neo-liberalism and universal hostility to, and scepticism of, the Left. These events created a set of global and local conditions that presented the new democratic government in South Africa with a two-fold development challenge, each governed by the opposing discourses: to meet the basic needs of the majority poor by providing adequate social services and redistributing opportunity and wealth, and concurrently to situate the nation competitively in the knowledge-intensive network society and the market-driven globalized economy. Pursuing a redistributive agenda shaped by the transformative discourse, needless to say, stands in direct ideological tension with the prevailing market-oriented framework of deregulation, fiscal constraint and minimalist government, shaped by the dominant 'global' discourse. This raises questions about the nature of the contemporary state and the constraints and contradictions it faces in addressing inequalities amidst the current global balance of forces. It also raises the issue of the feasibility of local mediation of the impacts of globalization and of developing and implementing alternatives to the neo-liberal orthodoxy. The discursive role of policy is examined in this light below.

Not surprisingly, the vital contribution of higher education to meet the nation's contemporary developmental challenges has been prominently foregrounded in policy documents – in particular, its critical role in preparing graduates and in producing relevant knowledge not only for effective participation in the global knowledge-driven economy but also for addressing the basic needs of the majority. To these ends, the new South African government developed a policy framework for higher education restructuring, embodied in the largely symbolic 1997 White Paper on higher education transformation (DoE 1997).

Over the last two decades the system has witnessed considerable changes that were in some respects skewed but nonetheless revolutionary, notably in student and institutional profiles (Cooper and Subotzky 2001). However, many of these changes were unanticipated and cannot be attributed only (or even primarily) to the effects of policy. They are instead the outcome of the complex interplay between institutional initiatives, societal needs (driven mainly by market forces) and policy – all framed by globalization discourses and practices (Cloete *et al.* 2002). In this context, many of the new developments were not necessarily transformative in nature, but shaped by market-oriented individual institutional interests, freely pursued in an increasingly competitive environment and in the absence of a regulatory policy framework. At the same time, despite emerging policy initiatives, other key systemic features have remained persistently unchanged, notably the 'race' and gender composition of academic staff.

This chapter explores this pattern of continuity and change that characterizes the transformation process in South African higher education and examines the combination of factors underlying it. Two features of the recent policy process provide the starting point of this analysis. First, the implementation of the national policy framework has been slow and uneven, and has currently become somewhat fragmented and diverted from addressing stated goals. Indeed, the 2001 National Plan for Higher Education (DoE 2001) acknowledges an 'implementation vacuum', which occurred between the White Paper and the National Plan. Second, concomitant to the macroeconomic policy trends mentioned above, a discernible shift occurred in higher education policy discourse – from an initial symbolic commitment to addressing equity and redistributive concerns to increasing emphasis on the global discourse of the market and efficiency. Furthermore, the ministry is currently preoccupied with a literal interpretation of transformation in the form of large-scale mergers. While this will undoubtedly transfigure the system, it is not clear how it will advance the range of policy goals captured in the White Paper. Driven mainly by political and policy exigencies, this measure constitutes what Fataar (2001) refers to as the 'narrowing' of the education policy trajectory.

The main contention is that systemic continuities, which preclude the translation of progressive symbolic policy into substantive implementation, are rooted in a number of related factors. These comprise persistent *structural* impediments,[2] as well as the complexity of higher education institutional change (in the light of which rationalist assumptions underlying the government's predilection for 'grand' transformative policy and planning appears naïve); and a range of *conjunctoral* factors, including the implementation vacuum (which is only partly attributable to inadequate capacity and resources) and the discursive shifts described above (driven by the power of the dominant global discourse and the government's ready adoption of this).

Understanding this pattern of change and continuity, as well as the implementation 'gap' and discursive policy 'shifts', requires aligning four analytic lenses, each of which inform the next. First, it is necessary to re-examine the nature of policy – in particular, distinguishing between symbolic and substantive policy, identifying the limits and indeterminacy of policy (and the policy research implications of this), and highlighting its discursive function. Second, given the limits to policy as a driver of change, it is necessary to systematically identify the other key drivers and trace their inter-relationship. Third, the obstacles to change and policy implementation must be identified. Fourth, a significant change factor, which tends to be under-played by other analysts, is how the dominant global discourse has foreclosed (and has been allowed to foreclose) the redistributive-transformative dis-course that forms one component of the two-fold development imperative of post-apartheid society. The case of South African higher education is thus informative not only because of the ambitious scale of the transformative agenda and what this suggests about the complex challenges of higher edu-cation systemic and institutional change, but also because of what it tells us about how prospects for translating progressive symbolic policy into substan-tive implementation have been reduced by the combination of structural persistence, limits to policy, market forces and fragility of redistributive-transformative aspirations in the face of the dominant global discourse.

Revisiting the nature of policy and change

The point of departure in this chapter, then, is to revisit key aspects of policy itself and its relation to change theory and strategy, with a view to providing key analytic constructs with which to account for the pattern of change and continuity in South African higher education. Here, I briefly examine the complexity of policy, significant types of policy, its limits and indeterminacy and some implications for managing change and researching policy.

Policy, it hardly needs stating, is a complex, multi-faceted, indeterminate and inevitably contested process. It comprises distinct types and involves several non-linear but related elements and a variety of agents and stake-holders in different settings. Amongst the voluminous expansion of policy research and analysis, interpretations of policy are varied and bedevilled by unstated assumptions and multiple meanings, with the result that much of this work remains theoretically thin. This is so not only in South Africa, where the pressure for large-scale policy formulation exacerbated this tendency, but elsewhere, as Ball (1993: 15) indicates:

> One of the conceptual problems currently lurking within much policy research and policy sociology is that more often than not analysts fail to define conceptually what they mean by policy. The meaning of policy is taken for granted and theoretical and epistemological dry rot is built into the analytic structures they construct. It is not difficult to find the term policy being used to describe very different 'things' at different points in the same study.

The various elements of the policy process are commonly regarded as sequential: prior research, identifying and choosing options, formulation, adoption, planning, implementation, evaluation and adaptation. In reality, they are related in complex ways, iterative, mediated or obstructed by con-text and by the diverse policy agents involved in the process. In South African debates these elements are often falsely dichotomized with the assumption that while policy formulation is sound (and indeed often admirably progressive), the problem simply lies in implementation, usually interpreted as a capacity problem (Cloete *et al.* 2002: 452). For this reason, these authors question the notion of a higher education implementation 'vacuum' precisely because this displaces the problem onto poor implementation, thus reinforcing the dichotomy. The thrust of my argument below is that good policy incorporates implementation and its multi-faceted demands, while understanding the inevitable indeterminacy and contingency of actual outcomes.

Different policy agents, situated in different institutional locations and driven by their own exigent interests and agendas, affect policy outcomes at different points. These are: government, parliament, the bureaucracy, organized business, civil society (organized labour, teacher and student organizations, academics, researchers and other stakeholders), foreign advisors and the donor community.

Policies can be classified in a number of ways. For the purposes of this chapter, it is important to distinguish between the following types:[3]

- *Distributive, redistributive or regulatory policies:* Distributive policies aim at favouring all groups in the allocation of resources and benefits, while redistributive policies distribute additional resources to one set of beneficiaries for equity reasons. Regulatory policies limit or direct behaviours of particular groups through conditional resource allocation.
- *Symbolic policy:* Several recent analyses have drawn attention to symbolic policy as a key construct to explaining the pattern of South African higher education transformation and policy process (see Jansen 2001, 2002; Subotzky 2001b; Cloete *et al.* 2002). Symbolic policies signify general values, principles and normative ideals with very little or no indication of implementation procedures or resource allocations. Symbolic policy captures aspirational goals sufficiently broadly, without operational details, in order to consolidate general consensus, which disguises the nature of the political settlements and trade-offs. It thus makes decisive breaks with the past and signals new directions (Cloete *et al.* 2002), which are especially important functions in post-conflict situations. It is widely accepted that the framework for higher education transformation captured in the 1997 White Paper is quintessentially symbolic in character (see below). Jansen (2001) regards symbolic policy as necessarily negative in that its political function to secure consensus masks any intent to implement. Against this, it can be argued that symbolic policy formation performs a legitimate function in securing consensus and in providing undisputed benchmarks (through stated values and goals) against which implementation can be evaluated.
- *Substantive policy:* By contrast, substantive policies deal with the concrete actions governments want to take, that is, the content of decisions. The distinction between symbolic and substantive policy is related to that

between the 'intrinsic' logic of policy, which captures broad values and interests, and the 'institutional' logic, which refers to the concrete conditions of implementation (see Young 2001). The successful implementation of symbolic policy, that is, its translation into substantive policy, rests on a number of enabling resource and conjunctural conditions. These are elaborated shortly.

- *Top-down or bottom-up:* Top-down policies are developed by an authoritative structure and distributed downwards through the system in a linear, hierarchical process, described by Elmore (1980) as 'forward mapping'. This assumes that those closest to the source of policy have greatest authority and influence, and that responding to problems in complex systems depends on clear lines of authority and control. By contrast, bottom-up policies build on existing practices and, through analysing the conditions at the coalface of implementation, seek to create conducive behaviours (compliance, knowledge, skills, capacities and resources, attitudes and perceptions) among practitioners to support successful implementation. This relates to Elmore's concept of 'backward mapping'. It assumes that those closest to the source of the problem have the greatest ability to influence it and that problem solving in complex systems depends not on hierarchical control but on maximizing discretion at the point where the problem is most immediate (Elmore 1980: 605). Backward mapping 'begins not with a statement of intent, but with a statement of the specific behavior at the lowest level of the implementation process' (Elmore 1980: 604). Effective policy, then, proceeds from identifying the sufficient conditions for successfully changing practice and then extrapolating backwards 'up' the system, and determining what is required through the structure of implementing agencies, asking at each level about the ability of the unit to affect the behaviour that is the target of the policy and what resources are required to have this effect. Here, policy implementation theory and change theory converge. Elmore's framework provides key insights about the limitations of top-down policy, which does not adequately address conditions required for successful implementation. Recent South African education policy is replete with examples of this, most notably the Curriculum 2005 fiasco, which has been fundamentally reviewed for these reasons. Elmore's concept, therefore, has significant implications for how policy is formulated and enacted, and how change is managed and strategized. Ball (1993: 19) comes to a similar position in stating that 'the enactment of texts relies on things like commitment, understanding, capability, resources, practical limitations, cooperation and (importantly) intertextual compatibility'.

Regarding the discursive function of policy, Ball's distinction between policy as *text* (representations that are encoded and decoded in complex ways) and policy as *discourse* (the way in which policy ensembles exercise power through a production of 'truth' and 'knowledge' as discourses) provides a key analytic tool by which to further our understanding of how dominant discourses have shaped the pattern of higher education policy in South Africa, with the effect of closing down the transformative redistributive discourse. These two elements of policy, though distinct, are implicit in each other. Drawing from Foucault, Ball argues that 'discourses are about what can be said, and thought, but also about who can speak, when, where and with what authority' (Ball 1993: 21). In these terms, 'the effect of policy is primarily discursive, it changes the possibilities we have for thinking "otherwise"; thus it limits our responses to change' (Ball 1993: 23). In this sense, discourses constitute objects, and in so doing conceal their own invention. Policies thus 'create circumstances in which the range of options available in deciding what to do are narrowed or changed, or particular goals or outcomes set' (Ball 1993: 19).

Another significant feature of policy is its indeterminacy. The outcomes or effects of policy depend on multiple variables and conditions embedded in the various contexts of policy-making (Ball 1993). Each of these involves interpretation and reinterpretation, struggle, compromise and 'ad hocery', the outcomes and settlements of which cannot be predetermined. Consequently, Ball argues that 'we cannot predict or assume how they will be acted on in every case in every setting, or what their immediate effect will be, or what room for manoeuvre actors will find for themselves. Action may be constrained differently (even tightly) but it is not determined by policy' (1993: 17). Further indeterminacy arises through the political process where 'policies shift and change their meaning; representations change, key interpreters . . . change' (Ball 1993: 17). Similarly, Muller (2003) draws attention to the mediating effect of context by distinguishing between *intended* policy, the *effects* of policy on practice, and the crucial intervening step, the *enacted* policy, the outcome of which is mediated by context. This resonates with Elmore's notion of backward mapping and implies not only the necessity to focus on practitioners' required behaviours to maximise effective implementation, but also to offsetting of assumptions that effective implementation relies on a top-down policy process – which, as we shall see, constitutes government's current approach.

Following from this, the limits to the effectiveness of policy as a change mechanism become evident. Given the post-apartheid transformative and redistributive imperatives mentioned at the outset, the South African policy community – both government and analysts – understandably perhaps placed heavy reliance on modernist, centralized 'grand' policy and planning as drivers of change (Subotzky 2003a). As Muller (2003: 13) observes 'South African commentary dwells over-much on the intended policy, investing it with an importance that is rarely borne out empirically. We tend naturally to expect that the policy can and should have its intended impact, and are invariably surprised when it doesn't'. The White Paper and the National Plan were conceptualized as instruments for what Cloete *et al.* (2002) identify as 'comprehensive' or 'big-bang' theory for system-wide transformative steerage, which carries the expectation of 'transformation at once'. Embedded in this policy and planning framework are implicit (and ungrounded) rationalist assumptions about the effectiveness of strong centralized policy in steering change. Besides the current discursive frowning on modernist centralist strategies, evidence shows that these assumptions are questionable because change is a complex indeterminate process driven by multiple agents and agencies, which casts doubt on the extent to which policies and plans lead to anticipated outcomes. Cloete *et al.* (2002: 448) capture this key point thus:

> Changes in the day-to-day realities of higher education are related to a complex set of interactions between government, society and higher education institutions, as affected by globalization. Consequently the changes are not simply the result of specific policies or deliberate actions by a single agency such as the government, the market or a higher education institution ... Social institutions and social actors have a much greater role in change than is generally anticipated in government policy reform.

In contradistinction to grand 'comprehensive' policy, Cloete *et al.* (2002) identify the need for a different kind of change strategy, which they call 'differentiated policy'. While consensus is easily attained consultatively at the level of symbolic policy, such an approach is needed to deal with the contested details of implementation. It involves 'trade-offs between competing interests, on the basis of indicators or specific criteria, with the intention of addressing targeted problems or sub-sectors' (Cloete *et al.* 2002: 448). Particular institutional targets would be identified against systemic benchmarks, as well as a regulatory environment that pressures and encourages progress towards these. Based on the information-rich interaction between government, institutions and society, they argue, this will be more effective in facilitating change and implementing policy. This view draws from Carnoy's vision of a network state which is 'made of shared institutions, and enacted by bargaining and interactive iteration all along the chain of decision-making' (cited in Cloete *et al.* 2002: 185). This is a state 'whose efficiency is defined in terms of its capacity to create and sustain networks – global, regional, and local, and through these networks, to promote economic growth and develop new forms of social integration' (Cloete *et al.* 2002: 185). This approach, with its underlying vision of a networked state and its goal of information-based iterative relations generating new forms of 'social integration' provides a refreshing antidote to top-down centralist policy. However, in presenting such a brave new world of negotiated information-based social cohesion, it may optimistically underestimate the depth of social divisions, conflictual interests and asymmetrical capacities among developing country governments, institutions and stakeholders, especially given the knowledge intensity of this approach.

The limits to policy and planning apply at the institutional level as well. The new worldwide emphasis on innovative entrepreneurialism in an increasingly competitive environment has generated the need for centralized institutional strategic planning. While institutional capacity to develop and implement strategic plans is critical to the success of the transformation process, recent research (Rhoades 2000) suggests that even where abundant capacity is evident, the effectiveness of management planning initiatives to achieve change cannot be assumed. Rhoades concludes that several key premises of current university strategic management thinking amount to little more than 'myths'. It is now common that higher education institutions are complex, loosely coupled organizations, comprising multiple centres of power, authority and interests, which give rise to intricate dynamics of formal and informal decision making and contestations. In addition, faculty often have stronger cosmopolitan allegiances to their disciplinary networks than to their local institutions. It is often through these linkages that independent initiatives arise in the substructures of departments and centres. These both subvert centralized managerial planning objectives and realize institutional goals in spite of, and not because of, them. Within these complex dynamics, intricate overt and covert strategies are utilized to facilitate decision making and to effect or obstruct change. This is especially so given growing concentrations of power in executive management and the increasing tensions between corporate and collegiate styles of management. For these reasons, it is often strategically counterproductive to reveal such strategies as part of the culture of disclosure and consciousness-raising associated with the current vogue of the 'learning organization' This insight suggests the notion of 'strategic organizational non-learning' as a way of describing these kinds of clandestine manoeuvres to achieve change (Breier and Subotzky 2003). Instead of the often assumed institution-wide model of co-ordinated change, based on a consensual singleness of purpose, a much more politicized model of institutional change emerges: one that acknowledges contestation, conflicting interests and Machiavellian strategies (Breier and Subotzky 2003). In the light of these complex linkages and change dynamics, rationalist assumptions about the extent to which change is effected through central steerage and strategic planning must be tempered.

This leads to the final point about policy: it is inevitably contested and political in nature. Indeed, in many languages, there is no distinction between the terms 'policy' and 'politics'. As resources are universally constrained, making policy is always subject to tensions, contradictions and competing priorities. This has been succinctly captured as follows:

> Policy is constituted and reconstituted within a continuum of activities from the textual to the practical. Within these processes of constitution and reconstitution, outcomes arise which are both intended and unintended. These are complex. As regimes of practices and trends, they could be coherent in so far as the intended and the unintended are in alignment, or they could be structured in manifest contradiction. The contradiction could, moreover, present itself as the assertion of one or other hegemonic ideological or value framework.
>
> (Soudien *et al.* 2001: 79)

However, these insights and the bulk of recent definitive policy theory derive from analyses that focus on power relations and discursive contestations as conceptualized within the framework of the nation state. The contemporary challenge is to reconceptualize the nature of policy in relation to the current global balance of forces – fertile ground for further inquiry, drawing from empirical evidence in developing countries. This raises the tension between the worldwide trend towards minimal government as part of market-driven global discourse, and the need for strong interventionist government in developing countries to offset the negative impact of market-driven globalization, linked to the transformative discourse.

To conclude: successfully translating symbolic policy into substantive policy requires specific conditions and overcoming obstacles. These are set out in the next section. Following Elmore's concept of 'backward mapping' and the notion of the mediating effect of context, effective implementation also entails understanding and identifying the range of facilitating or obstructive 'behaviours' in each context: the various roles, interests, motives, resistances, priorities, capacities, technical skills, knowledge and discretionary ability to deal with contingencies. Successful implementation involves attaining adequate compliance, based either on sufficient ideological consensus and shared belief in the symbolic value, substance and planning strategies of policy, or on sanctions. In the developing country context especially, political will to counter hegemonic discourses and to address inequalities through sound redistributive alternatives is also necessary.

Overcoming policy naivety is a final necessary condition, through understanding the constraints of change and the limits and indeterminacy of policy, especially regarding the limits of 'grand' policy and planning, outlined above. In explaining the apparent gap between symbolic policy and implementation, Muller (2001) identifies the realization that symbolic policy cannot deliver on implementation as a sign of policy maturity. As indicated, the bulk of South African higher education policy making and analysis has to date been naively based on rationalist assumptions. Failure to recognize the complex dynamics of implementation and change, and role in this of stakeholders and practitioners in their particular contexts, is the result of what Ball (1993: 19) calls 'the privileging of the policy maker's reality' as opposed to the need to adjust policy to context. The danger is that, in the absence of mature policy insights, top-down implementation strategies are falsely interpreted as political 'resistance' which, as Ball argues, is far too crude a substitute for nuanced understanding of the process. In turn, this will tend to simply goad government into tighter top-down control to override what it perceives as heretical sectional interest in opposition to national policy priorities. This will lead to what Cloete *et al.* (2002: 21) refer to as the 'widening gap between politics and political programmes on the one side, and the dynamics of public sectors such as higher education on the other'. As we shall see, this tendency is currently evident in the increasing tensions and mutual suspicion between the South African Minister and the higher education sector.

Agents and obstacles of change in higher education

Having identified the overriding assumption that centralized policy and planning is the key driver of the transformative post-apartheid policy process in South Africa, it is important now to identify and frame the various agents and drivers and inhibitors of change other than government policy.

Cloete *et al.* (2002) make an important contribution to the debate by utilizing a framework comprising 'the triangular relationships between the state, institutions and society and the effects of globalization on these relationships' (Cloete *et al.* 2002: 19) to analyse South African higher education policy. This analytic triangle, which represents a 'network of co-ordination', 'locates change within a complex interaction between the state, society and institutions, within the context of globalization' (Cloete *et al.* 2002: 5). This provides a useful analytic lens with which to focus 'not only on implementation but on the social actors involved, and the ways in which interactions between actors and relevant social institutions affect the outcomes of the policy process'. In this perspective, change in higher education is seen as 'not only the outcome of higher education policy implementation, or of market interactions, or of academic deliberations ... [but] is the result of many interactions between many actors leading to many different interpretations of reality in higher education' (Cloete *et al.* 2002: 6). Within this framework, these authors analyse the unanticipated aspects of change, in particular the impact of globalization and the range of institutional responses and behaviour in terms of resource dependence theory and neo-institutional theory.

While this framework usefully identifies the key agentive clusters involved in the change process, further elaboration of aspects of this will provide greater levels of understanding of the limits and possibilities of change. For example, informed by contemporary theories of organizational change and learning, further exploration of the ongoing impact of globalization and marketization on higher education institutions will reveal a richer and more complex set of intra-institutional change processes. Emerging trends towards the entrepreneurial model of innovation and relevance and managerialism amidst the proliferation of corporate, transnational and virtual institutional types have created a complex new range of interactions and contestations between managers, academics, their various disciplinary networks and increasingly, the networks of social and commercial partners and stakeholders. These contestations are a manifestation of the growing tension between the managerialist and collegiate cultures, with new and sometimes radical patterns of assertive and covert organizational change strategies undertaken by the new management regime (see Breier 2002; Subotzky 2003b; Van Vught 2002).

Muller (2003) provides exactly such an elaboration, focusing on the endogenous role of science itself and institutional life in shaping change in response to exogenous change imperatives. Muller argues that policy analysis has not paid sufficient attention to the dynamics of these two dimensions of institutional life. This renders (especially strong) institutions 'far more durable and resistant to external pressures to change than either policy analysts or market pessimists usually give them credit for' (Muller 2003). Universities' response to exogenous pressures for restructuring – from government policy, society or market – is largely based on 'features internal to the science system (the structures of disciplines, their state of innovation) and internal to the university institutions (their intellectual and managerial capacity or capital)' (Muller 2003: 2). The consequence for policy and change management is that shifting both science and institutions is best achieved 'via steering, rather than by plans or money. Both may be important, but the institution of science keeps its own council, a fact that the social engineers of central policy are all too prone to forget' (Muller 2003: 2). This is an interesting and important analytic perspective to bear in mind – in relation to both our theoretical understanding of institutional change, policy and the sociology of science and to the policy process itself. Its veracity will need to be tested through empirical studies.

Other areas of fruitful elaboration of the Cloete *et al.* model are the dynamics of student choice and the shifting dynamics of aid to higher education in the light of globalization and the market ethos. Students (through their choices) and aid policy (embedded in the nexus foreign policy and trade) are both key drivers of change in higher education but remain underresearched in the South African context.

A final area of elaboration concerns the main theme of this chapter: the discursive effect of policy, already described. Cloete *et al.* (2002: 22) identify the way in which what they call the 'national' issues of equity and redress have been dominated by 'global' concerns for efficiency and effectiveness. In so doing, they acknowledge the dominance of global discourse over the local. However, they are also wary of attributing the lack of progress towards transformative goals to a simple conspiracy theory-based account of the role of global capitalism in blocking equitable transformation, and the ANC's sell-out of its anti-apartheid ideals. Without succumbing to this conspiratorial explanation, it will be apparent that the analysis in this chapter, drawing mainly from Ball's account of policy, places greater emphasis on the discursive role of policy than these authors do, in (partly) explaining the apparent ideological shift of the new South African government towards neo-liberal conservatism and a concern for efficiency in higher education policy.

Extrapolating from all the above considerations, the following framework of levels of change dynamics and interactions emerges:

- *At the global, international and sub-regional level:* the various discourse and practices associated with globalization and internationalization, including the role of multilateral and bilateral development assistance agencies.

- *At the national and regional levels:* the various sectors of the state; national, provincial and local government (including the ruling party and its relations with its political allies); parliament and statutory bodies; civil society and community organization; organized business; the organized higher education sector.
- *At the institutional and sub-institutional level:* executive leadership and management and institutional policies; organized academic leadership and structures at institutional and sub-institutional level; informal individual academic initiatives; organized non-academic structures; organized and informal staff and student structures and activities; individual student choice.
- *At cross-cutting levels:* the domain of science and knowledge.

Complementing this, the following brief framework of the obstacles to the implementation of policy and to change is set out. This is not meant to be an exhaustive account or a composite model, but an illustrative range of factors drawn from the current analysis. As is apparent from the description below, these factors vary according to *context* (different institutional and other locations) and *time/moment.* Of course, the absence of these obstacles means that they can facilitate change when they are present.

- *Structural impediments:* particularly as a developing country and given its apartheid history, South Africa faces a range of particularly sharp structurally rooted obstacles to change, embedded in unequal socio-economic relations. These impediments will vary according to different contexts, institutional locations and time.
- *Resources and capacity:* human, technical, time (needed for realistically paced transformation and to avoid unrealistic 'grand' policy) and informational resources and capacity at the level of government, stakeholder bodies and institutions. Although fiscal constraint is ubiquitous, given South Africa's relatively strong base, lack of resources is not (and should not be regarded as) a major obstacle.
- *Interpretation and operationalization of policy by various policy agents:* The extent of policy naivety and policy maturity. The latter entails a more nuanced understanding of the nature of policy and the connection between the various elements identified above. An important aspect of this is systemic and institutional policy overload: the extent of simultaneous demands without the proper operational sequencing of priorities. There are currently something like 30 higher education change initiatives emanating from the South African government (Muller 2003).
- *Discursive environment:* the extent to which particular discourses dominate or are subordinate in various government and institutional locations. Following Ball (1993), this will determine what choices, ideas and options are allowed or foreclosed, according to the prevailing political balance of forces and power relations at particular moments and in specific contexts. This is embedded in both background macro-economic/political, as well

as foreground educational values, discourses, theories, current trends and 'fashions' in policy and practice. It relates to the extent to which government and other policy agents demonstrate political will or reluctance, that is, whether they are politically prepared to make decisive choices. This would shape, for example, interpretations of the appropriate role of the state, across the spectrum from interventionist to minimalist. An important element of this is political compliance or resistance from various agents in central and decentralized bureaucracy and institutions. A prominent example here are the shifts in meaning of equity and transformation that have occurred in the South African higher education context. As indicated, the two principal discourses framing this analysis of current South African higher education are the 'global' and the transformative-redistributive. The analysis then depends crucially on the periodization of policy, identifying key moments when shifts occur. For example, the moment when the balance of forces shifted from the ANC to corporate interests during the informal negotiations leading up to the first elections in 1994 (Terreblanche 2003). The notion of 'settlement' is crucial to how discursive and political conflicts are negotiated in different contexts at different times by policy agents. This process results in a particular balance of forces and discursive moment.

- *Contingent and individual factors:* this ranges from unanticipated institutional crises to the initiatives and behaviours of particular policy agents in different contexts and moments. This would include the biographical and temperamental particularities of key agents at different times, for example, particular ministers or leaders at particular moments in their terms of office or career paths. In the case of academics, this often relates to the process of their winning their reputational credibility as scientists.[4]

A final point on theorizing policy and policy research: elaborating these kinds of analytic frameworks points to the need for greater theoretical complexity in policy research. Ball (1993) identifies the then prevailing theoretical poverty of policy research, as a result of which, he concludes, we cannot yet really talk about an 'applied policy sociology'. In the South African context, the bulk of policy research has been largely operational in nature or has comprised analyses that are not extensively theory-based. Ten years later, Ball's (1993: 11) challenge remains before us:

> The *complexity* and *scope* of policy analysis – from an interest in the workings of the state to a concern with contexts of practice and the distributional outcomes of policy – precludes the successful single-theory explanations. What we need in policy analysis is a toolbox of diverse concepts and theories – an applied sociology rather than a pure one (original emphasis).

Ball thus makes an appeal for composite theories that accommodate 'localised complexity'. The challenge, in his view, 'is to relate together analytically the ad hocery of the macro with the ad hocery of the micro without losing sight of the systematic bases and effects of *ad hoc* social actions: to look for the iterations embedded in the chaos' (Ball 1993: 15). Drawing from Ozga, Ball argues that it is necessary to bring together structural, macro-level analysis of education systems and education policies and micro-level investigation, especially that which takes account of people's perception and experiences. Ball links this to the need to rethink the simplicities of the structure/agency dichotomy and, drawing from Harker and May, to 'account for agency in a constrained world' (Ball 1993: 15). Consequently, he contends that 'Policy analysis requires an understanding that is based not on constraint *or* agency but on the changing relationships between constraint *and* agency and their interpenetration. Furthermore, such an analysis must achieve insight into both overall and localized outcomes of policy' (Ball 1993: 21). The methodological implications of this for Ball is to conduct policy trajectory and implementation studies across the various 'contexts' of policy making that he identifies, namely the contexts of influence, policy text production, practice, outcomes and political strategy.

An important elaboration of current policy theory would be to build on frameworks that emerged in the 1980s and 1990s, which were based on relations within the nation state and to re-examine these in the light of globalization. This would theoretically clarify how change actually occurs or is inhibited in this broader context and across the macro, meso and micro levels. Some recent work addresses these issues (see, for example, Marginson and Rhoades 2002 on the mediating effect of the national). At the institutional level, the utilization of neo-institutional and organizational theory (Cloete *et al.* 2002; Muller 2003) are other instances. At the sub-institutional level, there is a need for studies on the micro-politics of social and institutional relations in for example equity and gender studies (see Subotzky 2001a).

The final section of the chapter examines the patterns of change and continuity in emerging higher education policy in South Africa, utilizing these analytic perspectives on policy, change and key agents in higher education. Before this, however, it is necessary to sketch the background macro-economic trends and government choices that frame higher education policy in South Africa. As indicated, the policy formulation process in post-apartheid South Africa has been particularly challenging, not only because of the scale of the social reconstruction agenda, but also because of the contradictory competing discourses of redistributive transformation and the new globalized world order. How did the global discourse come to dominate the transformative? A comprehensive answer to this crucial question lies beyond the scope of this chapter and is the subject of further inquiry in which the author is currently involved. Nonetheless, it is possible to trace some relevant trends in this regard.

Origins and emerging dominance of the global discourse in the political economy of South Africa

It has already been mentioned that South Africa's emergence as a new democracy in the 1990s coincided with the intensification of global economic, cultural and social relations. As the anti-apartheid struggle intensified and the various internal and external crises facing the apartheid government deepened, it became apparent that the period of political negotiation and transition was approaching. Anti-apartheid activists began to envisage a new democratic government and society. Some, especially those in exile (including the current president), who were exposed to global trends and foreign government thinking, envisaged the new South African nation from the outset in relation to the new global order. Others focused much more inwardly on the transition to democracy. There was at times considerable animosity and contestation between these two streams, which persisted through the negotiation and transition periods into the new government.

The consistent and sometimes militant socialist tenor of the anti-apartheid struggle raised serious concern among the (mainly white) middle class and business community about the effects of likely redistributive and redress measures on the market and thereby on their privilege. However, during the first meeting between 'enlightened' Afrikaners and the ANC in Dakar in 1987 pressure was brought to bear for a moderate and conciliatory political-economic approach that would affirm the importance of foreign and local investment to kickstart growth and thereby assure business confidence and the role of the (mainly white) business class in the new South Africa. Subsequently, during formal and informal meetings after 1990 between the ANC and business leaders, the balance of power shifted from the ANC to the corporate sector, with the global perspective prevailing among key figures of the government-in-waiting (Terreblanche 2003). In so doing, the global discourse began to take precedence over the transformative redistributive one, and measures such as the nationalization of certain industries, which were prominently part of the struggle discourse, became – in a very short space of time – discursively marginalized. An additional factor was that, by the late 1980s, the apartheid government had already embarked on a series of structural adjustments and fiscal constraint measures in compliance with the orthodoxy of the Bretton Woods institutions. By the time the new government took office in 1994, therefore, the global discourse had already taken root and had considerable support within the broad catholic organization of the ANC and its political allies.

The immediate post-apartheid era presented additional political, organizational and capacity constraints for transformative redistributive policy. The ruling party was clearly circumscribed in transforming the bureaucracy by protective 'sunset clauses' and by the conditions attached to the Government of National Unity (GNU), which comprised of the ANC and the

National Party (the ruling party under apartheid). However, the extent to which this was a factor is offset by the prior history of the ANC's global orientation prior to the elections in 1994. By the time the National Party withdrew from the GNU in 1996 and ostensively provided the political space for government to assert its redistributive-transformative agenda, government had already prioritized the global discourse above redistribution.

During the lead-up to the first elections, there were strong and demonstrative aspirations among the mass democratic movement for redistributive policies to offset the ravages of apartheid and to complement the political victory with a programme of socio-economic development that would manifestly benefit the majority poor. This was captured in the government's 1994 Reconstruction and Development Programme (RDP) – a people-centred programme committed to meeting the basic needs of the majority of the population. It was, crucially, premised on growth through redistribution. While there was constant rhetorical commitment to the RDP goals of meeting basic needs, severe delivery problems and organizational haphazardness resulted in the dismantling of the RDP ministerial portfolio and the effective closure of the programme itself. This was a reflection that behind the scenes, the notion of redistribution was being discursively banished.

While retaining a broad moral and political commitment to redistribution and reconstructive development, government instituted a range of monetarist macro-economic and fiscal policy measures, thereby positioning itself squarely within the prevailing neo-liberal paradigm of deregulated markets and capital flows and fiscal restraint. It thus created deep contradictions in relation to its redistributive commitment. To name a few: while offering relief to the low income groups, the proportional tax burden was increasingly shifted from companies to individuals in order to create conducive conditions for investment. In efforts to reduce the budget deficit, state expenditure on social services, though high proportionally, was restrained. Consequently, services are still inadequate to meet the priority needs of the poor, despite some redistributive reallocations from richer provinces to poorer ones. Ongoing trade and exchange control deregulation created conditions conducive to foreign investment and the free flow of capital, but have made the economy vulnerable to short-term speculation, the negative effects of which have impacted more directly on the poor. While the privatization of state enterprises provides for the injection of huge capital for development, the ownership of parastatal organizations is increasingly passing to foreign interests and linked to this, major South African firms have been allowed to relocate overseas, with a huge outflow of assets. Finally, although social spending is up, the last few budgets have provided huge individual tax cuts and massive military spending – at a time when social services are inadequate and the needs greatest. While financial resources are not the only problem (indeed some social welfare budgets have not been spent due to lack of absorptive capacity), allocating these resources would help build the required capacity for effective service delivery.

A turning point in the process occurred around 1995–96, by which time the ascendancy of the global discourse within two key ministries was assured: the Treasury and the Department of Trade and Industry. Ironically headed by prominent previous activists, both of these departments appear to have exerted considerable influence within government to bring about a decisive shift towards a global orientation in macro-economic policy. This manifested in the emergence of the government's 1996 Growth, Employment and Redistribution (GEAR) strategy. In direct contradistinction to the RDP, this was premised on redistribution through growth and structural adjustments. It aims at job creation and budget deficit reduction through a projected growth rate based on increasing foreign investment. The GEAR strategy is thus consistent with World Bank macro-economic principles of reduced spending and deregulation. The redistribution element in its title is, therefore, somewhat anomalous. To date, apart from successes in the reduction of the budget deficit, its targets have not been reached. Under sustained pressure from its Tripartite Alliance partners (the Congress of South African Trade Unions and the South African Communist Party), the ANC agreed to modify GEAR targets, but remained committed throughout to its framework. Even the Church was asked at one point to oppose the GEAR policy on the grounds that this policy favours the global development path at the expense of RDP concerns and the interests of the poor. Since then, GEAR has been the target of ongoing criticism by the Alliance and others, but the ANC leadership has sustained the hegemony of this discourse and policy orientation nonetheless.

Given the socialist leaning of the African National Congress during the years of anti-apartheid resistance, the unanticipated moderateness of its emerging macro-economic policy was (and still is) somewhat surprising. These developments represent significant ideological shifts in government policy from its previously overt and symbolic unconditional commitments to redistribution. As mentioned, a range of socio-economic indicators signal the uncomfortable fact that the overall effect of nine years of new government rule has been the decline in the living standards of the majority of the population (Terreblanche 2003) and the narrowing of opportunity, despite some successes in social services. In spite of becoming a 'well behaved economy' in the light of investors and the Bretton Woods institutions, and in spite of the economic 'fundamentals' all being in place, the expected catalyst to economic growth has not occurred. Even if it did, in the current global market milieu, the moderate expected growth would be insufficient to generate the kind of development needed to address the extent of grinding poverty and other social problems experienced by the majority of the population.

The key question, of course, is why has this discursive shift from transformation and redistribution to a global market orientation occurred so dramatically and unexpectedly? Expectations were high that South Africa – given its progressive anti-apartheid history, its relatively well developed infrastructure, its favourable position as a donor target, its pressing development needs – might well have provided a success case in charting a third way between the market-driven global path and a genuinely redistributive path. Why did the government not pursue such alternatives, as did countries like Malaysia (in regulating exchange control) and Brazil (in producing generic HIV/AIDS drugs in opposition to WTO regulations)? How could its prominent original progressive and redistributive intent become so backgrounded? How do previous staunch activists now in the current government leadership construct their realities and mediate the manifest contradictions facing a developing country nation state in the current global configuration?

Within the scope of this chapter it is of course not possible to be anything more than conjectural about these complex issues. Addressing them adequately is, as indicated, the focus of proposed systematic research that would require developing adequate analytic tools to understand the constraints and opportunities facing the contemporary nation state in the globalized context, facing government in relation to policy implementation challenges and facing the ANC itself as an ex-liberation movement, now in power. Cloete *et al.* (2002) are right in stating that they cannot be explained just as conscious 'sell-out' to previous ideals or we may add, a simple lack of political will or capacity.

Several recent analyses have begun to address these issues (see Motala and Pampallis 2001; Motala and Singh 2001; Kraak and Young 2001; Jansen and Sayed 2001; Gerwel 2002; Alexander 2002). Among these Kraak (2001: 3)[5] accounts for the shift in terms of 'policy ambiguity and slippage', which is the outcome of the interplay between discourse, state power and history. In his view, a process of slippage has occurred from the 'policy idealism' of the early 1990s to 'policy mediation and adaption' after state power had been attained in the post-1994 period, and further to 'policy doubt and retraction' once the limits of state power and the complexities of governance were encountered. The ambiguity arises from lack of clarity and a series of contestations around key issues: the role of globalization and economic modernization in reconstructing higher education, equity, the status of institutional differentiation and the political will to adopt a developmental interventionist position. In so doing, he highlights the tension between opposing discourses which characterized the policy formulation process since the post-1990 period: the 'high skills' thesis, popular democratic ideals and stratification. These tensions cause policy slippage. Muller (2001) questions the notions of ambiguity and slippage, arguing that the false expectation that symbolic policy could produce substantive outcomes was an expression of policy naivety. The lack of implementation is not so much a matter of policy analysts shifting their views or government not being able to grasp the nettle, but arise from the complexities of educational reform. Greater appreciation of this and greater reflection and critique represents policy maturation.

The issues clearly have to do with government perceiving a lack of genuine alternatives to dominant global practices, coupled with a fear of ostracism from global economic, financial and diplomatic networks if 'messages' about the heretical pursuit of such alternatives were broadcast. This points again to the dominance of the global discourse. Drawing once more from Ball (1993: 21), discourse is about 'what can be said, and thought, but also about who can speak, when, where and with what authority'. It changes the possibilities we have for thinking 'otherwise' and thus limits the range of our actions. In the current context, leftist aspirations and alternatives to globalization discourses are regarded as naïve nostalgic iterations of the struggle of the past. These are seen to be anachronistic in relation to the hard realities of day-to-day government and of the globalizing political economy. In this view, globalization is (largely if not totally) inevitable and unchallengeable. The prevalence of this view among ex-activist government leadership in South Africa bears testimony to the persuasive power of the neo-liberal global discourse.

The end result has been the backgrounding of transformative redistributive discourse and policies. To appease popular aspirations, recourse has consistently been taken to symbolic policy that captures the transformative values and goals of equity, redress, access and democracy. In the field of higher education, the White Paper fulfilled this symbolic purpose, but subsequent policy formulation has backgrounded these goals. I now turn in the final part of this chapter to trace the pattern of these issues in the process of higher education policy in South Africa.

The higher education policy process in South Africa

Progressive engagement in higher education policy formulation in South Africa commenced after the unbanning of resistance organisations in 1990. Initial studies provided the first systematic accounts of the inequitable, dysfunctional and fragmented system inherited from apartheid. Faced with the extent of these systemic distortions, the need not merely to reform (regarded a pejorative term associated with late apartheid tinkering), but to fundamentally restructure the system became readily apparent.

In response, the National Education Policy Initiative of 1991/92 provided a range of policy options across the sector as a whole, including higher education. The tension between equity and development formed the central conceptual conundrum in the then current discourse and debates. Understandably at that time, given the stark inequalities between the advantaged white and disadvantaged black institutions, policy goals were directed towards a strict sense of equity as parity and equality. This translated into the goal of a single, co-ordinated system in terms of which the multiple historical advantages concentrated among white institutions would be dismantled, and equally high quality black ones created. Any persistent form of institutional differentiation was equated with apartheid discrimination.

In the lead-up to the first democratic elections in 1994, the ANC government-in-waiting was provided by policy think-tanks and the Education Policy

Units with a policy framework to incorporate in its manifesto, and an implementation plan to guide the new minister (which was never really utilised). After the election, the new minister identified two priorities in higher education. The first was to establish the consultative process for developing a comprehensive policy framework and legislative instruments for transforming the higher education system – which was done through setting up of the National Commission on Higher Education (NCHE). The second priority involved establishing the required new bureaucratic and statutory structures for transformation (see below).

The NCHE process was intended to be widely consultative for obvious political reasons. Throughout the process, however, tensions emerged between experts and stakeholders and also between the commissioners and intellectuals involved in the research on the one hand and the ANC, its affiliates, the ministry and the Department of Education (DoE) on the other, particularly over the governance recommendations. In the ministry's view, these provided too much power to the proposed Higher Education Council and its stakeholders' representatives and diminished the regulatory role of the state (see Mathieson 2001: 57–59 for an informative 'insider' account of this). Despite this, the final 1996 NCHE report was highly regarded both locally and internationally as a comprehensive engagement with the complexities of higher education transformation. Tensions surfaced again in the subsequent process of producing the Green and White Papers during 1996 and 1997. These were consultative only in the sense that submissions were invited, and remained internally constructed government documents. In comparison to the richness of the NCHE document, the Green Paper and draft White Paper failed, as Mathieson (2001: 57–59) argues, 'to capture the vision for an integrated and transformed higher education system that had been achieved by the NCHE'.

In particular, pronounced ideological contestations and discursive tensions were apparent in the process of formulating the White Paper. This was evident in the wide fluctuations in emphasis on equity and efficiency in the various drafts of the White Paper. This was the result of two factors. First, NCHE members were invited to participate in the drafting of the Green Paper as individuals, detached from their previous accountability to the NCHE and its consultative process. Some clear departures from the NCHE recommendations arose as a result. Second, a crude economic technicism entered the discourse of the draft White Paper mainly through the conduit of foreign advisors present in the DoE at the time (including a senior education advisor from the World Bank). These influences were subsequently mediated by the timely intervention of progressive local educationists who carefully shaped the final version of the White Paper. The result was a well mediated and balanced document, reflecting discursive settlement on all the key issues of contestation outlined above: equity and development; equity and institutional differentiation; a clear recognition of institutional disadvantage and the need for redress; and emphasis on both global and local development concerns. As a result, the White Paper enjoyed almost universal support in the South African higher education community. Few would question the democratic legitimacy of the various values, principles and goals that comprise the broad framework for higher education transformation set out in the document. This is clearly the result of its broadly symbolic character, without any substantive elements, wherein the devil of contested detail lies.

Broad national consensus on the general framework of the White Paper did not, however, preclude selective reading of the document in support of particular institutional and stakeholder interests. Indeed, its very breadth allowed particular interpretations that generated unanticipated outcomes contrary to national policy intentions. The most prominent example of this was the wholesale shift to modularized inter-disciplinary programmes and academic restructuring at various institutions on the basis of the White Paper's endorsement of a 'programme-based', rather than an institutionally-based system. Despite much debate at the time, this recommendation was singularly lacking in clarity or guidelines. These institutional initiatives, in turn, were interpreted by the DoE as a 'too literal' reading of the White Paper's intentions. Research conducted on the process since then revealed that the widespread application of inter-disciplinarity into the curriculum has been somewhat counterproductive, with most programmes retaining their disciplinary cores, despite being purveyed as interdisciplinary in form, and the intended flexibility and portability obstructed rather than enhanced (Ensor 2002). The unintended result of the restructuring, however, was less portability and flexibility of student choice. In some instances, the pendulum swung too far towards inter-disciplinarity with the result that core disciplinary majors were decimated – a situation that was rapidly reviewed and reversed. This is one of a number of areas of progressive policy intent, based on somewhat uncritical policy borrowing, which now appear to be much more complicated and even counterproductive in implementation (Muller 2000; Subotzky 2003).

For the purposes of this chapter, the important point is the broad, inclusive, settlement-type symbolic nature of the White Paper that emerged as a solution to the discursive contestation at the time and in answer to the need for a comprehensive framework for higher education transformation that enjoyed widespread consensus.

Turning symbolic policy into substantive policy and effective implementation, as indicated, is a function of a number of enabling conditions and is governed by the limitations and opportunities within concrete contextual conditions. It does not flow from goals and principles, which was the unstated assumption at the time of writing of the White Paper. The question arises whether we have expected more than symbolic policy at the time that the White Paper was formulated? If not, what were the constraints precluding this and the choices available?

Part of the answer is that, after the 1994 election, the Ministry of Education faced the immediate mammoth organizational task of unifying the splintered apartheid and homelands education structures. What followed was a series of symbolic frameworks in the form of White Papers and other policy documents. The compelling political reason for establishing these frameworks was that they were consultative in nature. This is particularly so in a society so sharply divided, with such a high degree of systemic fragmentation. An overarching framework of principles, values and goals was necessary in order in order to establish broad initial consensus and from there, it was assumed, to proceed to the more detailed level of substantive policy formulation and implementation. In the immediate post-election period, government was concerned to establish its ideological and political credentials. This was driven by the need, not to win support (which was demonstrated in the overwhelming scope of its electoral victory), but to demonstrate immediate visible progress from the inherited apartheid system. As it was not possible to deliver on large-scale transformation, political recourse was taken in formal and symbolic policy-making – especially towards the Tripartite Alliance partners (Jansen 2001). In higher education, this was particularly important, given the strongly institutionalized sectional and stakeholders, interests involved. In very few instances did educational policies indicate clear concrete implementations steps, with the result that the policy terrain has been characterized by dramatic policy announcements and the production of sophisticated policy documents (many of which are widely admired internationally) but which make no or little reference to the modalities of implementation. Where they do, they tend to be last-minute improvised adjuncts and not the advanced planning tool they should be (Jansen 2001: 274).

As mentioned, after the White Paper the next priority in taking the transformation process forwards was the establishment of the required bureaucratic and statutory structures required by the White Paper and Higher Education Act in the form of the Higher Education Branch of the DoE, the Council on Higher Education (CHE) and its Higher Education Quality Committee. After its establishment, the Branch was rapidly inundated with two sets of unforeseen priorities. These were first dealing with the sudden institutional crises in historically disadvantaged institutions, precipitated by the unanticipated drop in student numbers and (in some cases severe) management and financial problems, and second dealing with regulating the private higher education sector, which included several court cases and an amendment to the Higher Education Act. Both were tremendously time-consuming and deviating. Other priorities included the incorporation of the colleges and establishing the preparatory three-year rolling planning processes, in terms of which institutions were required to produce indicative plans for student enrolments in various fields and programmes and institutional development plans.

Besides this, the new minister, who took office in 1999, revealed his intention to prioritize the restructuring of the system. This became known as the 'size and shape' issue, and was aimed at arriving at an optimum number and range of institutions for the system to fulfil its obligations. This was required, in his view, because a highly irrational and duplicative set of distinctly advantaged and disadvantaged institutions, strictly divided into a binary system of universities and technikons, were established as part of what he, in a memorable turn of phrase, calls the 'geo-political imagination of apartheid planners'. On such a radical issue, he was obliged need to consult widely and mandated the CHE to engage the sector and make recommendations. The 2000 draft and final CHE reports were highly controversial in setting up a fairly rigid institutional typology that served to reinforce historically institutional advantage. Strong sectoral opposition was voiced and the matter was referred to the minister, who incorporated his response into the National Plan for Higher Education, released in early 2001. This issue is addressed further below.

Before discussing this key document, I track some key changes and continuities in the system that occurred in the implementation vacuum and, linking back to the sections on policy and change agency, make some comments about the drivers and impediments to change. The purpose here is not to provide a comprehensive account of all patterns of change and non-change, but to highlight some of the key issues of the chapter.

First, between the 1997 White Paper and Higher Education Act and the 2001 National Plan, a range of institutional responses, initiatives and in some cases non-responses (due to internal crises) emerged. This can be interpreted as a set of responses to external conditions during the 'implementation vacuum' caused by the absence of a comprehensive regulatory framework. For the advantaged and capacitated institutions, this meant entrepreneurially seizing market opportunities (typically through satellite campuses, technology-based distance education programmes and business ventures to commercialize knowledge and services) or positioning themselves strategically within the market by developing innovative inter-disciplinary programmes and undertaking academic restructuring (the excesses and problems associated with this were highlighted above). Some institutions also began to structure themselves on the entrepreneurial model (Clark 1998a), setting up executive management teams and executive deans in charge of decentralized faculty entities. For some historically disadvantaged institutions, on the other hand, the implementation vacuum carried negative consequences. The postponement of a proposed new funding formula (which was expected to incorporate a fairer distribution of public funds and redress measures) and the absence of a substantive redress policy despite sustained ongoing symbolic commitment to this, was particularly problematic in this regard.

A four-fold typology of these responses has been developed by Cloete and Bunting (2000) and Cloete *et al.* (2002), linked to student enrolment patterns and approaches to knowledge in the form of teaching and research activities. These authors analysed institutional responses in terms of those that consolidated or expanded their domains, those that were seeking to identify their domains and those that were prevented from these three options by being paralysed in management and financial crises. In addition, a substantial growth in private higher/further education providers occurred, including collaborative partnerships among and between private and public, local and international institutions.

Change in this area of higher education was driven principally by institutional strategic and market-related initiatives in the domains of teaching and knowledge production, influenced by the globalization-related trends of entrepreneurialism and commercialization, the use of IT for diversified delivery and inter-disciplinary programmes.

A second major area of change is that, over a period of about 15 years, the student composition radically changed, with a huge increase in African enrolments in the system as a whole and in historically disadvantaged institutions particularly. While this was revolutionary at the aggregate level, the pattern remained somewhat skewed at lower levels of disaggregation, with black and female students remaining clustered in traditional fields and lower qualification levels (see Cooper and Subotzky 2001; Cloete *et al.* 2002 for details). Enrolments at some historically disadvantaged institutions dropped significantly, mainly as a result of student fee problems, but to some extent also the result of the attractiveness of previously white universities to which academically able students were now gaining access. Over the past two years, enrolment patterns have shifted, again, with growth among some disadvantaged institutions and increases in white students. These patterns of student choice are largely unresearched and unknown, though it is clear that perceptions of institutional reputation and financial considerations are paramount.

In stark contrast, staff composition regarding race and gender changed very little, especially at the senior academic and management levels, despite initiatives associated with the promulgation of the Employment Equity Act. Research output remains dominated by white males. A range of obstacles prevented significant progress in this regard, including structurally-rooted impediments (shortage of black and female entrants in key fields), institutional culture and subtle obstacles at the level of institutional micropolitics (see Howell and Subotzky 2002; Subotzky 2001a). The extent to which the promulgation of the Act is impacting on employment equity remains to be seen. Changes in the South African academic workplace as a result of globalization trends appear to be following worldwide trends, with heightened managerial-collegiate tensions, increasing pressure for commercialization of knowledge and services, and growing part-time staff utilization, to name a few (Webster and Mosoetsa 2001).

In terms of national policy and planning, most of these initiatives and changes were unanticipated – bearing out the point made earlier that significant changes in the higher education system occurred in spite of policy and not because of it. The institutional initiatives were somewhat suspiciously regarded by the ministry in that they constituted an unregulated proliferation of programmes, delivery sites and partnerships driven by sectional institutional interests that threatened the coherence of the goal of a planned and co-ordinated system and in turn the national interest. As a result, the policy and legislative framework has become fairly strongly regulative in character. Likewise, relations between the ministry and the sector have at times become increasingly strained, with the minister demonstrating diminishing patience with individual institutional interests.

These characteristics are reflected in the National Plan for Higher Education, released in 2001, four years after the White Paper. It is a strongly interventionist document, indicating stronger centralized control of the system. The minister made it clear that with the publication of the plan, the long process of consultative macro-policy formulation was now over and the time for decisive intervention and delivery had arrived. Systemic governance in South Africa is a paradoxical combination of strong interventionism and minimalism. The former is linked to the idea of 'grand' policy, transformative discourse and perhaps even to the government's socialist roots, while the latter relates to the global discourse. The interventionist character of the plan and the ministry is paradoxical in that it largely fosters market-like behaviour through the planning process, while transformation and equity – the goal of the 'traditional' interventionist role – are not foregrounded. This is the result of the closing down of the discursive space in which the role of state in supporting redress was narrowed (see below). An example of minimalism is the new funding formula's indication that the subsidy now comprises 'state funding in the last resort'. The framework for systemic governance in South Africa was established in the White Paper in the form of the notion of co-operative governance: the aspiration towards a co-operative relationship between state and higher education in which institutional autonomy and public accountability would be mutually accommodating. As indicated, this has recently come under strain, both at the systemic and institutional levels.

Other examples of interventionism include the new programme mix, which addresses the proliferation of higher education programmes by an increasing range of providers, without planning and adequate safeguards to ensure the quality of provision. This is a clear indication of the assumption of that the state has a strong role to play in regulating what is perceived as the *laissez-faire* operation of the market. Ironically, it was the government's own management and interpretation of the policy process which created the conditions for certain institutions' seizing market opportunities during the regulatory vacuum. Also, the non-voluntary mergers signal a shift 'from co-operative governance to coerced co-operation' (Cloete *et al.* 2002: 484). Another indicator of greater interventionism is that stronger powers have been vested in the minister through recent legislation and amendments, reflecting a strong directive role (Cloete *et al.* 2002). Following the notions of backward mapping and the mediating role of context, this shift in government-stakeholder relations has consequences for policy implementation. Consultation cannot be regarded linearly as a single phase in the policy process. Without appropriate participatory involvement by stakeholders in consultative policy-making and implementation, they will be unlikely to comply with government's stronger interventionism. Legal and bureaucratic obstructions to implementation will arise.

The National Plan provides the detailed framework and operational steps to implement the goals of the White Paper. Among other things, it establishes targets for increased participation and graduation rates, for reshaped enrolments by field of study and for staff equity. It also provides for the restructuring of the institutional landscape through mergers, but without reducing the number of institutional sites and capacity for expanded participation. The plan establishes three main policy levers of change. First, the iterative national and institutional three-year rolling planning process, which is linked to the ministry's 'Programme and Qualifications Mix' process, in terms of which ministerial funding for approved programmes is allocated. Second, the new quality assurance framework is in the process of being operationalized, and third, a new funding framework is being developed, though here too a long delay in implementation is evident.

Beyond this, in terms of the plan a ministry-appointed National Working Group was mandated to make recommendations about the optimal way to reduce the current 35 institutions to 22. Thus the minister focused his preoccupation on the size and shape of the system to the reduction in institutional numbers. From the outset, however, it was never clear how this reduction would necessarily advance the policy goals of efficiency (mergers are not a cheap option), effectiveness and systemic equity (despite numerous mergers between previously advantaged and disadvantaged institutions). In the absence of a compelling rationale, the minister's single-minded insistence on system pruning appears to be primarily motivated by the political need to achieve demonstrable change. He appears personally intent, in the twilight of his career, to stamp his change on the system by removing the anomalies of apartheid planning at all costs. With an election year looming next year, and given persistent demands for meaningful socio-economic transformation, the need for visible transformation is understandable. However, mergers absorb enormous energy and resources, with little certainty of cost benefits. This highlights the danger of policy being primarily motivated politically, rather than educationally. In this view, mergers represent a reductionist quantitative narrowing of the goal of higher education transformation and as such mistake means for (essentially political) ends. Nonetheless, the system will radically change (we will have 11 universities, 5 technikons and 6 hybrid comprehensives), with new institutions and regional institutional clusters, in some cases with radically different student populations. Whether these changes will effectively enhance the achievement of broader goals remains to be seen.

A number of factors and conditions can be seen to have contributed to the gap between the formulation of the White Paper and the implementation of its framework for transformation. The National Plan acknowledges clearly that the central policy goal of the White Paper, namely the development of a single, national, diverse, co-ordinated higher education system, remains 'unachieved'. This is largely due to the fact that it has adopted an 'incremental approach to the development and implementation of the [necessary] key policy instruments' (DoE 2001: 8). Although the three-year rolling planning process commenced in 1998, this was 'developed in the context of the broad transformation agenda and policy goals signalled in the *White Paper*, rather than a clear set of implementation and funding guidelines linked to a *National Plan*' (DoE 2001: 8). This clearly locates the White Paper and the initial three-year rolling plans in the domain of symbolic policy as opposed to substantive elements of implementation and funding guidelines linked to the National Plan. According to the plan, the incremental approach was adopted for three reasons. First, the lack of systemic person-power, capacity and technical skills; second, the absence of an adequate information base, as well as analyses and understanding of systemic and institutional trends; and third, the need to develop a consultative and inter-active planning process as part of co-operative governance partnerships with institutions.

From the DoE's perspective, the prior phase of policy development *was* necessary. It would not have been possible to develop the substantive and procedural aspects of policy as they have now been captured in the National Plan any earlier. In addition, as indicated, various organizational and politi-cal challenges facing new government – the realities of governance, trans-forming the bureaucracy and capacity constraints, and the need to consult on the 'size and shape' issue – also limited implementation possibilities. Policy naivety, as Muller (2001) suggests, also contributed to the implemen-tation gap through a lack of a clear grasp of the complexities of policy and implementation and, indeed, the distinction between symbolic and substan-tive policy. Indeed, it appears that the realization that White Paper did not constitute an adequate strategy for implementation only arose in hindsight through the DoE's subsequent implementation experience.

An important element in the policy process has been the shift in meanings and tensions around certain key concepts. The notions of equity and devel-opment and the assumed tension between them were figural in the early policy debates of the 1990s. Within this, different notions of each of these terms evolved and held discursive sway at various times. Regarding equity, there was, as already mentioned, early emphasis on equity as equality or strict parity, in terms of which, for example, the differences between previously black and white institutions would be eradicated in post-apartheid South Africa, with the capacity of black institutions being built up to that of white ones, using a single (research) institutional model as the benchmark. During the National Commission on Higher Education, the principle of institutional differentiation was debated, and building on other theoretical foundations (see Subotzky 2001a), the notion of equity as accommodating and address-ing difference in an emancipatory way emerged. This notion of equity avoids the traditional tension with excellence and is, indeed, a means to that end – a point that builds on contemporary accounts of the value of diversity in education (Subotzky 2001a).

As the influence of the global discourse was increasingly felt, the notions of equity and redress have become threatened. Cloete *et al.* (2002: 458–9) offer a fascinating account of how the redress question was handled intern-ally in government. This reveals fractures and divisions among and within government departments, including the higher education branch of the DoE and the increasingly prominent role played by the Treasury in social policy formulation.

Similarly, Barnes (2003) traces the shifts in meaning and interpretation of redress to the point where, in the most recent draft version of the funding framework, it is entirely absent, having been subsumed into the funding mechanism and merger process and changing its meaning in the process – that is, detached from any notion of redistribution, a notion that does not enjoy prominence in the current discursive moment. Thus, the notion of redress has become almost entirely discursively foreclosed, a prominent example of the dominance of the global discourse.

Conclusion: towards an explanation of change and non-change

We have seen that, as a new developing country democracy, South Africa faces formidable challenges in meeting its dual development imperative: engaging in the global economy and knowledge society, and simultaneously addressing the basic socio-economic development needs of the poor. Addressing the latter is particularly challenging, given the current dominance of the global discourse over the redistributive-transformative one.

Higher education has a crucial role to play in both of these goals. To this end, a symbolic framework of systemic transformation was established. For a variety of reasons, the implementation of this framework has been partial, though paradoxically there are a large number of simultaneous change initiatives under way. As a result, the current system is characterized by some radical changes alongside persistent continuities, by a gap between symbolic and substantive policy, and by a discernible shift towards the global discourse.

The current system is fairly strongly centrally driven by an interventionist national plan. Within the overall framework for change, institutions currently face a bewildering array of policy and planning initiatives and change imperatives, leading to a crippling demand overload. Not only do they face multiple aspects of higher education change, but they are also subject to labour legislation and employment equity stipulations. Clearly lacking in this overall transformation agenda is the sequential alignment of policy and planning priorities. While the temptation to adopt 'grand' policy approaches must be resisted, without sensible policy co-ordination and prioritization, multiple demands will simply exhaust capacity, energy and compliance, resulting in resistance to implementation. Within this, the system is currently preoccupied with the landscape pruning process.

The focus of this chapter has been to trace and offer an account of these patterns of change, drawing from a fresh look at policy and what drives and inhibits change. This analysis highlights the tension between the global market-driven discourse and the redistributive-transformative discourse. Given the formidable challenges facing South Africa as a middle-income developing country in the new global scheme of things, it suggests that some form of discursive mediation between these positions is necessary as a basis for developing effective public and higher education policy, to meet the nation's contemporary dual development demands. It also suggests that a far richer understanding of the nature of policy and change is required among all policy agents, in order to develop and successfully operationalize such policies. The South African case, with all the dramatic intensity of recent changes and the promise that it still holds symbolically worldwide for achieving these aims, therefore remains an informative and interesting one. The real interest lies in how successfully this can be translated into substantive policy and practice.

Notes

1 The reasons for this are complex, and form the subject of a proposed collaborative study in which the author is involved.
2 I am indebted to Professor Johan Muller of the University of Cape Town, in a personal communication, for highlighting the importance of this point.
3 This typology draws from a variety of sources: many informal conversations on this topic in the Education Policy Unit at the University of the Western Cape over the past decade; from teaching material developed by the previous Director, Professor Saleem Badat; from Subotzky 2001; and from Dudley and Vidovich 1995: 14–15 and Taylor *et al.* 1997: 33–35. Further distinctions may be made between *rational policy* (guidelines for policy development independent of practice), *incremental policy* (which depends on previous or existing policies), *procedural policy* (indicates how decisions are to be implemented) and *material policy* (which shows commitment to implementation through the allocation of resources). Of course, policies cannot be neatly classified in one or other of these distinct categories. In practice, they are typically a combination of the categories and/or their components (Taylor *et al.* 1997).
4 I am indebted to Professor Johann Mouton of Stellenbosch University for this insight.
5 This account is derived from J. Gamble's synopsis of a symposium presented at the conference *Globalization and Higher Education: Views from the South*, Cape Town, 27–29 March 2001.

References

Adelman, C. (2001) The Medieval Guild in Cyberclothes: International Dimensions of Industry Certification in Information Technology, *Tertiary Education and Management*, 7(3): 277–92.

Albright, B.N. (1997) Of Carrots and Sticks and State Budgets, *Trusteeship*, the journal of the Association of Governing Boards of Colleges and Universities, March/April: 18–23.

Albright, B.N. (1998) The Transition from Business as Usual to Funding for Results: State Efforts to Integrate Performance Measures in the Higher Education Budgetary Process. Denver, Colorado: State Higher Education Executive Officers.

Alexander, N. (2002) *An Ordinary Country: Issues in the Transition from Apartheid to Democracy in South Africa*. Scottsville: University of Natal Press.

Allen, H. (1999) Workload and productivity in an era of performance measures. NEA Almanac, pp. 27–44, Washington, DC: National Education Association.

Altbach, P.G. (1991) The academic profession, in P.G. Altbach (ed.) *International Higher Education: An Encyclopedia*. New York: Garland Publishing, Inc.

Altbach, P.G. (ed.) (1996) *The International Academic Profession: Portraits from Fourteen Countries*. Princeton: Carnegie Foundation for the Advancement of Teaching.

Altbach, P.G. (2001) Academic Freedom: International Realities and Challenges, *SRHE International News*, No. 46, November 2001, London, p. 13.

Archer, L., Hutchings, M., Ross, A. *et al.* (2003) *Higher Education and Social Class*. London: Routledge Falmer.

Askling, B. (2001) In Search of New Models of Institutional Governance: Some Swedish Experiences, *Tertiary Education and Management*, 7(2): 163–80.

Austin, A.E. (1990) Faculty cultures, in B.R. Clark and G. Neave (eds) *The Encyclopedia of Higher Education*. Oxford: Pergamon Press.

Australian Bureau of Statistics, ABS (2000a) Research and Experimental Development: All sector summary Australia, 1998–9, *Catalogue* No. 8112.0. Canberra: ABS.

Australian Bureau of Statistics, ABS (2000b) The Labour Force, *Catalogue* No. 6203.0. Canberra: ABS.

Australian Bureau of Statistics, ABS (2000c) Transition from Education to Work, *Catalogue* No. 6227.0. Canberra: ABS.

Australian Science and Technology Council, ASTEC (1987) *Education and National Needs*. Canberra: Australian Government Publishing Service.

Australian Vice-Chancellors' Committee, AVCC (2000) Statistical data on trends in the Australian government funding of higher education.

Bain, O. (1997) Cost of higher education to students and parents in Russia: Tuition policy issues, Buffalo, NY: The Center for Comparative and Global Studies, State University of New York at Buffalo [unpublished paper].

Bakonsky, R. (2002) La promotion de la qualité dans l'étude des langues, Rumania, Thematic Network Project in the Area of Languages 2, Subgroup 3 – Quality enhancement in language studies, National reports, Universität zu Köln.

Baldwin, P., Minister for Higher Education and Employment Services (1991) *Higher Education: Quality and Diversity in the 1990s*. Canberra: Australian Government Publishing Service.

Ball, S. (1993) What is policy? Text, trajectories and toolboxes. *Discourse*, 13(2): 14–27.

Banta, T.W. *et al.* (1993) *Making a Difference: Outcomes of a Decade of Assessment in Higher Education*. San Francisco: Jossey-Bass.

Banta, T.W. *et al.* (1996) Performance Funding Comes of Age in Tennessee, *Journal of Higher Education*, 67(1) January/February: 23–45.

Bargh, C. *et al.* (2000) *University Leadership: The Role of the Chief Executive*. Buckingham: Open University Press.

Barnes, T. (2003) Towards the formulation of a Redress Policy: Draft Research Report for the Council on Higher Education. Cape Town: Education Policy Unit, University of the Western Cape.

Barr, N. (1989) *Student Loans: The Next Steps*. Edinburgh: Aberdeen University Press.

Barry, D. and M. Elmes (1997) Strategy Retold: Toward a Narrative View of Strategic Discourse, *The Academy of Management Review*, 22(2): 429–52.

Bauer, M., Askling, B., Gerard-Marton, S. and Marton, F. (1999) *Transforming Universities: Changing Patterns of Governance, Structure and Learning in Swedish Higher Education* (Vol. 48). London: Jessica Kingsley.

Bauer, M. and Henkel, M. (1999) Academic Responses to Quality Reforms in Higher Education: England and Sweden Compared, in M. Henkel and B. Little (eds) *Changing Relationships between Higher Education and the State*. London: Jessica Kingsley.

Becher, T. (1987) The disciplinary shaping of the profession, in Clark, B.R. (ed.) *The Academic Profession: National, Disciplinary, and Institutional Settings*. Berkeley: University of California Press.

Becher, T. and Trowler P. (2001) *Academic Tribes and Territories: Intellectual Enquiry and the Cultures of Disciplines*. London: Society for Research into Higher Education and Open University Press.

Besters-Dilger, J. (2002) National Report on Quality Enhancement in Language Studies, Austria, Thematic Network Project in the Area of Languages 2, Subgroup 3 – Quality enhancement in language studies, National reports, Universität zu Köln.

Bett Report (1999) Independent Review of Higher Education, Pay and Conditions, London: HMSO.

Biglan, A. (1973) The characteristics of subject matter in different academic areas, *Journal of Applied Psychology*, 57(3): 195–203.

Blašková, S. (2003) Thematic Network Project in the Area of Languages 2, Subgroup 3 – Quality enhancement in language studies, National reports, Slovakia, Universität zu Köln.

Blight, D., Davis, D. and Olsen, A. (2000) The Globalisation of Higher Education, in Scott, P. (ed.) *Higher Education Re-formed*. London and New York: Falmer Press.

Breier, M. (2002) Organisational learning and non-learning: Emerging strategies of organisational change. Paper presented at the 2nd SANTED Formative Research Seminar Strand, 5–7 December 2002.

Breier, M. (forthcoming) The Recruitment and Recognition of Prior Informal Experience in the Pedagogy of Two University Courses in Labour Law. PhD thesis, Department of Education, University of Cape Town.

Brennan, J. (ed.) (1992) *Towards a Methodology for Comparative Quality Assessment in European Higher Education*, London: Twente, Hanover: CNAA, CHERS, HIS.

Brennan, J. *et al.* (1996) *Changing Conceptions of Academic Standards*. London: Open University, Quality Support Centre.

Brennan, J. (1997a) *Standards and Quality in Higher Education*. London: Taylor and Francis.

Brennan, J. (1997b) Authority, Legitimacy and Change: the rise of quality assessment in higher education, *Higher Education Management*, 9: 1.

Brennan, J., Fedrowitz, J., Huber, M. and Shah, T. (eds) (1999) *What Kind of University?* Buckingham: Open University Press.

Brennan, J. and Shah, T. (2000a) Quality assessment and institutional change: Experiences from 14 countries, *Higher Education*, 40(3): 331–49.

Brennan, J. and Shah T. (2000b) *Managing Quality in Higher Education*. Buckingham: Open University Press.

Broderick, M. (2003) Quality Enhancement in Language Studies, Ireland, Thematic Network Project in the Area of Languages 2, Subgroup 3 – Quality enhancement in language studies, National reports, Universität zu Köln.

Brooks, A. and Mackinnon, A. (2001) *Gender and the Restructured University*. Buckingham: Open University Press.

Brown, J.S. (2000) Growing up digital: how the web changes work, education, and the way people learn, *Change*, March/April: 11–20.

Brunner, J. (1997) From state to market coordination: the Chilean case, *Higher Education Policy*, 10(3/4): 225–37.

Buchanan, M. (1997) One Law to Rule Them All, *New Scientist* 2107, 8 November.

Buchert, L. and King, K. (1995) *Learning from Experience: Policy and Practice in Aid to Higher Education*. The Hague: Centre for the Study of Education in Developing Countries.

Bull, G. (1994) Teaching and Learning, in G.M. Bull, C. Dallinga-Hunter, Y. Epelboin, E. Frackmann, D. Jennings (eds) *Information Technology: Issues for Higher Education Management* (pp. 15–22). London: Jessica-Kingsley.

Burke, J.C. and Serban, A.M. (1998) Performance funding for Public Higher Education: Fad or Trend?, *New Directions for Institutional Research*, no. 97. San Francisco: Jossey-Bass.

Callender, C. and Kemp, M. (2000) *Changing Student Finances: Income, Expenditure, and the Take-up of Student Loans Among Full- and Part-time Higher Education Students in 1998/99*. London: Department for Education and Employment.

Casey, C. (1995) *Work, Self and Society after Industrialism*. London: Routledge.

Castells, M. (1996) *The Information Age: Economy, Society and Culture*. Oxford: Blackwell Publishers.

Castells, M. (2000) Materials for an exploratory theory of the network society, *British Journal of Sociology*, vol. 51 No 1.

Chapman, B. and Smith, D. (1994) The Higher Education Contribution Scheme after five years, *Current Affairs Bulletin*, University of Sydney, 71(4): 27–34.

Chevaillier, T. (1998) Moving away from central planning: using contracts to steer higher education in France, *European Journal of Education*, 33(1): 65–76.

Chiarloni, A. *et al.* (2003) Italian Report on Foreign Language Teaching in the Educational System with Social Reference to Higher Education, Thematic Network Project in the Area of Languages 2, Subgroup 3 – Quality enhancement in language studies, National reports, Universität zu Köln.

Christal, M.E. (1998) 1997 SHEEO Survey on Performance Measures. Denver, Colorado: State Higher Education Executive Officers.

CIHE (Council for Industry and Higher Education) (1997) Widening Participation in Lifelong Learning: A Progress Report. London: The Council.

CIHE (1999) Graduate Opportunities, Social Class and Age. London: The Council.

Clark, B.R. (1983) *The Higher Education System: Academic Organization in Cross-National Perspective*. Berkeley: University of California Press.

Clark, B.R. (1985) Listening to the professoriate, *Change*, 17(5): 36–43.

Clark, B.R. (1987a) *The Academic Life: Small Worlds, Different Worlds*. Princeton: The Carnegie Foundation for the Advancement of Teaching.

Clark, B.R. (1987b) *The Academic Profession: National, Disciplinary, and Institutional Settings*. Berkeley: University of California Press.

Clark, B.R. (ed.) (1993) *The Research Foundations of Graduate Education. Germany, Britain, France, United States, Japan*. Berkeley: University of California Press.

Clark, B.R. (1996) Substantive Growth and Innovative Organization: New Categories for Higher Education Research, *Higher Education*, 32: 417–30.

Clark, B.R. (1998a) *Creating Entrepreneurial Universities: Organizational Pathways of Transformation*. Oxford: Pergamon.

Clark, B.R. (1998b) The Entrepreneurial University: Demand and Response, *Tertiary Education and Management*, 4(1): 5–16.

Clark, B.R. (2000) The entrepreneurial university: New foundations for collegiality, autonomy, and achievement. Paper presented to the IMHE General Conference, Paris, France, 11–13 September.

Clark, B.R. and Neave, G. (eds) (1990) *The Encyclopedia of Higher Education*. Oxford: Pergamon Press.

Clarke, C. (2003a) Foreword to DfES 2003, The Future of Higher Education, Cm 5735.

Clarke, C. (2003b) speech, in Keep, E. (2003) Higher Education Expansion and the Evidence on Economic Demand for Graduates – Another Failure of Evidence-based Policy Making to Materialise? presentation to SRHE/ESRC Seminar, May 2003, London.

Clarke, J. and Newman, J. (1997) *The Managerial State: Power, Politics and Ideology in the Remaking of Social Welfare*. London: Sage.

Cloete, N. *et al.* (eds) (1997) *Knowledge, Identity, and Curriculum Transformation in Africa*, Cape Town: Maskew Miller-Longman.

Cloete, N. and Bunting, I. (2000) *Higher Education Transformation: Assessing Performance in South Africa*. Pretoria: CHET.

Cloete, N. *et al.* (eds) (2002) *Transformation in Higher Education: Global Pressures and Local Realities in South Africa*. Landsdowne: Juta and Company.

Coaldrake, P. and Stedman, L. (1999) *Academic Work in the Twenty-First Century: Changing Roles and Policies*, 99H. Higher Education Division. Australia: Commonwealth of Australia.

Cockett, R. (1995) *Thinking the Unthinkable: Think-tanks and the economic counter-revolution, 1931–1983.* London: Fontana Press.

Cohen, A. (1998) *The Shaping of American Higher Education.* San Francisco: Jossey-Bass.

Colclough, C. and Manor, J. (1991) *States or Markets? An Assessment of Neo Liberal Approaches to Education Policy.* Oxford: Clarendon Press.

Commission of the European Communities (1993) *Quality Management and Quality Assurance in European Higher Education: Methods and Mechanisms.* Brussels: European Commission, Education, Training and Youth, Studies no. 1.

Cooper, D. and Subotzky, G. (2001) *The Skewed Revolution: Trends in South African Higher Education 1988–(1993).* Bellville: Education Policy Unit, UWC.

Cowen, R. (1996) Performativity, Post Modernity and the University, *Comparative Education,* 32(2): 245–58.

Crosson, F. (1987) The philosophy of accreditation, *North Central Quarterly,* 62(2).

Crow, S.D. (2002) Engaging the Future by Restructuring Expectations. Keynote address, Annual Meeting, North Central Association, Higher Learning Commission. Chicago, IL: NCA.

Cunningham, S., Ryan, Y., Stedman, L. *et al.* (2000) *The Business of Borderless Education,* AGPS Canberra. http://www.detya.gov.au/highered/eippubs.htm#00-3.

Currie, J. and Newson, J. (eds) (1998) *Universities and Globalization: Critical Perspectives.* Thousand Oaks and London: Sage.

CVCP (Committee of Vice Chancellors and Principals) (1998) *From Elitism to Inclusion: good practice in widening access to higher education.* London: The Committee.

Daniel, H.-D., Schwarz, S. and Teichler, U. (1999) Study costs, student income and public policy in Europe, *European Journal of Education,* 34 (1): 7–21.

Darling, J. (1994) *Child-centred Education and its Critics.* London: Chapman.

Davies, J.L. (1997) The Evolution of University Responses to Financial Reduction, *Higher Education Management,* 9: 1.

Dawkins, J., Minister for Employment, Education and Training (1987) *Higher Education: A Discussion Paper.* Canberra: Australian Government Publishing Service.

Dawkins, J., Minister for Employment, Education and Training (1988) *Higher Education: A Policy Statement.* Canberra: Australian Government Publishing Service.

De Boer, H. (1998) Vom partizipatorischen System zum Managerialism? Internationale Trends in der Leitung von Hochschulen, in D. Müller-Böling and J. Fedrowitz (eds) *Leitungsstrukturen für autonome Hochschulen* (pp. 59–83). Gütersloh: Bertelsmann Foundation.

De Boer, H. (2001) On Limitations and Consequences of Change: Dutch University Governance in Transition, *Tertiary Education and Management,* 7(2): 163–80.

De Corte, E. (ed.) (2003) *Excellence in Higher Education.* Proceedings from a symposium held at the Wenner-Gren Centre, Stockholm, 31 May–1 June 2002, London: Portland Press.

Deem, R. (1998) New Managerialism in Higher Education – the Management of Performances and Cultures in Universities, *International Studies in the Sociology of Education,* 8(1): 47–70.

Deem, R. (2003a) Gender, Organisational Cultures and the Practices of Manager-Academics in UK Universities, *Gender, Work and Organisation,* 10(2): 239–59.

Deem, R. (2003b) Managing to Exclude? Manager-Academic and Staff Communities in Contemporary UK Universities, in M. Tight (ed.) *International Perspectives on Higher Education Research: Access and Inclusion.* Elsevier Science JAI: 103–25.

Deem, R. and Johnson, R.J. (2000) Managerialism and University Managers: Building New Academic Communities or Disrupting Old Ones?, in I. McNay (ed.) *Higher Education and Its Communities*. Buckingham: Open University Press: 65–84.

Deem, R. and Ozga, J. (2000) Transforming Post Compulsory Education? Femocrats at Work in the Academy, *Women's Studies International Forum*, 23(2): 153–66.

Department for Education and Skills (2001) *Skills in England*, London, DfES, London HMSO.

Department for Education and Skills (2003a) *The Future of Higher Education*, Cm 5735, London HMSO.

Department for Education and Skills (2003b) *The Future of Higher Education*, DFES White Paper. London: HMSO.

Department of Education (DoE) (1997) *Education White Paper 3: A Programme for the Transformation of Higher Education*. General Notice 1196 of 1997, Pretoria.

Department of Education (DoE) (2001) National Plan for Higher Education. Pretoria: DoE.

Department of Education, Training and Youth Affairs, DETYA (1995) Higher Education Students: Time Series Tables. Canberra: DETYA.

Department of Education, Training and Youth Affairs, DETYA (1998) The Characteristics and Performance of Higher Education Institutions, Occasional Paper. Canberra: DETYA.

Department of Education, Training and Youth Affairs, DETYA (1999a) Selected Higher Education Staff Statistics 1998. Canberra: DETYA.

Department of Education, Training and Youth Affairs, DETYA (1999b) Selected Higher Education Finance Statistics, 1998. Canberra: DETYA.

Department of Education, Training and Youth Affairs, DETYA (1999c) Education Participation Rates, Australia – 1997. Canberra: DETYA.

Department of Education, Training and Youth Affairs, DETYA (2000a) Students 1999: Selected Higher Education Statistics. Canberra: DETYA.

Department of Education, Training and Youth Affairs, DETYA (2000b) Research Expenditure: Selected Higher Education Statistics 1998. Canberra: DETYA.

Dill, D., Massy, W.F., Williams, P.R., and Cook, C.M. (1996) Accreditation and academic quality assurance: can we get there from here?, *Change*, September/October.

Dill, D. and Teixeira, P. (2000) Program diversity in higher education: an economic perspective, *Higher Education Policy*, 13: 99–117.

Dill, W. (1998) Specialized accreditation: an idea whose time has come? Or gone?, *Change*, July/August: 18–25.

Du Gay, P. (ed.) (1998) *Production of Cultures/Cultures of Production*. London: Sage.

Du Gay, P. and Salaman, G. (1992) The Cult(Ure) of the Customer, *Journal of Management Studies*, 29(4): 616–33.

Easterby-Smith, M. *et al.* (eds) (1999) *Organisational Learning and the Learning Organisation*. London: Sage.

Eaton, J. (2001) Regional Accreditation Reform, *Change*, 33(2): 39–45.

Eggins, H. (ed.) (1997) *Women as Leaders and Managers in Higher Education*. Buckingham: SRHE/Open University Press.

Eggins, H. (2000) Old Verities, New Realities: The Academic Community in the 21st Century. Public Lecture given at the University of Strathclyde, 16 March.

Eicher, J.-C. (1998) The costs and financing of higher education in Europe, *European Journal of Education*, 33 (1): 31–9.

Elias, P. and Purcell, K. (2003) The early careers of graduates, presentation to SRHE/ ESRC Seminar, May 2003, London.

El-Khawas, E. (1993) External Scrutiny, US Style: Multiple Actors, Overlapping Roles, in T. Becher (ed.) *Governments and Professional Education*. London: SRHE/Open University Press.

El-Khawas, E. (1998) Strong State Action but Limited Results: Perspectives on University Resistance, *European Journal of Education*, vol. 33(3): 317–30.

El-Khawas, E. (2001) *Accreditation in the United States: Origins, Developments and Future Prospects*. Paris: UNESCO/International Institute for Educational Planning.

Elmore, R. (1980) Backward mapping: Implementation research and policy decisions. *Political Science Quarterly*, 94(4): 601–15.

Enders, J. (ed.) (2001) Employment and Working Conditions of Academic Staff in Europe. Frankfurt am Main: Gewerkschaft Erziehung und Wissenschaft.

Enders, J. and Teichler, U. (1997) A victim of their own success? Employment and working conditions of academic staff in comparative perspective, *Higher Education*, 34: 347–72.

Ensor, P. (2002) Curriculum, in Cloete, N., Fehnel, R., Gibbon, T., Maassen P., Moja T., and Perold, H. (eds) *Transformation in Higher Education: Global Pressures and Local Realities in South Africa*. Landsdowne: Juta and Company.

Epelboin, Y. (1994) Research and National Networking, in G.M. Bull, C. Dallinga-Hunter, Y. Epelboin, E. Frackmann and D. Jennings (eds) *Information Technology: Issues for Higher Education Management* (pp. 23–7). London: Jessica-Kingsley.

Etzkowitz, H. and Leydesdorff, L. (1997a) Introduction: Universities in the Global Knowledge Economy, in H. Etzkowitz and L. Leydesdorff (eds) *Universities and the Global Knowledge Economy* (pp. 1–8). London: Pinter.

Etzkowitz, H. and Leydesdorff, L. (eds) (1997b) *Universities and the Global Knowledge Economy*. London: Pinter.

Ewell, P. (1994) Tennessee, in S.S. Ruppert (ed.) *Charting Higher Education Accountability: A Sourcebook on State Level Performance Indicators*. Denver: Education Commission of the States, pp. 147–66.

Ewell, P.T. (1997) Strengthening Assessment for Academic Quality Improvement, in M.W. Peterson, D.D. Dill and L.A. Mets (eds) *Planning and Management for a Changing Environment: A Handbook on Redesigning Postsecondary Institutions* (pp. 360–81). San Francisco: Jossey-Bass.

Exworthy, M. and Halford, S. (eds) (1999) *Professionals and the New Managerialism in the Public Sector*. Buckingham: Open University Press.

Fairweather, J. (2000) Diversification or homogenisation: how markets and governments combine to shape American higher education, *Higher Education Policy*, 13: 79–98.

Fane, G. (1984) Education Policy in Australia, EPAC Discussion Paper 85/08. Canberra: Economic Planning Advisory Council.

Fataar, A. (2001) Engaging the narrowing education policy trajectory in South Africa. *South African Review of Education*, 6: 19–30.

Fedrowitz, J., Krasny, E. and Ziegele, F. (eds) (1999) *Hochschulen und Zielvereinbarungen*. Gütersloh: Bertelsmann Foundation.

Ferlie, E., Ashburner, L., Fitzgerald, L. and Pettigrew, A. (1996) *The New Public Management in Action*. Oxford: Oxford University Press.

Fulton, O. (1996a) Differentiation and diversity in a newly unitary system: the case of the UK, in V.L. Meek, L. Goedegebuure, O. Kivinen and R. Rinne *The Mockers and the Mocked: Comparative perspectives on differentiation, convergence and diversity in higher education* (pp. 163–87). Oxford: Pergamon.

Fulton, O. (1996b) Mass Access and the End of Diversity? The Academic Profession in England on the Eve of Structural Reform, in P. Altbach (ed.) *The International Academic Profession: Portraits from Fourteen Countries.* Princeton, USA: Carnegie Foundation for the Advancement of Teaching.

Fulton, O. (1998) Unity or Fragmentation, Convergence or Diversity? The Academic Profession in Comparative Perspective in the Era of Mass Higher Education, in W.G. Bowen and H. Shapiro (eds) *Universities and Their Leadership.* Princeton: Princeton University Press.

Fulton, O. (2001) Academic Staff in the United Kingdom, in J. Enders (ed.) *Employment and Working Conditions of Academic Staff in Europe.* Frankfurt am Main: Gewerkschaft Erziehung und Wissenschaft.

Gellert, C. (ed.) (1999) *Innovation and Adaptation in Higher Education: The Changing Conditions of Advanced Teaching and Learning in Europe* (vol. 22). London: Jessica Kingsley.

Gerwel, J. (2002) Inaugural Memorial Lecture to the Harold Wolpe Memorial Trust, Cape Town, 19 September.

Gewirtz, S. *et al.* (1995) *Markets, Choice and Equity in Education.* Buckingham: Open University Press.

Gibbons, M. *et al.* (1994) *The New Production of Knowledge: The Dynamics of Science and Research in Contemporary Societies.* London: Sage.

Gibbons, M. (1995) The University as an Instrument for the Development of Science and Basic Research: The Implications of Mode 2 Science, in D.D. Dill and B. Sporn (eds) *Emerging Patterns of Social Demand and University Reform: Through a Glass Darkly* (pp. 90–104). Oxford: Pergamon.

Gibbons, M. (1998) Higher education relevance in the 21st century. Paper presented to the UNESCO World Conference on Higher Education, Paris, France, 5–9 October.

Giddens, A. (1990) *The Consequences of Modernity.* Stanford, California: Stanford University Press.

Giddens, A. (2001) The Great Globalization Debate, Zellerbach Distinguished Lecture, University of California, Berkeley, 25 October.

Glazer-Raymo, J. (1999) *Shattering the Myths: Women in Academe.* Baltimore: The Johns Hopkins University Press.

Goddard, A. (2001) Labour can't find the right formula, *Times Higher Education Supplement* 29 June.

Goddard, A. (2003) £750,00 Wage Rise for Those at the Top, *Times Higher Education Supplement.* London, 7 February: 8–9.

Goldstein, H., Maier, G. and Luger, M. (1995) The University as an Instrument for Economic and Business Development: U.S. and European Comparisons, in D.D. Dill and B. Sporn (eds) *Emerging Patterns of Social Demand and University Reform: Through a Glass Darkly* (pp. 105–33). Oxford: Pergamon.

Goldstein, H.A. and Luger, M.I. (1997) Assisting Economic and Business Development, in M.W. Peterson, D.D. Dill and L.A. Mets (eds) *Planning and Management for a Changing Environment: A Handbook on Redesigning Postsecondary Institutions* (pp. 521–47). San Francisco: Jossey-Bass.

Goodchild, L. (1989) The turning point in American Jesuit higher education: The standardization controversy between the Jesuits and the North Central

Association, 1915–40, in L. Goodchild (ed.) *ASHE Reader on the History of Higher Education*, Needham Heights, MA: Ginn Press: 425–44.

Gornitzka, A., Kyvik, S. and Larson, I.M. (1998) The Bureaucratisation of Universities. *Minerva*, 36: 21–47.

Graduate Careers Council of Australia, GCCA (1999) Annual survey of graduate outcomes. Melbourne: GCCA.

Green, D. (2002) Research, Knowledge Transfer and the Regional Contribution, presentation to the Modern Universities Conference, 17 September 2002, Leeds Metropolitan University.

Green, K. (1999) When wishes come true: colleges and the convergence of access, lifelong learning, and technology, *Change*, March/April: 11–15.

Guillen, M.F. (2001) Is Globalization Civilizing, Destructive or Feeble? A Critique of Five Key Debates in the Social Science Literature, *Annual Review of Sociology*, No. 27, pp. 235–60.

Gumport, P.J. and Pusser, B. (1999) University Restructuring: The Role of Economic and Political Contexts in J. Smart (ed.) *Higher Education: Handbook of Theory and Research*. New York: Agathon.

Gumport, P.J. and Sporn, B. (1999) Institutional Adaptation: Demands for Management Reform and University Administration in J. Smart (ed.) *Higher Education: Handbook of Theory and Research* (Vol. XIV, pp. 103–45). New York: Agathon.

Gumport, P.J. (2000) Academic restructuring: Organizational change and institutional imperatives, *Higher Education*, 39(1): 67–91.

Guri-Rosenblit, S. (1999) The agendas of distance teaching universities: Moving from the margins to the center stage of higher education, *Higher Education*, 37(3): 281–93.

Guskin, A.E. (1994) Reducing student costs and enhancing student learning Part II: restructuring the role of faculty, *Change*, September/October: 16–25.

Halsey, A.H. (1992) *Decline of Donnish Dominion: The British Academic Professions in the Twentieth Century*. Oxford: Clarendon.

Hampel, R.L. *et al.* (1996) History and Educational Reform, *History of Education Quarterly*, 36(4): Winter.

Harley, S. (2002) The Impact of Research Selectivity on Academic Work and Identity in UK Universities, *Studies in Higher Education*, 27(2): 187–206.

Harman, G. (1998) Quality assurance mechanisms and their use as policy instruments: major international approaches and the Australian experience since 1993, *European Journal of Education*, 33(3): 331–48.

Harvey, D. (1989) *The Condition of Post-Modernity*. Malden: Blackwell.

Hayek, F. (1944) *The Road to Serfdom*. London: Routledge and Kegan Paul.

Heller, D.E. (1999) The effects of tuition and state financial aid on public college enrolment, *The Review of Higher Education*, 23(1): Fall, pp. 65–89.

Henkel, M. and Little, B. (eds) (1999) *Changing Relationships Between Higher Education and The State* (vol. 45). London: Jessica Kingsley.

Henkel, M. (2000) *Academic Identities and Policy Change in Higher Education*. London: Jessica Kingsley.

Herbst, J. (1997) Essay Review of Rohrs and Lenhart op. cit. *History of Education Quarterly* 37(1): Spring.

Hernes, G. and Martin, M. (2000) Trends in the management of university-industry linkages: what challenges are ahead? Paper presented to the IMHE General Conference, Paris, 11–13 September.

Higher Education Funding Council for England (2001), Higher Education – Business Interaction Survey, Bristol: HEFCE.

Hoare, D., Chair of Committee (1995) Higher Education Management Review, report of the committee of inquiry. Canberra: Australian Government Publishing Service.

Holtta, S. (1998) The funding of universities in Finland: towards goal-oriented government steering, *European Journal of Education*, 33(1): 55–63.

Hood, C. (1995) Contemporary Public Management: A New Global Paradigm?, *Public Policy and Administration*, 10(2): 104–17.

House of Commons (2001a) Higher Education: Access. Fourth Report of the Education and Employment Committee. London: Stationery Office HC 205.

House of Commons (2001b) Higher Education: Student Retention. Sixth Report of the Education and Employment Committee. London: Stationery Office HC 124.

Howell, C. and Subotzky, G. (2002) Obstacles and Strategies in Pursuing Staff Equity: A Regional Study of the Five Western Cape Higher Education Institutions Draft Research Report for Western Cape Higher Education Research Project.

Inter-American Development Bank, Sustainable Development Department (1997) Higher Education in Latin America and the Caribbean, a strategy paper, p. 6.

Itzin, C. and Newman, J. (eds) (1995) *Gender, Culture and Organisational Change*. London: Routledge.

Jansen, J.D. (2001) Explaining non-change in education reform after apartheid: political symbolism and the problem of policy implementation, in Jansen, J.D. and Sayed, Y. (eds) *Implementing Education Policies: The South African Experience*. Cape Town: UCT Press.

Jansen, J.D. (2002) Political symbolism as policy craft: explaining non-reform in South African education after apartheid, *Journal of Educational Policy*, 17(2): 199–215.

Jansen, J.D. and Sayed, Y. (eds) (2001) *Implementing Education Policies: The South African Experience*. Cape Town: UCT Press.

Jary, D. and Parker, M. (1998) *The New Higher Education: Issues and Directions for the Post-Dearing University*. Stoke on Trent: University of Staffordshire.

Jeliazkova, M. and Westerheijden, D.F. (2002) Systemic adaptation to a changing environment: Towards a next generation of quality assurance models, *Higher Education*, 44(3–4): 433–48.

Jemmott, N.D. and Morante, E.A. (1993) The College Outcomes Evaluation Program, in Banta, T.W. *et al.* (1993) *Making a Difference: Outcomes of a Decade of Assessment in Higher Education*, pp. 306–21, San Francisco: Jossey-Bass.

Johnstone, D.B. (1972) *New Patterns for College Lending: Income Contingent Loans*. New York: Teachers College Press.

Johnstone, D.B. (1986) *Sharing the Costs of Higher Education: Student Financial Assistance in the United Kingdom, the Federal Republic of Germany, France, Sweden, and the United States*. New York: College Entrance Examination Board.

Johnstone, D.B. (1991) The costs of higher education, in P.G. Altbach (ed.) *International Higher Education: An Encyclopedia*, Vol. 1, pp. 59–89. New York: Garland Publishing, Inc.

Johnstone, D.B. (1992) Tuition fees, in Burton R. Clark and Guy Neave (eds) *The Encyclopedia of Higher Education*, Vol. 2, pp. 1501–9, London: Pergamon Press. *High Tuition-High Aid Model of Public Higher Education Finance: The Case Against.*

Albany: Office of the SUNY Chancellor [for the National Association of System Heads].

Johnstone, D.B. (1993a) *The High Tuition High Aid Model of Public Higher Education Finance: The Case Against.* Albany: Office of the SUNY Chancellor [for the National Association of System Heads].

Johnstone, D.B. (1993b) The costs of higher education: Worldwide issues and trends for the 1990s, in Altbach, P.G. and Johnstone, D.B., *The Funding of Higher Education: International Perspectives.* New York: Garland Publishing.

Johnstone, D.B., Arora, A. and Experton, W. (1998) The Financing and Management of Higher Education: A Status Report on Worldwide Reform, Washington, DC: The World Bank. [Prepared in conjunction with the October 1998 UNESCO World Conference on Higher Education, Paris, 5–8 October, 1998].

Kane, T. (1995) *Rising Public College Tuition and College Entry: How Well do Public Subsidies Promote Access to College?* Cambridge: National Bureau of Economic Research.

Keep, E. (2003) Higher Education Expansion and the Evidence on Economic Demand for Graduates – Another Failure of Evidence-based Policy Making to Materialise? presentation to SRHE/ESRC Seminar, May 2003, London.

Kells, H.R. (1992) *Self-regulation in Higher Education: A Multinational Perspective on Collaborative Systems of Quality Assurance and Control,* London: Jessica Kingsley.

Kemp, D., Minister for Education, Training and Youth Affairs (1999a) *Knowledge and Innovation: A Policy Statement on Research and Research Training.* Canberra: Commonwealth of Australia.

Kemp, D., Minister for Education, Training and Youth Affairs (1999b) Proposals for Reform in Higher Education, Cabinet Submission [confidential paper leaked to media and circulated]. Canberra: Australian Government.

Kikert, W. (1991) *Steering at a Distance; a New Paradigm of Public Governance in Dutch Higher Education.* University of Essex: European Consortium for Political Research.

Kirkpatrick, I. and Lucio, M. (1995) *The Politics of Quality in the Public Sector: The Management of Change.* London: Routledge.

Kogan, M. (1998) University-state relations: a comparative perspective, *Higher Education Management,* 10(2): 121–35.

Kogan, M. (1999) Academic and administrative interface, in M. Henkel and B. Little (eds) *Changing Relationships between Higher Education and the State* (pp. 263–79). London: Jessica Kingsley.

Kogan, M. and Hanney, S. (2000) *Reforming Higher Education.* London: Jessica Kingsley.

Kraak, A. (ed.) (2000) *Changing Modes: New Knowledge Production and its Implications for Higher Education in South Africa.* Pretoria: Human Science Research Council.

Kraak, A. (2001) Policy Ambiguity and Slippage: Higher Education under the New State 1994–2000. Presentation in Symposium 11: Higher Education Policy in South Africa at the international conference Globalisation and Higher Education: Views from the South, Cape Town, March.

Kraak, A. and Young, M. (eds) (2001) *Education in Retrospect: Policy and Implementation Since 1990.* Pretoria: Human Sciences Research Council, in association with the Institute of Education, University of London.

Lauridsen, K. (2002) National Report for Denmark on Quality Enhancement in Language Studies, Thematic Network Project in the Area of Languages 2,

Subgroup 3 – Quality enhancement in language studies, National reports, Universität zu Köln.

Layzell, D.T. and Caruthers, J.K. (1995) Performance Funding at the State Level: Trends and Prospects. Paper presented to the 1995 Annual Meeting, Association for the Study of Higher Education, Orlando, Florida, 2 November.

Lazerson, M., Wagener, U. and Shumanis, N. (2000) What makes a revolution? Teaching and learning in higher education, 1980–2000, *Change*, May/June: 12–19.

Leslie, L. and Brinkman, P. (1989) *The Economic Value of Higher Education*. New York: Macmillan Publishing Company.

Levine, A. (1997) How the academic profession is changing, *Daedalus*, 126: 1–20.

Lillie, E. (2003) Higher Education, Languages and Quality in the United Kingdom, Thematic Network Project in the Area of Languages 2, Subgroup 3 – Quality enhancement in language studies, National reports, Universität zu Köln.

Lucas, L. (2001) The Research Game: A Sociological Study of Academic Research Work in Two Universities. Unpublished PhD thesis, Dept of Sociology, Coventry. University of Warwick.

Lüdi, G. (2002) Thematic Network Project in the Area of Languages 2, Subgroup 3 – Quality enhancement in language studies, National reports, Switzerland, Universität zu Köln.

Luke, C. (2001) *Globalization and Women in Academia: North/West – South/East*. Mahwah, New Jersey: Lawrence Erlbaum Associates.

Lyotard, J.F. (1984) *The Postmodern Condition: A Report on Knowledge*. Manchester: Manchester University Press.

Maassen, P. (2000) The Changing Roles of Stakeholders in Dutch University Governance, *European Journal of Education*, 35(4): 449–64.

Mace, J. (2000) The Rae and University Efficiency, *Higher Education Review*, 32(2): 17–35.

Marginson, S. (1993) *Arts, Science and Work: Work-related Skills and the Generalist Courses in Higher Education*. Canberra: Australian Government Publishing Service.

Marginson, S. (1995) Markets in higher education: Australia, *Academic Work*: 17–39.

Marginson, S. (1997) Steering from a distance: power relations in Australian higher education, *Higher Education*, 34, September: 63–80.

Marginson, S. (1997a) *Markets in Education*. Sydney: Allen and Unwin.

Marginson, S. (1997b) *Educating Australia: Government, Economy and Citizen*. Cambridge and Melbourne: Cambridge University Press.

Marginson, S. (1997c) Imagining Ivy: Government and private universities in Australia since 1985, *Comparative Education Review*, 46(4): 460–80.

Marginson, S. (1997d) Competition and contestability in Australian higher education, 1987–1997, *Australian Universities Review*, 40(1): 5–14.

Marginson, S. (1999) Diversity and convergence in Australian higher education, *Australian Universities Review*, 42(1): 12–23.

Marginson, S. (2000a) *Monash: The Remaking of the University*. Sydney: Allen and Unwin.

Marginson, S. (2000b) Research as a managed economy: the costs, in T. Coady (ed.) *Why Universities Matter: A Conversation about Values, Means and Directions*, pp. 186–213. Sydney: Allen and Unwin.

Marginson, S. and Considine, M. (2000) *The Enterprise University: Power, Governance and Reinvention in Australia*. Cambridge and Melbourne: Cambridge University Press.

Marginson, S. and Rhoades, G. (2002) Beyond national states, markets, and systems of higher education: A glonacal agency heuristic. *Higher Education*, 43: 281–309.

Martin, L., Chair of Committee (1964) Tertiary Education in Australia, report of the Committee on the Future of Tertiary Education in Australia. Melbourne: Australian Universities' Commission.

Massy, W.F. and Zemsky, R. (1994) Faculty discretionary time: departments and the academic ratchet, *Journal of Higher Education*, 65: 1–22.

Mathieson, S. (2001) Contestations around the formulation of the White Paper on Higher Education, in Jansen, J. D. and Sayed, Y. (eds) *Implementing Education Policies: The South African experience*. Cape Town: UCT Press.

McInnis, C. (1999) *The Work Roles of Academics in Australian Universities*, June. Australia: Higher Education Division, Commonwealth of Australia.

McInnis, C. (2000a) Promoting academic expertise and authority in an entrepreneurial culture. Paper presented to the IMHE General Conference, Paris, France, 11–13 September.

McInnis, C. (2000b) The impact of new technologies on academic work. Paper presented to the Anniversary Symposium of the Center for the Study of Higher Education, State College, PA, 24–25 June.

McInnis, C. (2000c) The Work Roles of Academics in Australian Universities, Evaluations and Investigations Program 00/5. Canberra: Department of Education, Training and Youth Affairs.

McMahon, W. (1988) Potential resource recovery in higher education in the developing countries and the parents' expected contribution, *Economics of Education Review*, 7(1).

Meek, V.L. (2000) Diversity and marketisation of higher education: incompatible concepts?, *Higher Education Policy*, 13: 21–39.

Meek, V.L., Goedegebuure, L. and Huisman, J. (2000) Understanding diversity and differentiation in higher education: an overview, *Higher Education Policy*, 13: 1–6.

Meek, V.L. and Wood, F. (1997) Higher Education Governance and Management, an Australian Study, Evaluations and Investigations Program. Canberra: Australian Government Publishing Service.

Meek, V. L. and Wood, F. (1998) Managing higher education diversity in a climate of public sector reform, Evaluations and Investigations Program, 98/5. Canberra: Australian Government Publishing Service.

Middlehurst, R. (1993) Leading Academics. Buckingham: Open University Press.

Middlehurst, R. (1999) Quality enhancement in principle and practice: A case study in leading change. *Tertiary Education and Management*, 5(1).

Middle States Commission on Higher Education (2002) *Characteristics of Excellence in Higher Education*. Philadelphia: MCHE.

Mignot Gerard, S. (2003) Who are the actors in the government of French universities? The paradoxal victory of deliberative leadership, *Higher Education*, 45(1): 71–89.

Millns T. and Piatt W. (eds) (2000) *Paying for Learning: the future of individual learning accounts*. London: Institute for Public Policy Research.

Mintzberg, H. (1979) *The Structuring of Organisations*. Engelwood Cliffs, New Jersey: Prentice Hall.

Mintzberg, H. (1983) *Structures in Fives*. London: Prentice Hall.

Mok, K.-H. (2000) Reflecting globalisation effects on local policy: Higher education reform in Taiwan, *Journal of Education Policy*, 15(6): 637–60.

Mollis, M. and Marginson, S. (2000) The assessment of universities in Argentina and Australia, between autonomy and heteronomy, *Higher Education*, 43: 311–30.

Moore, K.M. (1998) Thinking about advanced learning systems. Paper presented to Consortium of Higher Education Researchers Annual Meeting, Kassel, Germany, 1–2 September.

Morey, A.I. (1999) The growth of for-profit education in the United States. Paper presented to the Japan/U.S. Teacher Education Consortium's Eleventh Annual Meeting, Honolulu, Hawaii, 2–4 August.

Morgan, A.W. (2000) Importing organizational reform: The case of lay boards in Hungary, *Higher Education*, 40(4): 423–48.

Morley, L. (2001) Subjected to review: Engendering quality and power in higher education, *Journal of Education Policy*, 16(5): 465–78.

Mortimer, K.P. (1999) Governance in the 21st century university: The world is changing faster than the governance system can accommodate. Paper presented to the Six-Nation Presidents' Summit, Hiroshima, Japan, 20–21 September.

Moses, I. (1993) The development of knowledge and skills of academic staff, *Higher Education Management*, 5:2.

Motala, E. and Pampallis, J. (eds) (2001) *Education & Equity: The impact of state policies on South African education*. Sandown: Heinemannn Publishers.

Motala, E. and Singh, M. (2001) Introduction, in Motala, E. and Pampallis, J. (eds) (2001) *Education & Equity: The impact of state policies on South African education*. Sandown: Heinemannn Publishers.

Muller, J. (2000) *Reclaiming knowledge*. London: Routledge-Falmer.

Muller, J. (2001) Presentation in Symposium 11: Higher Education Policy in South Africa at the international conference Globalisation and Higher Education: Views from the South. Cape Town, March.

Muller, J. (2003) Knowledge and the limits to institutional restructuring: the case of South African Higher Education. Unpublished paper.

Muller, J., Cloete, N. and Badat, S. (eds) (2001) *Challenges of Globalization: South African debates with Manuel Castells*. Cape Town: Maskew Miller Longman.

Muller, J. and Subotzky, G. (2001) What knowledge is needed in the new millennium? *Organization*, 8(2): 163–82.

Müller-Böling, D. (1997a) Neue Medien – Hoffnungsträger für die Hochschulentwicklung?, in I. Hamm and D. Müller-Böling (eds) *Hochschulentwicklung durch neue Medien. Erfahrungen, Projekte, Perspektiven* (pp. 25–44). Gütersloh: Verlag Bertelsmann Stiftung.

Müller-Böling, D. (1997b) Zur Organisationsstruktur von Universitäten, *Die Betriebswirtschaft*, 57(5): 603–14.

Müller-Böling, D. (1998) University Governance as Conflictual Management, in D. Müller-Böling, E. Mayer, A.J. MacLachlan, J. Fedrowitz (eds) *University in Transition. Research Mission – Interdisciplinarity – Governance* (pp. 231–45). Gütersloh: Bertelsmann Foundation.

Müller-Böling, D., Mayer, E., MacLachlan, A.J. and Fedrowitz, J. (eds) (1998) *University in Transition. Research Mission – Interdisciplinarity – Governance*. Gütersloh: Bertelsmann Foundation.

Murray, K. Chair of Committee (1957) Report of the Committee on Australian Universities. Canberra: Commonwealth Government Printer.

National Commission on Higher Education (NCHE) (1996) *A framework for transformation*. Pretoria: NCHE.

National Committee of Inquiry into Higher Education (1997) *Higher Education in the Learning Society*. HMSO.

Neave, G. (1998) Growing pains: the Dearing Report from a European perspective, *Higher Education Quarterly*, 52(1), January.

Neave, G. (2000) Diversity, differentiation and the market: the debate we never had but which we ought to have done, *Higher Education Policy*, 13: 7–21.

Neave, G. (2002) Anything goes: or, How the accommodation of Europe's universities to European integration integrates an inspiring number of contradictions, *Tertiary Education and Management*, 8(3): 181–97.

New England Association of Schools and Colleges, Commission on Higher Education (2002) *Standards of Accreditation*. Bedford, MA: NEASC.

Newman, F. and Couturier, L. (2002) . . . and a new Compact with Their States, *The Chronicle of Higher Education*, 18 October, B13.

Newton, J. (2000) Feeding the beast or improving quality? Academics' perceptions of quality assurance and quality monitoring, *Quality in Higher Education*, 6(2): 153–63.

Newton, J. (2002) Barriers to effective quality management and leadership: Case study of two academic departments, *Higher Education*, 44(2): 185–212.

North, J. (1999) Post-tenure review: rehabilitation or enrichment? *AAHE Bulletin*, 51(8): 10–13.

North Central Association (2002) *New Policies and Policy Revisions most recently approved by the Board of Trustees of the Higher Learning Commission*. Chicago, IL: NCA.

Nowotny, H. (1995) Mass higher education and social mobility: a tenuous link, in D.D. Dill and B. Sporn (eds) *Emerging Patterns of Social Demand and University Reform: Through a Glass Darkly* (pp. 72–89). Oxford: Pergamon.

OECD (1987) Structural Adjustment and Economic Performance. Paris: OECD.

OECD (1989) Education and the Economy in a Changing Society. Paris: OECD.

OECD (1997) Thematic Review of the First Years of Tertiary Education – Comparative Report: Summary and Conclusions Paris: the Organisation.

OECD (1998) Redefining Tertiary Education. Paris: OCED.

OECD (2000) Education at a Glance: OECD indicators. Paris: OECD.

Ozga, J.T. and R. Deem (2000) Colluded selves, new times and engendered organisational cultures: The experiences of feminist women managers in UK higher and further education. *Discourse*, 21(2): 141–54.

Papadopoulos, G. (1994) *Education 1960–1990: The OECD Perspective*. Paris: The Organisation.

Paris, D.C. (1995) *Ideology and Educational Reform: Themes and Theories in Public Education*. Boulder: Westview Press.

Parry, G. (2001a) Academic Snakes and Vocational Ladders. Fourth Philip Jones Memorial Lecture. Leicester: National Organisation for Adult Learning.

Parry, G. (2001b) Reform of Higher Education in the United Kingdom, in B. Nolan (ed.) *Public Sector Reform: An International Perspective*. Basingstoke: Macmillan: 117–32.

Pechar, H. (2002) Accreditation in higher education in Britain and Austria: Two cultures, two time-frames, *Tertiary Education and Management*, 8(3): 231–42.

Perkin, H. (1987) The academic profession in the United Kingdom, in B.R. Clark (ed.) *The Academic Profession*. Berkeley: University of California Press.

Peter, M. and Roberts, P. (1999) Globalisation and the crisis in the concept of the modern university, *Australian Universities Review*, 42(1): 47–55.

Peterson, M. and Augustine, C. (2000) Organizational practices enhancing the influence of student assessment information in academic decisions, *Research in Higher Education*, vol. 41, no. 1, pp. 21–52.

Peterson, M.W., and Dill, D.D. (1997) Understanding the competitive environment of the postsecondary knowledge industry, in M.W. Peterson, D.D. Dill and L.A. Mets (eds) *Planning and Management for a Changing Environment: A Handbook on Redesigning Postsecondary Institutions* (pp. 3–29). San Francisco: Jossey-Bass.

Pigden, C.R. (1997) Submission to the New Zealand Ministry of Education in response to the September 1997 Green Paper. A Future Tertiary Education Policy for New Zealand http://www.minedu.govt.nz/data/tertiary/review97

Power, M. (1997) *The Audit Society.* Oxford: Oxford University Press.

Poynter, J. and Rasmussen, C. (1996) *A Place Apart – The University of Melbourne: Decades of challenge.* Melbourne: Melbourne University Press.

Prahalad, C.K. and Hamel, G. (1990) The core competence of the corporation, *Harvard Business Review* (May-June): 79–91.

Quality Assurance Agency, http://www.qaa.ac.uk/public/publications.htm

Ranson, S. and J. Stewart (1994) *Management for the Public Domain – Enabling the Learning Society.* London: Macmillan.

Reed, M. (1995) Managing Quality and Organisational Politics: Tqm as a Governmental Technology, in I. Kirpatrick and M. Martinez-Lucio (eds) *The Politics of Quality in the Public Sector.* London: Routledge: 44–64.

Reed, M. (1999) From the 'Cage' to the 'Gaze': The dynamics of organisational control in late modernity, in G. Morgan and L. Engwall (eds) *Regulation and Organisations: International Perspectives,* 17–49. London: Routledge.

Reed, M. (2002) New managerialism, professional power and organisational governance in UK universities: A review and assessment, in A. Amaral, G.A. Jones and B. Karseth (eds) *Governing Higher Education: National Perspectives on Institutional Governance.* Dordrecht, Netherlands: Kluwer Academic Publishers.

Reed, M. and Deem, R. (2002) New managerialism: The manager-academic and technologies of management in universities – looking forward to virtuality?, in K. Robins and F. Webster (eds) *The Virtual University? Information, Markets and Managements,* 126–47. Oxford: Oxford University Press.

Rhoades, G. (2000) Who's doing it right? Strategic activity in public research universities. *The Review of Higher Education,* 24(1): 41–66.

Rhoades, G. and Sporn, B. (2002a) New models of management and shifting modes and costs of production: Europe and the United States, *Tertiary Education and Management,* 8: 3–28.

Rhoades, G. and Sporn, B. (2002b) Quality assurance in Europe and the U.S.: Professional and political economic framing of higher education policy, *Higher Education,* 43(3): 355–90.

Robbins, L., Chair of Committee (1963) Higher Education, report of the Committee on Higher Education. London: HMSO.

Robins, K. and Webster, F. (eds) *The Virtual University? Information, Markets and Managements,* 126–47. Oxford: Oxford University Press.

Robinson, P. and Piatt, W. (2000) *The Foundation Degree and the Expansion of Higher Education.* London: Institute for Public Policy Research, November.

Rohrs, H. and Lenhart, V. (eds) (1995) *Progressive Education Across the Continents: A Handbook.* Frankfurt am Main: Peter Lang.

Ryanearson (2000) www.fathom.com

Sadlak, J. (1998) Globalization and Concurrent Challenges for Higher Education, in P. Scott (ed.) *The Globalization of Higher Education* pp. 100–107. Buckingham: Open University Press.

Sajavaara, K. (2003) Quality enhancement in higher education language studies in Finland, thematic network project in the area of languages 2, subgroup 3 – Quality enhancement in language studies, National reports, Universität zu Köln.

Salmi, J. (2000) Tertiary education in the twenty-first century: challenges and opportunities. Paper presented to the IMHE General Conference, Paris, France, 11–13 September.

Schmidt, P. (1999) A State transforms colleges with performance funding, *The Chronicle of Higher Education*, 2 July: A26–8.

Schmidt, P. (2002a) Dashed hopes in Missouri, T*he Chronicle of Higher Education*, November 29: A18.

Schmidt, P. (2002b) Most states tie aid to performance, despite little proof that it works, *The Chronicle of Higher Education*, February 22: A20.

Schmidtlein, F.A. (1999) Assumptions underlying performance-based budgeting, *Tertiary Education and Management*, 5(2): 159–74.

Scott, P. (1995) *The Meanings of Mass Higher Education*. London: Society for Research on Higher Education and the Open University Press.

Scott, P. (1997a) The changing role of the university in the production of new knowledge, *Tertiary Education and Management*, 3(1): 5–14.

Scott, P. (1997b) Changes in knowledge production and dissemination in the context of globalization, in Cloete, N., Muller, J., Makgoba, M.W., and Ekong, D. (eds) *Knowledge, Identity and Curriculum Transformation in Africa*, Cape Town: Maskew Miller-Longman.

Scott, P. (1998a) Massification, Internationalization and Globalization, in P. Scott (ed.) *The Globalization of Higher Education* pp. 108–29. Buckingham: Open University Press.

Scott, P. (ed.) (1998b) *The Globalization of Higher Education*. Buckingham: Open University Press.

Selingo, J. (2003) The disappearing state in public higher education, *The Chronicle of Higher Education*, February 28: A20.

Senge, P.M. (2000) Die Hochschule als lernende Gemeinschaft, in S. Laske, T. Scheytt, C. Meister-Scheytt, C.O. Scharmer (eds) *Universität im 21. Jahrhundert: Zur Interdependenz von Begriff und Organisation der Wissenschaft* (p. 509). München: Rainer Hampp.

Sequeira, F. (2002) Quality enhancement in higher education language studies, Portugal, thematic network project in the area of languages 2, subgroup 3 – Quality enhancement in language studies, National reports, Universität zu Köln.

Shattock, M. (1999) Governance and management in universities: the way we live now, *Journal of Education Policy*, 14(3): 271–82.

Shattock, M. (2001) The academic profession in Britain: A Study in the failure to adapt to change, *Higher Education*, 41(1–2).

Sheehan, B. and Welch, T. (1994) International survey of the academic profession: Australia. Unpublished paper for the Carnegie international study of the academic profession. Melbourne: University of Melbourne.

Sheehan, P. and Tikhomirova, G. (1998) The nation in the global economy, in P. Sheehan and G. Tegart (eds) *Working for the Future: Technology and Employment in the Global Knowledge Economy*, pp. 87–126. Melbourne: Victoria University Press.

Simon, B. (1994) *The State and Educational Change: Essays in the History of Education and Pedagogy*. London: Lawrence and Wishart.

Sjolund, M. (1998) Strategic management in research funding, *Higher Education Management*, 10(2): 107–19.

Skurvydiene, I. and Juceviciute, R. (2002) National report on quality enhancement in language studies, Lithuania, thematic network project in the area of languages 2, subgroup 3 – Quality enhancement in language studies, National reports, Universität zu Köln.

Slaughter, S. (1998) National higher education policies in a global economy, in J. Currie and J. Newson (eds) *Universities and Globalization* pp. 45–70. London: Sage.

Slaughter, S. and Leslie, L.L. (1997) *Academic Capitalism: Politics, Policies and the Entrepreneurial University*. Baltimore: Johns Hopkins University Press.

Smith, A. and Webster, F. (eds) (1997) *The Postmodern University? Contested Visions of Higher Education in Society*. Buckingham: Open University Press.

Snow, C.P. (1959) *The Two Cultures and the Scientific Revolution*. Cambridge: Cambridge University Press.

Soudien, C., Jacklin, H. and Hondiey, H. (2001) Policy values: problematising equity and redress in education, in Jansen, I. and Sayed, Y. (eds) *Implementing Education Policies: The South African Experience*, pp. 78–91. Cape Town: UCT Press.

South Carolina Commission on Higher Education (2001) *Performance Funding at a Glance*. Columbia, SC: SCCHE.

Sporn, B. and Miksch, G. (1996) Implementing an information strategy – The case of the Vienna University of Economics and Business Administration, in O. Imhe (ed.) *Managing Information Strategies in Higher Education* (pp. 121–131). Paris: OECD.

Sporn, B. (1999a) *Adaptive University Structures: An Analysis of Adaptation to Socioeconomic Environments of US and European Universities*. London: Jessica Kingsley.

Sporn, B. (1999b) Current issues and future priorities for European higher education systems, in P.G. Altbach and P.M. Peterson (eds) *Higher Education in the 21st Century: Global Challenges and National Responses* (pp. 67–77). MD: Annapolis Junction: Institute of International Education.

Sporn, B. (1999c) Towards more adaptive universities: Trends of institutional reform in Europe, *Higher Education in Europe*, XXIV(1): 23–34.

Sporn, B. (2001) Building adaptive universities: Emerging organizational forms based on experiences of European and US universities, *Tertiary Education and Management*, 7(2): 121–34.

Stanley, E. and Patrick, W. (1998) Quality assurance in American and British higher education: A comparison. *New Directions for Institutional Research*, #99. San Francisco: Jossey Bass.

Stensaker, B. (2000) Quality as discourse: An analysis of external audit reports in Sweden 1995–1998, *Tertiary Education and Management*, 6(4): 305–17.

Stern, D. and Nakata, Y. F. (1991) Paid employment among US college students, *Journal of Higher Education*, 62:10 (January/February), pp. 25–43.

Stiglitz, J. (2002) *Globalization and its Discontents*. London: Penguin Books.

Stromquist, N. and Monkman, K. (eds) (2000) *Globalization and Education*, Lanham, Maryland: Rowman and Littlefield Publishers.

Subotzky, G. (1999) Alternatives to the entrepreneurial university: New modes of knowledge production in community service programmes, *Higher Education*, 38(4): 401–40.

Subotzky, G. (2001a) Addressing equity and excellence in relation to employment: What prospects for transformative change in South Africa? *Equity and Excellence in Education*, 34(3): 56–9.

Subotzky, G. (2001b) Understanding the current situation in higher education. Background paper prepared for the CHE Annual Report 2000–(2001). Bellville: EPU, UWC.

Subotzky, G. (2003a) Higher education's contribution towards reconstructing South African society: Constraints, challenges and cautionary tales. In proceedings of the University of Toronto 175th Anniversary Symposium: *Creating Knowledge, Strengthening Nations: The Changing Role of Higher Education*, Toronto, September.

Subotzky, G. (2003b) Draft regional report on innovations in higher education in Southern Africa. Prepared for the Working Group on Higher Education of the Association for the Development of Education in Africa. Bellville: Education Policy Unit.

Subotzky, G. and Cele, G. (2003) New modes of knowledge production and acquisition: Peril or promise for developing countries? In proceedings of the conference *African Universities in the 21st Century*. University of Illinois, Urbana-Champaigne, April.

Swan, T. (2002) Thematic network project in the area of languages 2, subgroup 3 – Quality enhancement in language studies, National reports, Norway, Universität zu Köln.

Symes, C. (1996) Selling futures: a new image for Australian universities? *Studies in Higher Education*, 21(2): 133–47.

Szabó, K. (2002) National report on quality enhancement in language studies in Hungary, thematic network project in the area of languages 2, subgroup 3 – Quality enhancement in language studies, National reports, Universität zu Köln.

Teichler, U. (1998a) Massification: a challenge for institutions of higher education, *Tertiary Education and Management*, 4(1): 17–27.

Teichler, U. (1998b). The role of the European Union in the internationalization of higher education, in P. Scott (ed.) *The Globalization of Higher Education* pp. 88–99. Buckingham: Open University Press.

Teichler, U. (1999) Internationalisation as a challenge for higher education in Europe, *Tertiary Education and Management*, 5(1): 5–23.

Teichler, U. (2001) Mass higher education and the need for new responses, *Tertiary Education and Management*, 7(1): 3–7.

Terenzini, P.T. and Pascarella, E.T. (1994) Living with myths: undergraduate education in America, *Change*, Jan/Feb.

Terreblanche, S. (2003) *A history of inequality in South Africa 1652–2002*. Scottsville: University of Natal Press.

Tierney, W.G. (ed.) (1997) *The Responsive University: Restructuring for High Performance*. Baltimore: Johns Hopkins University.

Tierney, W.G. (1999) *Building the Responsive Campus: Creating High Performance Colleges and Universities*. Thousand Oaks, California: Sage.

Times Higher Education Supplement (1999) Performance indicator tables, 3 December: I–XII.

Tocatlidou, V. (2003) Thematic network project in the area of languages 2, subgroup 3 – Quality enhancement in language studies, National reports, Greece, Universität zu Köln.

Tolbert, P.S. (1985) Institutional environments and resource dependence: Sources of administrative structure in institutions of higher education, *Administrative Science Quarterly*, 30: 1–13.

Tost Planet, M. (2002) Quality enhancement in language studies, Spain, thematic network project in the area of languages 2, subgroup 3 – Quality enhancement in language studies, National reports, Universität zu Köln.

Toudic, D. (2002) Enhancement in the area of languages, France, thematic network project in the area of languages 2, subgroup 3 – Quality enhancement in language studies, National reports, Universität zu Köln.

Trow, M. (1989) American higher education – past, present and future, *Studies in Higher Education*, 14:1.

trow, m. (1993) managerialism and the academic profession: The case of England. Berkeley, USA: University of California at Berkeley.

Trowler, P. (1998) *Academics Responding to Change: New Education Frameworks and Academic Cultures*. Buckingham: Open University Press.

Tudor, I. (2002) Quality enhancement in higher education language studies, Belgium, thematic network project in the area of languages 2, subgroup 3 – Quality enhancement in language studies, National reports, Universität zu Köln.

Tuning Educational Structures in Europe, http://odur.let.rug.nl/TuningProject/background.asp

Turner, D. (1996) Changing patterns of funding higher education in Europe, *Higher Education Management*, 8:1.

Tyack, D. and Cuban, L. (1995) Tinkering toward Utopia: A century of public school reform. Cambridge MA: Harvard University Press.

Tysome, T. (1995) Academics keep CAT in the bag, *Times Higher Education Supplement* 21 July.

Universitas 21 (2002) Report presented at Global Experience Conference, October 2002, Singapore: Universitas 21.

Universität zu Köln, www.uni-koeln.de/elc/tnp2/reports.html

UniversitiesUK (2001) New directions in higher education funding – Funding Options Review Group Final Report, March. London: UniversitiesUK.

Urbanikowa, J. (2002) National report on quality enhancement in language studies, Poland, thematic network project in the area of languages 2, subgroup 3 – Quality enhancement in language studies, National reports, Universität zu Köln.

Van den Bosch, H. and Teelken, C. (2000) Organisation and leadership in higher education. Learning from experiences in the Netherlands, *Higher Education Policy*, 13(4): 379–97.

Van der Wende, M. (2002) Higher education globally: towards new frameworks for research and policy, *The CHEPS Inaugural Lectures 2002*, Enschede: Universiteit Twente.

Van Vught, F. (ed.) (1989) *Governmental Strategies and Innovation in Higher Education*. London: Jessica Kingsley.

Van Vught, F. (1994) Policy models and policy instruments in higher education: The effects of governmental policy-making on the innovative behavior of higher education institutions, in J. Smart (ed.) *Higher Education: Handbook of Theory and Research* Vol. X, pp. 88–125. New York: Agathon.

Van Vught, F. (1999) Innovative universities, *Tertiary Education and Management*, 5(4): 347–55.

Van Vught, F. (2002) Entrepreneurial universities: Governance, management and organisational change. In Entrepreneurial higher education institutions seminar report, pp. 5–14. Sunnyside: Centre for Higher Education Transformation.

Varghese, N.V. (2000) Diversification of sources of funding in higher education. Paper presented to the IMHE General Conference, Paris, 11–13 September.

Veld, R. J. i.t. (1981) Survival during the Eighties, *International Journal of Institutional Management in Higher Education*, 5(2): 97–107.

Vogelberg, K. (2002) Thematic network project in the area of languages 2, subgroup 3 – Quality enhancement in language studies, National reports, Estonia, Universität zu Köln.

Voskova, M. (2002) Quality enhancement in higher education language studies, Czech Republic, thematic network project in the area of languages 2, subgroup 3 – Quality enhancement in language studies, National reports, Universität zu Köln.

Wagenaar, R. (2002) Tuning educational structures in Europe. Presentation for the pre-Berlin Conference, Working on the European Dimension of Quality, Amsterdam, March 12–13, http://www.jointquality.org/content/nederland/Tuning_Presentation.doc

Wande, W. (2002) Quality enhancement in language studies in Sweden, thematic network project in the area of languages 2, subgroup 3 – Quality enhancement in language studies, National reports, Universität zu Köln.

Watson, D. and Bowden, R. (2001) Can we be equal and excellent too? The new Labour stewardship of higher education 1997–2001. Education Research Centre Occasional Paper, June. Brighton: University of Brighton

Watson, L. (2000) Survey of private providers in Australian Higher Education 1999, Evaluations and Investigations Program 00/4. Canberra: Department of Education, Training and Youth Affairs.

Webb, J. (1999) Work and the new public service class, *Sociology*, 33(4): 747–66.

Webster, E. and Mosoetsa, S. (2001) At the Chalk Face: Managerialism and the Changing Academic Workplace. Background paper commissioned for Cloete, N. *et al.* (eds) (2002) *Transformation in higher education: Global pressures and local realities in South Africa.* Landsdowne: Juta and Company.

West, R., Chair of Committee (1998) Learning for Life, Final Report of the Review of Higher Education Funding and Policy. Canberra: Australian Government Publishing Service.

Western Association of Schools and Colleges (1998) *Invitation to Dialogue: Principles for the Next Handbook of Accreditation.* Oakland, CA: WASC.

Western Association of Schools and Colleges (2001) *Handbook of Accreditation.* Alameda, CA: WASC.

Western Association of Schools and Colleges (2002) *Substantive Change Resources.* Alameda, CA: WASC.

Whitehead, S. (2001) Women as Managers: A Seductive Ontology, *Gender, Work and Organisation*, 8(1): 86–107.

Williams, G. (1998a) Advantages and disadvantages of diversified funding in universities, *Tertiary Education and Management*, 4(2): 85–93.

Williams, G. (1998b) Current debates on the funding of mass higher education in the United Kingdom, *European Journal of Education*, 33(1): 77–87.

Woodhall, M. (1988) Designing a student loan programme for a developing country: The relevance of international experience, *Economics of Education Review*, 7(1): 153–61.

Woodhall, M. (1989) *Financial Support for Students: Grants, Loans, or Graduate Tax?* London: Kogan Page.

Woodhall, M. (1992) Changing sources and patterns of finance for higher education: A review of international trends, *Higher Education in Europe*, 17(1): 141–49.

World Bank (1994) *Higher Education: Lessons of Experience.* Washington, DC: The World Bank.

World Bank (2000) *Higher Education in Developing Countries: Peril and Promise.* Washington D.C.

Wran, N., Chair of Committee (1988) Report of the Committee on Higher Education Funding. Canberra, Department of Employment, Education and Training.

Wright, R. (1994) *The Moral Animal.* London: Little Brown.

Yorke, M. (1996) *Indicators of Programme Quality.* London: HEQC.

Yorke, M. (2000) Developing a Quality Culture in Higher Education, *Tertiary Education and Management,* 6(1): 19–36.

Young, M. (2001) Higher Education Policy in South Africa. Symposium Presentation at the Conference Globalization and Higher Education: Views from the South, hosted by the SRHE/Education Policy Unit, University of the Western Cape, Cape Town, March.

Ziderman, A. and Albrecht, D. (1995) *Financing Universities in Developing Countries.* Washington, DC: The Falmer Press.

Index

n/ns indicates note(s). Numbers in *italics* refer to tables

The Society for Research into Higher Education

The Society for Research into Higher Education (SRHE), an international body, exists to stimulate and coordinate research into all aspects of higher education. It aims to improve the quality of higher education through the encouragement of debate and publication on issues of policy, on the organization and management of higher education institutions, and on the curriculum, teaching and learning methods.

The Society is entirely independent and receives no subsidies, although individual events often receive sponsorship from business or industry. The Society is financed through corporate and individual subscriptions and has members from many parts of the world. It is an NGO of UNESCO.

Under the imprint *SRHE & Open University Press*, the Society is a specialist publisher of research, having over 80 titles in print. In addition to *SRHE News*, the Society's newsletter, the Society publishes three journals: *Studies in Higher Education* (three issues a year), *Higher Education Quarterly* and *Research into Higher Education Abstracts* (three issues a year).

The Society runs frequent conferences, consultations, seminars and other events. The annual conference in December is organized at and with a higher education institution. There are a growing number of networks which focus on particular areas of interest, including:

Access	FE/HE
Assessment	Graduate Employment
Consultants	New Technology for Learning
Curriculum Development	Postgraduate Issues
Eastern European	Quantitative Studies
Educational Development Research	Student Development

Benefits to members

Individual

- The opportunity to participate in the Society's networks
- Reduced rates for the annual conferences
- Free copies of *Research into Higher Education Abstracts*
- Reduced rates for *Studies in Higher Education*

- Reduced rates for *Higher Education Quarterly*
- Free online access to *Register of Members' Research Interests* – includes valuable reference material on research being pursued by the Society's members
- Free copy of occasional in-house publications, e.g. *The Thirtieth Anniversary Seminars Presented by the Vice-Presidents*
- Free copies of *SRHE News* and *International News* which inform members of the Society's activities and provides a calendar of events, with additional material provided in regular mailings
- A 35 per cent discount on all SRHE/Open University Press books
- The opportunity for you to apply for the annual research grants
- Inclusion of your research in the *Register of Members' Research Interests*

Corporate

- Reduced rates for the annual conference
- The opportunity for members of the Institution to attend SRHE's network events at reduced rates
- Free copies of *Research into Higher Education Abstracts*
- Free copies of *Studies in Higher Education*
- Free online access to *Register of Members' Research Interests* – includes valuable reference material on research being pursued by the Society's members
- Free copy of occasional in-house publications
- Free copies of *SRHE News* and *International News*
- A 35 per cent discount on all SRHE/Open University Press books
- The opportunity for members of the Institution to submit applications for the Society's research grants
- The opportunity to work with the Society and co-host conferences
- The opportunity to include in the *Register of Members' Research Interests* your Institution's research into aspects of higher education

Membership details: SRHE, 76 Portland Place, London W1B 1NT, UK Tel: 020 7637 2766. Fax: 020 7637 2781. email: srheoffice@srhe.ac.uk world wide web: http://www.srhe.ac.uk./srhe/
Catalogue: SRHE & Open University Press, McGraw-Hill Education, McGraw-Hill House, Shoppenhangers Road, Maidenhead, Berkshire SL6 2QL. Tel: 01628 502500. Fax: 01628 770224. email: enquiries@openup.co.uk – web: www.openup.co.uk

HIGHER EDUCATION AND THE LIFECOURSE

Maria Slowey and David Watson (Eds.)

As we enter the twenty-first century it is increasingly clear to professionals at all levels of formal and informal education that we need to refresh the concept of lifelong learning. Most importantly, the concept needs to be expanded so that it is lifelong and lifewide, concerned not just with serial requirements of those already engaged, but also with the creation of opportunities for those who have not found the existing structures and processes accessible or useful.

The volume is structured around resulting arguments about policy and practice in three parts. The first focuses on the lifelong dimension, addressing in particular the changing nature of the student population. The second investigates the lifewide connections between higher education and other areas of social and economic life. The final section draws together a structural analysis, as well as research on changing needs of learners, to set out some key implications for higher education.

Contents

417pp   0 335 21377 4 (Paperback)   0 335 21378 2 (Hardback)

RESEARCHING HIGHER EDUCATION
ISSUES AND APPROACHES

Malcolm Tight

This book couples an authoritative overview of the principal current areas of research into higher education with a guide to the core methods used for researching higher education. It offers both a configuration of research on higher education, as seen through the lens of methodology, and suggestions for further research.

Contents

Case studies and tables are separately listed after the main contents pages – Part I: Recently Published Research on Higher Education – Introduction – Journals – Books – Part II: Issues and Approaches in Researching Higher Education – Researching Teaching and Learning – Researching Course Design – Researching the Student Experience – Researching Quality – Researching System Policy – Researching Institutional Management – Researching Academic Work – Researching Knowledge – Part III: The Process of Researching Higher Education – Method and Methodology in Researching Higher Education – Researching Higher Education at Different Levels – The Process of Researching – References

417pp   0 335 21117 8 (Paperback)   0 335 21118 6 (Hardback)

BEYOND ALL REASON
LIVING WITH IDEOLOGY IN THE UNIVERSITY

Ronald Barnett

A major work . . . provocative, unsettling and profoundly challenging. I think it should be prescribed reading for all vice-chancellors.
>   Colin Bundy, Director of the School of Oriental and African Studies,
>   University of London

Ron Barnett's latest book lives up to, and possibly exceeds, the high standards he has set himself in his previous books – which are now established as the premier series of reflective books on higher education.

Beyond All Reason argues that ideologies are now multiplying on campus and that, consequently, the university as a place of open debate and reason is in jeopardy. The book examines, as case studies, the ideologies of competition, quality, entrepreneurialism and managerialism. All of these movements have a positive potential but, in being pressed forward unduly, have become pernicious ideologies that are threatening to undermine the university.

Ronald Barnett argues that it is possible to realize the university by addressing the ideals present in the idea of the university, and so developing positive projects for the university. These 'utopian ideologies' may never be fully realized but, pursued seriously, they can counter the pernicious ideologies that beset the university. In this way, it is possible for the idea of the university to live on and be practised in the twenty-first century.

Beyond All Reason offers a bold optimistic statement about the future of universities and offers ideas for enabling universities to be 'universities' in the contemporary age. It will be of interest and value not just to students of higher education but also to vice-chancellors, administrators, academics generally and those who care about the future of universities.

Contents
Introduction – Part 1: The end of the matter – The ends of reason – A complex world – The states of higher education – The end of ideology? – Part 2: Pernicious ideologies – 'The entrepreneurial university' – Anything you can do – Never mind the quality – 'The academic community' – Part 3: Virtuous ideologies – Communicating values – Engaging universities – Uniting research and teaching – Reasonable universities – Prospects – Appendices – Notes – Bibliography – Index – The Society for Research into Higher Education.

192pp   0 335 20893 2 (Paperback)   0 335 20894 0 (Hardback)

THE GLOBALIZATION OF HIGHER EDUCATION

Peter Scott

This book describes and analyses the links between the growth of mass higher education systems and the radical processes of globalization which include not only round-the-clock, round-the-globe markets and new information technologies but revolutionary conceptions of time and space. Higher education is implicated as creator, interpreter and sufferer of these trends. *The Globalization of Higher Education* attempts to make sense of the connections between the expansion (and diversification) of higher education – including the increasing emphasis on international collaboration and the recruitment of international students – and the development of global politics, markets and culture. It offers a variety of perspectives, including those of national policies (from the UK, Europe and South Africa), of the European Union, of the Commonwealth, and of UNESCO.

This is a first, significant attempt to put the transformation of higher education within the more general context of globalization.

Contents

Preface – Contemporary transformations of time and space – Internationalizing British higher education: students and institutions – Internationalizing British higher education: policy perspectives – Internationalization in Europe – Internationalization in South Africa – A commonwealth perspective on the globalization of higher education – The role of the European Union in the internationalization of higher education – Globalization and concurrent challenges for higher education – Massification, internationalization and globalization – Index – The Society for Research into Higher Education.

144pp   0 335 20244 6 (Paperback)   0 335 20245 4 (Hardback)